C000121711

# Not for All
## the Tea in China

Can I have my money
back ??
My Dear friend.

Chris Burrows

**Grosvenor House
Publishing Limited**

This book is published by
Grosvenor House Publishing Ltd
Link House
140 The Broadway, Tolworth, Surrey, KT6 7HT.
www.grosvenorhousepublishing.co.uk

A CIP record for this book
is available from the British Library

ISBN 978-1-83975-388-6

# Introduction

My father advised me, the only way to make money for yourself is by working for yourself. I took no notice. Lads never do take any notice of their fathers particularly when they're young? But eventually, I decided he was right, so here we go. I've done so many things in my life I think I should be 173 years old, not 73 years old.

I hope that some of what this book contains will amuse you. It amused me at the time and it's intended to amuse. I repeat, it's intended to amuse wherever possible. There were things, there were serious things, for example, my devotion to the Super Reds, Barnsley Football Club. You won't believe it, but I'm sat here wearing a red shirt right now. Yorkshire cricket, and of course the subject of the book really is travel. I'm devoted to it.

A very old and good friend of mine; who lent me the Dictaphone into which I am speaking now, said to me when he lent me the Dictaphone, *"I'm giving you this. I'm not lending it to you. It's yours to keep."* So you know now, here's one of those rare Yorkshiremen who cares very little about money. John, there must be something wrong with you. It wasn't my intention to mention names in full in the book but since we've found a Yorkshireman who doesn't know, or value, or think about what brass is worth, his name is John Hibbard and he comes from Birdwell. Birdwell is a suburb of Barnsley. And of course, he supports the Super Reds. I can't understand for the life of me why anybody doesn't support the Super Reds, I can't understand it quite frankly.

When he gave me the machine, the Dictaphone (I shouldn't call it a machine) – I'm so old-fashioned in many of the ways that I have. I was even listening to Vera Lynn yesterday believe it or not! 103 she is! Or she was. A real British treasure. John said to me, *"I've sat and listened to you list a load of stories you've told over the years; there's two or three that I'd like you to <u>make sure</u> that go into this exercise, this navigation, this voyage into the unknown, call it what you will, of your life."* Basically, this was intended to be from 50 years of age onwards when I went into self-employment, but I've cheated a bit. One or two other things are from before.

# Chapter One

To please John, and to thank him so much for the help he's given me, some of the ones that he wants to hear are in the book, and they're going to follow soon. John and I were both football referees for many, many years. I remember one day, we both, as he puts it, refereed a game at Grimsby. They were playing, I think, Newcastle, but I wouldn't be sure about the opposition. Just to correct you John - no we didn't. I refereed the game and you were one of the two linesmen. The beauty of that day was, well, the second linesman was a Sheffield Wednesday supporter, and that day John and I had foregone the opportunity of going to Hillsborough to watch Barnsley play Sheffield Wednesday because we were both officiating at Grimsby.

A Sheffield Wednesday supporter came into the dressing room. We didn't know him. We didn't know him at all, but his beliefs and his football support became very clear when he knew where we were from and he was bragging about how many they would beat us by that afternoon. The end of the game at Grimsby, I enquired of a man with a radio as to whether he knew the final score at Sheffield Wednesday, and he said, *"Yes. They've lost two-nil."* I've never seen a man get changed as quick in my life than that Wednesdayite did to get away from John and I.

I decided when I was 50-years old to have a go at following my dad's advice and having a go on my own. But you need all sorts of things. You just can't set up and set off. You need money. Money's not easy to come by. You have to borrow it. I needed a car, I needed this, I needed that, I needed the other. And above all else, of course, I needed customers. And I decided, in my wisdom, and I've no idea where it came from at the time, that the first call I was going to make would be about as far away from Barnsley as it possibly could be while remaining in England. It was in Barnstaple, in Devon. So, on that first Monday morning, I set off with a little trepidation, with a lot of hope, and a lot of belief, and I set off to drive in the general direction of the south-west of England. My thoughts were simple. I'd stop roughly half way, find a bed and breakfast, carry on, see the man in Barnstaple, drive back, because I was going to Birmingham the following day to see another possibility. It all sounds quite simple doesn't it when you say it quickly?

So that's what I did. I wandered down the country and I got down as far as a place in Northamptonshire. I saw a sign for a little village to the left, I don't know what it was called, and when I drive past these days, the sign isn't there any longer, but I always remember it began with the letter "J". So I drove into the village, and looked for a sign with '*B & B*' - I saw one. It was an old farmhouse-type place. I knocked on the door, a lady came to the door, and I said, *"Do you have a room for* tonight?" She said *"Yes, would you care to come and have a look, approve it, so that when you get back from where you're going to…"* I'd explained the full situation to her… *"You'll know what you're coming back to?"* So I said *"Yeah, that's fine. That's really good of you."* So, I followed her out, across the yard, up the stairs, above a barn or some building or other or whatever it was. When we get to the door, she unlocks it and we go into a room. Quite a large room, but very basic. Very basic indeed. It had two beds, a single and a double. And I said *"Yeah,"* because money was tight, I said, *"Yes, that'll do me fine. I'll see you later tonight."* I put my case down and I set off to go. She said, *"Just a minute. I have a question for you. Which bed will you be using?"* I said *"Why? Does it matter?"* and she said *"Yes. If you sleep in the single, it's £15 for the night and if you sleep in the double, it's £18 for the night."* So not forgetting my upbringing, I said *"£15"* and I slept in the double.

I carried on; I came back to the place with a "J". I had a meal. It was very nice. They had a son who I believe, if memory serves me rightly, was some sort of body-building fella, so I wasn't going to fall out with him. Next morning, set off, said, *"Bye-bye,"* never, ever went back. I went off to Birmingham to see a man who, over the years, did as much for Chris Burrows Lighting (that was the name of my business) than anybody else ever did. The value of his orders over the years, sixteen and a half years about in total, was… Well, I don't know, but it was a lot of millions. Let's put it this way, it was a lot of notes. And it was always a standing joke when I went to see him. Nice bloke he was, not in the best of health,

3

but a very nice man. I used to say to him... He had a picture on the wall of him shaking hands with Prince Charles at an annual Sikh dinner. And the standing joke was that I used to say to him, *"Who's the fella shaking the hand of Prince Charles?"* He always thought that was highly amusing. I never found out why. I didn't think it was particularly so, but he did and I hope you do too.

That little aside, that little whimsy comment, made me a lot of money and a lot of business over the years. A strange call, a strange place, but they're lovely people. They love their cricket, they love their football. They always want England to win except when they're playing India. I wonder why. I can't imagine why. He is a big supporter of Tottenham Hotspur. Tottenham Hotspur this, and Tottenham Hotspur that. Whether he's ever seen Tottenham Hotspur play at football, I haven't got the faintest idea, but Tottenham Hotspur are his team. His brother, who I didn't deal with much, but who I spoke to an awful lot, was a bit more local. He was in Birmingham and he supported Aston Villa. I learnt recently that his brother had passed away; a very sad loss.

He was <u>always</u> trying to persuade me, after the working hours, after I'd been to see him, to go to an Indian restaurant with him for a meal, for which he would pay, or so he promised. Now, anybody who knows me knows one thing when it comes to food. I don't like curry; I don't like the smell of curry and I don't want to go into a curry house. Thank you very much, it's not for me. But one evening, and it used to get well into the evening, the meetings went on and on so long, because he used to buy so much stuff, I had to give in and say *"Yes,"* and we walked across the road and down the street and we saw an Indian curry restaurant. Me not being very well up on the Sikh language, or whatever they speak, I was surprised to see the word *'Milan'* outside the door. And I thought, *"Well, there's a funny thing to do"* – name an Indian restaurant after a city in Italy. I couldn't understand that. And it was only many years later that somebody told me that apparently in their language, *'Milan'* means welcome. Anyway, I went in. I thought it was awful. Never been in one since and won't be going again, thank you. End of story.

Nonetheless, I thank him for everything he did for me and I wish him a long and very, very happy life; both for him, his son who is a very clever lad and his daughters... I think he's got two daughters. It showed me that there's no need for racism. I never thought of him as being black; it never even mattered... Never. It was only this curry thing that used to get me, but our next door neighbour eats curry and it's just as bad.

He was a lovely man; well he is a lovely man and I enjoyed, very much, his company.

At the beginning of the book, you'll have noticed that when anybody ever asked me to mention a couple of stories, well what I'll do, I'll slip them in every now and again, just when one comes to mind, shall we say.

But my favourite, such a favourite of mine... to me it was hilarious at the time. You may find it quite now;

I hope you do. I had a customer in Dublin, and I was going over to see him and coincidentally we got an enquiry from somebody else in southern Ireland, but not in Dublin, in Limerick. Now I'd never been to Limerick in my life, and I've never been since. So, I'd gone to see the customer in Dublin that we've got, did a bit of business, stayed the night in a hotel, get up the next morning and get on the train to Limerick. I think the station's called Heuston with an 'H' not Euston like it is in London, but Heuston with an 'H'. And I got on the train.

I'm telling you about such a funny day in my life. This was during the height of the troubles of course, in the north. And I got on this train in the south of Ireland and I'd gone into a newsagent because I was quite a bit early for the train, and I'd bought a Daily Mirror. I got on the train, and there were very few people on it when I got on it. But it turned out by the time we left, that it was packed.

The guard was walking around and he said to me, in of course, a very strong southern Irish accent *"Is that your newspaper?"* And I said *"Yes."* And he said *"Well I shouldn't let anybody see it because you might get shot."* Well. That encouraged me no end. I really enjoyed the journey. Of course, I did in fact enjoy the journey because this guard, he was a gem. He knew everybody on that train. Absolutely everybody. I'm sat at a table for four with three nuns. And these three nuns; who he knew as Sisters so and so and whatever their names were, were counting their beads or whatever they do. I'm sorry if

NOT FOR ALL THE TEA IN CHINA

I sound ignorant but I'm afraid I don't know the answer to what they do with them.

He came round, checking the tickets, and these Sisters gave him their tickets and carried on counting the beads. And he said, *"You don't need to count the beads Sisters... I think the driver knows where we're going."* Now – that I thought was hilarious at the time.

There was a woman across the way, she's got a little lad with her, she'd just apparently had another child, he knew, *"How are they all?"* *"What have you called the young baby?"* *"Oh, that's a lovely name"* et cetera, et cetera, et cetera. He knew everybody.

We got down to Limerick, well Limerick Junction to be precise. Got off there and then got on another... a little tiny train, into Limerick City. That's where the fun, well the funny bit, in my opinion, begins.

I come out of the station and I set off to see the customer; I can't remember his name; he was German. We never did any business; it was a complete waste of time going. Never mind. That happens a lot if you speak to salesmen. I go outside into the street; I haven't got my car with me, mind I'm on the train. I don't know where this place is. I'm going to Thomas Street in Limerick. I got to the taxi rank and I said to the taxi driver *"Thomas Street please."* He was a very decent, honest fella and he said *"It's only a couple of minutes away. It's not worth the fare. If you just look behind you, that's the High Street, you walk down there, five minutes, and you'll see it."* I thought that was a very honest bloke, he could have ridden me all around Limerick, charged me ten quid for it and I would never have known the better.

So I'm walking down the High Street or wherever it was called, and I see one of Limerick's finest walking towards me. Because I hadn't seen Thomas Street, I was getting a little worried. It was a little bit more than the five minutes that the taxi driver had described. The Irish... the local police – the Garda... I think that's the right way of pronouncing it, so he's coming towards me and I say *"excuse me, can I ask you something please?"* And of course, in a very, very, very broad accent he replied *"Yes indeed. What can I do for you sir? Are you over here on holiday are you?"* *"No, I'm here on business."* *"Oh I thought you'd brought the wife and kids"* and he went on and on and on. And all I'm trying to do is say to him *"where the hell is Thomas Street?"* Eventually he said, *"Well I'll have to be going"* and I said *"Listen I haven't asked you the question yet. Where is Thomas Street?"*

Now, if ever you've seen a fella turn round and know exactly what he's talking about, it was him. He should do; he's a local policeman. And he's looked down the street and he said to me – holding up his hand - and he said to me... and he started to count the fingers of his hand with his other hand, and he went... 1, 2, 3, 4 - on the left. And I thought *"Oh thank goodness for that. Thomas Street is the fourth on the left. Thank you very much officer, nice to have met you. Bye-bye."*

*"No! It's not the fourth on the left."* This confused me considerably. He counts to four and then he says it isn't the fourth. He said *"Oh, it's not the fourth; it's the one before…"* Now everything that I'd ever heard about the Irish and the way they are and the way they can speak flashed across my mind at that particular moment. I thought it was a gem. I looked at him, I don't know whether he meant it, I don't know if it was accidental, I don't know whether he intended to be funny or if it was just his way of speaking to anybody who asked. I had no real idea.

But he was right. It was the third on the left, was Thomas Street. So, if ever you are in Limerick and you're looking for Thomas Street, go down the High Street, five or six minutes, cross the road to the left. Don't take the fourth. Whatever you do, <u>don't take the fourth turn</u>! Because that's not Thomas Street; it's the one before.

While we're on the topic of Ireland, southern Ireland in particular, I always remember a friend of mine, a dear friend of mine who invited me to his wedding and it was in a town called – well I pronounced it Mulling-AR – I was told very recently that it is actually pronounced Mulling-A. My wife was invited too and we were all set to go off to Mullingar for this wedding.

Two or three days before the wedding (she'd spent a fortune on a hat and a dress and all the rest of it), was supposed to be, the hotel rings up that they'd booked us in to. *"Will you still be wanting the room on Saturday?"* *"Eh – yes, why do you ask?"* Well Jim, that's the bloke, my friend, had cancelled the wedding. *"Oh."* He'd cancelled the wedding and he never told any of the damn guests! He left the hotel to tell the guests.

So, we didn't go. If you want a happy ending, he married her many years later in a registry office ceremony. I think it was in Liverpool. Because I don't know whether they had registry offices in Dublin but it was easier to come here and do it. Strange. Strange fella. Strange people, the Irish.

The man never had any food in the house. He always used to ask me to stay overnight and I used to say *"you're very kind; you've saved me a hotel bill."* I'd say *"Well, we'll have a cup of tea"* and he's got the best bloody fridge in the world and the most expensive, but there was no milk in it. There was no nothing in it. There was never anything in it. There was never anything in it. Nothing <u>at all</u>. He had breakfast, lunch and dinner every day out, in a restaurant. Out in a restaurant. And he never put on an ounce. He's as thin today as he was then. And I'm not. If you follow me.

Ireland is a lovely place. Yes, it rains too much but the people are pleasant and nice and look after you. I enjoyed my time in Ireland, in the south.

In the north, hmm... a little different. I had one or two rather unfortunate experiences in the north which were all to do with terrorism and bombs and heaven knows what. I was once going to Belfast on the train from Dublin to see a customer and I said to him *"well I'll see you in the hallway of the station when I come off the platform*". "*No, no you won't. I'll give you the car number now*". It was a blue Ford something or other. So, I'm in the car park looking for him. I found him and I said "*why couldn't you come and...*" and I didn't realise, he was too frightened to leave the car. Frightened to leave the car alone because we might have been coming back to a car with a bomb underneath it. I wasn't exaggerating - and I'm not exaggerating.

We drove from the station in Belfast to his nice new warehouse on the outskirts. And there was quite a sight when we pulled through the gate, which was well... really well protected, barbed wire all over the place. Which was fine, but there was an absolutely crumpled, dishevelled blown-up mess of a van, his van, his delivery van, in the yard. And it looked relatively new – what was left of it. And I said to him well, "*So what's this?*", as you would. Because it's not something you see every day, or every year, or every lifetime either. And he said "*Well, the IRA blew it up last night*". "*Oh*". He said "*Now you can see why I just... I couldn't come to the railway station. They'd blown up the van, I wasn't having them blowing up me in the car.*"

So, we had a meeting and we did a bit of business and then he said, "*Come on, we'll go and have lunch.*" He was always inviting me out for lunch. And he took me somewhere, and as we were driving along there was this great big house on the left-hand side and it was absolutely ringed with troops. And I said "*who lives there?*" "*The local judge. The local judge from the High Court in Belfast, that's the protection he has to have, day-in, day-out.*"

We went for a meal and we came back out and you know you go to the door of the car to get in, and suddenly you find a man saying *"Oh, just a minute. Hang on."* He was on his hands and knees looking underneath. Other people were also coming out of the restaurant, on their hands and knees, looking underneath their cars. And they're all looking for bombs. *"Is this really going on in my country?"* And it was. And you understand why my wife was always, always concerned when I went to Northern Ireland on business. It was dangerous, and sometimes unpleasant.

I recall once, driving through this place called Cookstown, a strong... a very strong Protestant area - you could always tell from the flags. When I come back, I want to come back as a flag salesman in Northern Ireland, I'll tell you that. Cookstown is a strong... very, very strong Protestant area. I knew this because there were Union Jacks all over the place... and my customer, strangely enough, just on the outskirts of Cookstown was a catholic boy. I didn't care less. I only wanted to know whether he'd got any money to pay the bills. I wasn't bothered what religion he was. It never crossed my mind at all.

I remember, once... and the lad was called... Colin – Colm, that's right. Colm not Colin. And we were chatting about staff and I said to him *"is it difficult to get staff?"* Because it wasn't a big place and finding people that knew about the electrical industry wouldn't be that easy. He said *"Well, we've just appointed a new van driver."* *"Oh yeah, a new van driver, yeah. A local* lad?" "Well no, he lives fifty miles away." "Fifty miles away and he's your new van driver?" "Yeah." This look of incredulity must have spread across my face when I heard this and I said "Colm, do me a favour; tell me why you have to get a van driver from fifty miles away?" That would be like me living in Barnsley and getting a van driver from Harrogate, or even further away than that. There's no way.

He said "No, but we looked at all the addresses and we know the catholic ones. And so we had to get a catholic for the job." "Oh. Fine." I said "I never thought of that Colm." Never thought about it, never thought about it. But it was the world they actually lived in and probably still do now; it was the truth, if the truth were known.

I said earlier on, there were one or two sad occasions, and one example of that was outside his building. It was nothing to do with Ireland; it wasn't to do with the IRA or anybody else for that matter. Our meeting had gone on for quite a long time, it was about 6 / 6.15 in the evening when I came out and I'd got to drive down to Dublin where I was staying. Dublin from this place was two and a half hours maybe, but I wanted to stop somewhere to get a meal because I didn't think much to the restaurant in the hotel where I was staying. And I came out, got in the car and put the radio on.

I put the radio on and I'm listening and I can't believe a word that I'm hearing. And I thought this had happened in London until I realised that it had happened in France. It was the day Concorde crashed. And it told you the name of the small town in France, Gonesse, just outside Paris, where Concorde crashed. It may not seem significant to you now but to me then it was, because we were distributors; agents is a better word, for a small importing company and manufacturer north of Paris, near Charles de Gaulle airport. Gonesse was the town!!

And I heard the name and a shiver went straight down my back because Concorde had come down in the town where I had friends who were supplying me with goods on a daily basis – on a daily basis!!  And I'm sitting in the car there in Cookstown, and I immediately rang the number in France and got no answer. And that was a scary moment in my life. I ought to have thought better because of course it was half past 6 by now and that was half past 7 in Paris, in France. So, I ought to have thought better, but it frightened me.

The good news was, the day after, they rang up and said that they were all safe and well and the honest truth was that they didn't even know Concorde had crashed. They hadn't even heard it until one of the girls who worked there, her dad was a local policeman, rang up to see whether she was alright. And they'd never even heard it come down and you've seen films and newsreels – that's an old word for me – you've seen them all, and how they didn't hear that crash I will never know.

But thankfully, my friends were not among those on the ground who died.

I'm splitting Ireland and France up a little bit. I spent a lot of time in France as well but that's something I will come to further on. For the moment, from what I can recall... Oh no, I forget – there was another fella in a place called Bray, just to the south of Dublin. I won't tell you his name because he's one of the biggest crooks I ever met. But he had the oldest, tattiest warehouse jam-packed full of stock, that I have ever seen in my life. And the warehouse was falling to bits. They were all in tatty old clothes, really old cars; they didn't care tuppence about appearances of the building or of themselves.

I met the father in later life, found out that he'd got all the money and left... they'd got nothing and the sons are running the business for him. You had to go upstairs to get to the office, and there was a very creaky old staircase and one particular step gave you a sign that... or the thought in your mind that you may be about to descend downward in the world.

I'm a big lad and it scared me every time I went up and down those stairs. They always used to warn me and I always used to say *"But Tom..."* (His name was Tom) *"There's a simple answer..."* and with his usual Irish twang *"and what might that be Chris?"* and I said *"Well the answer's simple, get a builder and get the bloody thing mended man. Somebody's gonna get hurt, you're gonna get sued and you ain't gonna like it."* *"We'll do that."* he replied.

Well I went there for sixteen years, and sixteen years later they were still waiting for the builder to come and have a word with them. Obviously he had great difficulty in directions. But... that's the Irish for you.

And they were making a fortune. A lot more money than I ever made. But they wouldn't spend it. They wouldn't put the place right, at no price. And everybody who knew them laughed about it and thought they were mean and miserable and all the rest, but... they'll never alter. If they're in business now, and I assume they are, they'll never alter.

There were many other things that happened to me in Ireland that were funny... strange... different. It's only a few hundred miles across the sea but it's a world apart in terms of culture and the way people think and the way people act. Completely different. Completely.

# Chapter Two

I suppose before we go round this... Or start on this trip round the world meeting some weird and wonderful people, and going to some wonderful and weird places, really I ought to explain to you how, in a sense, it all began.

My father was from down south. Well, somebody has to be, as they say. He came up here to Yorkshire looking for work, and he found some work in Barnsley. Now Barnsley was a town, I'm reliably informed by people who knew him, and from himself, that he had scarcely heard of. Didn't know where it was, didn't know how to get there, but eventually he made it. He got a job working at a local school, not as a teacher, but just doing some plumbing work I believe. But he needed some digs, somewhere to stay, somewhere to lodge. He asked around and somebody said to him, *"Have you tried Mrs Birch?"* Well, it's funny in this country isn't it? You get somebody in front of you from 200 mile away, who's never been anywhere near Barnsley, and they turn round and say to them, *"Have you tried Mrs Birch?"* Well, heaven only knows how my dad would have known Mrs Birch. But anyway, he found Mrs Birch, and he went to the door, and he said, *"Have you got a room?"*

Now, it turned out that Mrs Birch, who became of course my grandmother, put up theatricals. There was a little local theatre called the Princess Theatre, and she put up theatricals, like comedians, and singers, and ventriloquists and acrobats, and all this type of thing, and they were usually there for the week and then they moved on to somewhere else. This particular week he had a bit of luck. When he went there, there wasn't anything going off at the theatre, so she'd got rooms to spare, and he asked could he have a room?

Now, I'm reliably informed that my grandfather-to-be, who had opened the door, didn't understand a word that my dad was talking about, sent for an interpreter. Now, an interpreter was somebody who was classed as having been south of Bawtry. Now, if you don't know where Bawtry is, then that's your bad luck and you should buy an AA atlas. But I'm led to believe that the person concerned actually had been as far afield as Newark. Now, anybody who'd been as far afield as Newark in those days, now they'd been about. Their opinions were worth listening to. They knew what they were talking about. They were the crème de la crème. Well, they wouldn't because they wouldn't have understood what I was talking about, but nonetheless they would have been the crème de la crème.

He stayed there, did a bit of work locally, and began to notice a rather attractive young lady was also staying there. But she wasn't staying there, it was Mrs Birch's daughter. Their Kathleen. In Yorkshire, you may not understand, but we call everybody *'our this'* and *'their that'*. It's a means of endearment, or it's supposed to be.

Now, '*their*' Kathleen was a good-looking lass, so I'm told, when she was in her 30s as she was then, and not married and with no children, and he took rather a shine to her.

Anyway, to cut a long story short, time went by, started going out with her, he ended up marrying her, and he moved them all to Leeds. He opened a little business in Leeds which grew to quite a considerable size, as the years went by, and then I turned up on the scene. I was born in Leeds. I don't admit it very often, but it's on my passport so it's very difficult to deny. But let's put it this way, when Barnsley beat Leeds at football, I'm usually the only one from Leeds that's laughing. To move on. He did well with his business and he moved out of town to a place near Wetherby. That's another one that those of you that haven't got an AA book had better buy it and have a look. Go up from Bawtry and it's on the same road, the A1.

Things went wrong with the business and he died when I was just twelve. My mother, well she was lost due to his sudden death, so she came back to Barnsley to her family. He had always encouraged me throughout the years that I did know him, which weren't many unfortunately. One thing I do believe very strongly, just going off the point a moment is a lad needs his father. He needs his father for advice and for help, and I grew up without it and I know what I missed, and I missed him a lot. We came back to Barnsley. My father always encouraged me to ask questions, talk about things, to talk to people and to like and to want to travel, and all my life, I've liked to do all those things. I've loved and loved and loved to speak to people, to know people, to find out about people, and to visit places, and to go places. It's the only way you learn. It's one of the guaranteed ways that you'll learn. That's why, when he died at twelve, I'd been to Rome, I'd been to Mannheim in Germany because he knew a German there who owned a big hotel called the Park Hotel. Still there, so I'm led to believe.

It was a big change for me to come back here because things here were more rough and ready. The lads in the school were a bit like my grandfather. He didn't understand my dad, and they didn't understand me. It's the old story of going home from school on the first night and mother saying, *"How did it go?"* and I said, *"Well, I don't know. I can't work it out, but there's a couple of lads in our class called Sithee and Sirree."* It's an old story. It's an old joke round here, but if you haven't heard it, well... there you go. You have now!!

As I say, he encouraged me to ask, to enquire and to visit and to travel. And that's why I think in later years I went into the selling game, which meant that I got to travel throughout this country, throughout Ireland, and then parts of Western Europe, France, Germany, Holland, Belgium et cetera, and Spain. And then eventually when I started my own business, the world became my oyster and I decided that I was going to go virtually everywhere. And what follows, or is going to follow, is a story of things, or loads of stories, of things that happened on those travels, because of those travels, and they will live with me forever. I hope you enjoy it. I hope you can put your own self in my shoes and understand what it was like. I hope you'll encourage your own children to be a bit more outgoing and ask about the world rather than ask about computers.

I don't know where we'll start. I'll give it a little bit of thought, pick a country, pick a time, and we'll take it from there.

# Chapter Three

The first time I ever went to Hong Kong was in 1997 or 95, I can't remember which. It's not important. I knew nothing about the place. Nothing about the place whatsoever. Well, it was still a British colony at the time. Patten, Chris Patten, the former Tory Minister, was the Governor. Within a year or so we were due to hand over back into the hands of the Chinese, which hasn't been a glorious day for the people of Hong Kong to say the very least. Anyway, never mind. Politics.

I went to a hotel, booked in, had a bite to eat, and got chatting to the bloke at the next table, who it turns out came from somewhere in Yorkshire. I can't remember where, and it's not really important for the purposes of this story. He said to me, *"Do you know that there is a Yorkshire Society in Hong Kong?"* and I said, *"No, I had no idea."* *"Would you like to go tonight? There's a meeting."* Well, I was tired. It had been a long journey and I was tired, but he was a very pleasant man. It was kind of him to ask me to go with him.

So, we went down... A very long escalator this hotel has got. Went down to the street level, got into a taxi. He had the address and he gave it to the taxi driver and off we go. Ten minutes' drive, we pull into a place and we were there. It was a flat green bowling club that they were obviously sharing with and I remember going in with him and we were greeted by somebody who was obviously in charge. He was a member, this friend of mine, this bloke I was with, and he introduced me as a guest. Perhaps there were 20 – 25 people in a sort of meeting room, and we sat down and we were all from various parts of the Broad Acres, and we sat and we chatted and we talked. We talked about politics. We talked about cricket. We talked about Geoff Boycott. We went back to cricket. We went back to politics. We talked about football. We put the world to rights. We went back to Geoff Boycott.

Eventually, the night came to an end. We'd had a few... He'd had three or four pints of John Smith's. I think they import it specifically for places like that in Hong Kong. And I'd had a couple of gin and tonics, followed by few glasses of rather nice French Malbec wine. Anyway, we get to about midnight, and apparently that's the witching hour. That's when they're all going to pull up roots and go home. The man who I'd shaken hands with when I came in, who was in fact the secretary of the organisation, stood up, microphone in hand, *"Ladies and..."* Sorry, not ladies and gentlemen, beg your pardon. Sexist organisation. No ladies at all, just gentlemen. *"Gentlemen, we will now have the national anthem and that will cease the evenings business,"* or entertainment or whatever words he chose to use. I thought, *"That's a bit of a surprise, the national anthem, but never mind."* I've got no feeling about the Royal Family at all. I just tolerate them. They're there and why not. Why and why not? Live and let live.

So we stand up and I'm waiting for, *"God save our gracious Queen,"* and all of a sudden on comes in full blast, *"Wheear 'ast tha bin sin ah saw thee."* In other words, they were playing *"On Ilkla Moor Baht 'at,"* which he called the national anthem. I can't argue with him to be honest with you. I thought he was probably right. Everybody sang quite gustily. We went through all... I think there are eight verses. I'm not sure. But I can promise you that before I went, and certainly now, I know all eight.

And back to the hotel for a few more... A little bit more lubrication shall we say in readiness for tomorrow's business. Never met the man again. Never saw him again. Only at breakfast the following morning, and then that was it, and gone, and finished, and if you ever get to read or hear about this, well, it was nice of you to take me out. I'm sorry I don't know your name, but it was a good night out. I had several good times in Hong Kong.

I remember getting there the first time and people had forewarned me about what it was like when you came into the old airport. The new airport wasn't built at this time. The old airport, which was called Kai Tak, and I've no idea what Kai Tak means... It's still there by the way. They've knocked all the buildings down and Kai Tak is now a driving school for bus drivers, for double decker buses. All the buses, by the way, are all double decker in Hong Kong, and I'm led to believe that the reason is that they import them all from this country. They obviously have to pass a test and they use the old runways because there's plenty of land, plenty of room, plenty of roadway, to teach the men to drive the buses. You can see it as you pass by in a taxi, because the buildings where passengers used to check in are no longer there, so you can see straight through into the driving school area.

I remember landing there, and people had said to me it's one of the hairiest landings in the world, but it's one of the safest airports in the world. And I knew what they meant the first time we went. We came in at such a low level, so near the buildings. Because Kai Tak airport was almost bang slap in the middle of Hong Kong. There you are, you're flying in, couple of hundred feet above the rooftops in some great big metal tube called an aeroplane, and if it hits anything, it's *"Goodnight Vienna,"* and that's the end of you. But I believe in all the years it was open, it never had a proper accident. I think once I did hear that they had a plane which overshot the runway and they had to tow it back before it... Because the front wheel was overhanging the water.

But that was the nearest anything came to a problem. They always used to say that you used to fly in-between the washing lines. In other words, you could see what colour knickers Mrs Chen was going to wear... Had worn yesterday or was going to wear tomorrow. It was so intimate and near. Everything was absolutely on top of you. When you came out of the airport, it was heaving with people. Absolutely heaving with people, and you've got to try and get a taxi to somewhere.

I remember one night coming back, about... I still think we were in control. I don't think Patten had gone at the time. When you got through the immigration and all the rest of it, the planes were so tightly packed it was unbelievable, absolutely unbelievable. You pick out which one is yours; you know the gate number and, you know, if you're there a few hours early, you can get a bite to eat or have a drink, or both. On this particular evening, I'd had something to eat and decided to go and have a drink afterwards round a bar, which was again very tight, not much room. Virtually out of the bar, straight onto the concourse, and there's the gates.

At the bar, the only seating was stools. Anybody who knows me will tell you I'm not best suited for stools, but I got on one. I managed to perch myself on one. I must have looked like a very large budgie on a very small swing, but anyway. I'm sat there and I'm minding my own business and a fella came up next me and he began chatting. Just everybody chatted at that time. Not like today. From his accent, he was French. I was talking to him, and he was a very interesting man to talk to, and I asked him what he was doing there, and he said, *"I've just been in to China."* *"Oh aye, China. You've been in to China have you?"* and on this particular visit, I hadn't gone beyond Hong Kong. *"I've been to China."* *"Can I ask you why? Is it something private? If it is, please tell me to mind my own business. If it isn't, just tell me what it was."* And he says, *"Yes, I've been signing up Chinese businessmen for the Moulin Rouge in Paris."* *"Oh?"* I was a little surprised because what I'd seen of China, or heard of China, the Moulin Rouge was a little bit racy for them, a bit risqué I think is a clever word.

And I said to him, *"Did you do well?"* *"Remarkably well. Signed up dozens at a couple of thousand quid a year for membership. When they come over to Paris, they can come in, they can watch the show, once, twice, three times in a day if they want. They can just stay there. They are members. I tell you what would be a good idea,"* he said, and he gave me his card, and on the card was his name, and I've lost it unfortunately. I seem to be good at losing things. Was his name, and underneath it said, in French but translated into English, *"Deputy Managing Director."* I'm talking to the number two in command at the Moulin Rouge in Paris, who is saying to me, *"Do you do any business in Paris?"* *"Yes."* *"Well, next time you're in Paris, come and look me up."*

Where are we? 2020 as I dictate this. Well, I haven't managed to go and see him yet and I don't know whether he'll still be with us, but... I never went, which was a very silly thing to do, and it's not long since I actually found the card and I threw it away to be honest with you. I threw it away and I never did take up that visit. But it was a very interesting story, very interesting man, and I could just see all these little Chinese fellas suddenly being confronted by these rather scantily-clad young ladies, prancing around the stage at the Moulin Rouge, and thinking, *"This is not much like China. This is not something we get at home."* A fascinating evening. Fascinating thoughts about the outcome and who would go and who... Tremendous, tremendously interesting man.

I had, in Hong Kong, to be serious, the most, well, how shall I put it...? Frightening experience, health-wise, of my life. I'd experienced some sort of pains in my chest, but typical man, done nothing about it. I'd arranged a trip to China (and then down to Hong Kong) two or three days before I was due to fly home.

# Chapter Four

I came out of the hotel that I was staying in to go by taxi to a very, very good Western Restaurant. It was about eight o' clock at night and it was still up to about 40°C, and the humidity was in excess of 90%. Now, this was too much for me. It really was. Anyway, I said to the porter fella, *"Here's a card, get the taxi driver to take me to this address,"* and off we set, bearing in one thing simply in mind, two things in mind, I don't speak Chinese, he didn't speak English. Away we go.

About halfway on the journey, I suddenly felt... Because I'd gone from the heat outside the hotel into the air conditioning of the taxi. I suddenly felt as if somebody was standing on my chest. It was terrible. I was scared to death. I thought I was having a heart attack. I wasn't, of course, but I thought that I was. I couldn't speak to the driver, so I had no alternative but to carry on as we were, just keep going, keep going and going, and get to the restaurant, go inside and see if things improved.

Well, I did all that, paid the driver, got inside the restaurant, and the guy who runs it is a very, very good friend of mine, Kieran Galway, they call him. Australian. An Aussie. Loves cricket. Loves his cricket. Absolutely loves his cricket. And, I went inside and he said to me,

*"You don't look at all well Chris."* I said, *"Well, you're spot on there Kieran. I feel absolutely lousy."* He says, *"Shall I get an ambulance?"* I said, *"No, get me a double gin and tonic."* And the double gin and tonic and the being inside in the air conditioned environment, helped me no end, and I came round, had the meal... Wouldn't miss my meal, wouldn't miss my dinner, and got through the evening with him giving me reminders of cricket scores and all the rest of it and how many times Australia have beaten England recently, just to rub it in.

But all the time I was having the meal, I was getting a little bit better. I was beginning to think about what happens at the end of the meal when I've got to come outside, back into the heat and humidity, and get a taxi back to my hotel, and it was really worrying me. I didn't need to have worried. I came back out and everything was okay, and I got back to the hotel.

A couple of days later, I took a flight home which again concerned me because I was thinking, *"What a journey! What if anything went wrong?"* But it didn't, and everything went okay, and I got home, but that was a frightening time. That was a scary moment. Earlier in the book I mentioned about putting yourself in my shoes. Well, put yourself in my shoes. You don't know what the hell's wrong with you. You feel as if it's heart attack. You don't know what to do. You're in a foreign country, 8,000 miles away from home. It's not easy. But I got home.

Another thing I can remember very vividly about the restaurant, a bit more cheerful this, as I said earlier,

Kieran is a great cricket fan, and whenever he knew I was going, he would put the cricket on in his office, on his computer; if England were playing Down Under, and of course as usual losing. He used to love to come out during the course of the meal and say, *"Ha-ha, another one lost. Another one out. Another one out. Another one out."* I don't know how many wickets we had. It's usually ten, but the way he told them, it was about 20.

But he was a great man, a lovely man. I hope he's doing well now. Interesting thing about him and I was that although we became very, very strong friends, he would never, ever call me anything else but Mr Burrows, until we got to about half past eleven at night, in which case he'd drop the mister and call me Chris, and he used to come to my table, which was always the same table, the bottom right-hand corner, where the Pattens' residence, the Governor's residence, was behind me over my right shoulder. He used to come to the table and we'd chat about things for an hour or so, and then I'd go and get a taxi and go to my hotel.

Funny thing was, his sidekick, his number two was called Ken. Now Ken was a Hong Kong lad, but he'd never been to China. I once asked him, *"Have you ever been to China Ken?"* *"No,"* was his very simple and quick answer. *"Do you want to go to China Ken?"* *"No,"* was again the same answer. He said, *"I am British. I have got a British passport. I was born in Leyton in East London. I am... That's where I go for my holidays and I don't want anything to do with*

*China.*" Well, that's telling it from the elbow, telling it from the shoulder. That really is being straight with me.

Interesting thing about Ken was, being Hong Kongese, he wasn't really into cricket at all, although they do play cricket in Hong Kong. But he was a great football fan. I don't know whether he was a football fan, or a fan of the football pools, which used to be quite a strong thing here, but I haven't seen much of it in recent years, but they still have the pools every weekend, on the English football that is, all the way through the winter months. Our winter months. It's their winter months as well. And, when... He knew I was interested in football and watched it over here. He used to come up when we got to half past eleven time when he could call me Chris, which I always felt very embarrassed about, but nonetheless, never mind.

My mother wouldn't have liked to hear everyone calling me Mr Burrows, because my mother always used to say, *"There was only one Mr Burrows, and that was your dad."* He used to come up and say, with a piece of paper in his hand, *"Can you give me your prediction for the results of these games in England on Saturday?"* and it would be, we would call it Division Three, what's it called these days? League One. You'd have really nothing else but guess work. I think the best I ever did out of the twelve fixtures that he composed as a weekend's list was four, so why he kept believing in me I'm not quite sure. But believe in me he did. I can only assume that he put a few quid on it based upon what I'd forecast, and based upon what I'd forecast, I think Ken must have come out of that a few quid poorer because I don't recall me getting many right.

I don't know what he does now. I know they've opened another branch in Hong Kong and I know he's the manager of it, but when I say I don't what he does know, I don't know who his football tipster is, but it certainly isn't me. That was Kieran and Ken.

# Chapter Five

Carrying on with Hong Kong, I remember going once across there, going to see a company, a customer... a supplier, by the name of Luen Yick. That wasn't his name, that was the name of the company. Ken something or other was his English name. I remember going to see him and oh, he was having a go at me about the standard of the hotel that I was staying at in Hong Kong, that I was paying too much. *"You're paying too much Chris. You're paying too much."* I said, *"Well, where do you recommend then?"* And he said, *"Well, just write this down and the next time you come, stay here."* And I wrote down... he got me to write down, BP House. BP, as in British Petroleum... House.

Well, I went home and the next time I was going out there, I said to my travel agent, *"Can you find on your computer somewhere called BP House in central Hong Kong and book me two or three nights?"* Three nights I think it was. And she says, *"Yes, I've found it. I've booked it,"* and out I go. Out I fly. I get out there and I get in a taxi and I say to the taxi driver, who spoke some English because the older ones certainly do. *"BP House please."* *"Where? Never heard of it."* I said, *"BP House, it's called. It's the name of a hotel, I'm staying there."* He said, *"Well I haven't ever taken anybody to a hotel called BP House."* As we're parked on the side of the road trying to find out where this place is, a policeman turns up and he says to this policeman, obviously in Chinese, Cantonese it would be in Hong Kong, *"This bloke here wants to go to BP House. I've never heard of it."* Policeman says, straightaway, *"Straight through the lights, it's on the left."* I didn't understand it, but I could see from the instructions, it was straight through the lights, which is Austin Road, and it was on the left-hand side. So we go.

We pull up at this very big building, probably seven or eight floors high, and he said... I looked and it said, *"BP House."* I said, *"Well, it's here. We're here."* I got out and said *"Thank you very much,"* and paid him. I went in and it still hadn't twigged on me what I'd done. I walked in and there was a great big statue in the middle of the hallway. It wasn't to Mao Tse-tung or Chiang Kai-shek, or anybody else for that matter. It was to Baden-Powell. BP stood for Baden-Powell. It was the name of a hotel named after Baden-Powell, who was the creator of the Scout movement, and everybody there was probably aged, at the most 24-25, and I was certainly in my mid-50s, and I was welcomed at the reception with the most strange look as to why a man of my age who was in business would be staying there.

Everything was awful really. The rooms were for children. The meals were getting hold of a tray and go around and pick up... get what you want, and that was about it. It was a very, very poor job. But, as whatchamacallit did tell me, it was cheap. It was very cheap. But it was extremely embarrassing to tell people who were other suppliers when they were saying, *"Well, where do you want to go back to in a taxi?"* when they were coming down to the street side to help you get a taxi, get back, *"BP House."* Nobody had ever heard of it, and I had to show the drivers all the time where it was.

If ever you're in Hong Kong and anybody recommends that you should stay at BP House, just bear in mind that BP has got nothing to do with British Petroleum or any other secret connotation of letters. It's Baden-Powell. It's for Boy Scouts, Girl Guides and those a bit younger. In other words, young students. A little bit of an embarrassment, but you live and you learn. I never went back, and I never will ever again I don't suppose. I've never ever heard anybody else ever speak to me and tell me that they've even heard of it, never mind stayed there. But I have. Three nights. Because I was booked in and I'd got to stay because, well... I didn't want to go round looking for another place. And anyway, I'd paid for it.

Hong Kong is a wonderful place. An old friend of mine once said about Hong Kong, and I believe he was very correct and true in what he said, that the British didn't colonise Hong Kong, they civilised Hong Kong. In many ways looking back, it's a pity we didn't get the rest of China and Mao get Hong Kong. It would be a better world that we are now currently living in, and maybe we wouldn't have Coronavirus for a start. But, yes, that's what he used to say. Frank his name was. We didn't colonise them, we civilised them. And I think he's right. I think he was true and correct.

The last few times that I went, prior to retiring, the Chinese influence was starting to take effect in quite a big way. The English spoken at the desk in the hotels was nothing like as good as it was ten years prior, and things were altering. If you have watched the television, it's all suddenly come out into the streets. They're being told what to do by the Chinese, they don't like it, and I think that, put a guess on it, 70% of them, and I don't think I'm being... I don't think I'm exaggerating here. I think 70% of them, given the opportunity, would come back to British rule and forget the Chinese. These two systems in one country, or whatever it's called, is most definitely not working. There is no doubt whatsoever that the Chinese are imposing their will on people who don't want it, and don't need it. Now you've got it in the streets, people are firing rubber bullets, and the next thing is going to be real bullets, and where are we going to end up? It will be a sad day, but Hong Kong, as I say, is a great place. It's a great place to go to. It's a great place to be in. And I loved almost every minute of the time that I was there.

# Chapter Six

Let's move on from the delights of Hong Kong to what I would describe as being the exact opposite. Certainly, I don't know about today because I haven't been for many years, but certainly when I went it was exactly the opposite. It's a European country. It's an ex-Soviet country. It's Latvia. Now, I went three times to Latvia, which as they say round here is three times too many. But, business is business. You go where it's available. They supplied us. We paid them. That was really the end of it.

There was a flight to Latvia, to the capital city, Riga. I don't know about now, but in those days it was from Gatwick, so it was a bit of a bind to get down there. It was about two and a half hours, I remember, the flight to Riga. I remember waiting at the gate, sitting at the gate at Gatwick, and there was a chappy there who I was talking to who was working for a British bank in Riga. He was a Scotsman. This was Easter time here, and the weather was quite nice, and the temperature was a reasonable 19 or 18, or something like that. I'd just gone in ordinary clothes. He was there in overcoat, scarf and gloves, and he said, *"Is that what you're wearing to go to Riga?"* I said, *"Yes."* He said, *"I think you're in for a surprise. I don't think you've done your homework about the weather."* I said, *"Well, it's not that far away. I didn't think it would be that much different."* He said, *"Well, I can promise you one thing. Different it is, in one word, cold."*

We get on the plane, and they're all very nice people. Jet off, off we go, and we land at the airport at Riga. I think it had three gates at the time. It wasn't very big. As we came into land, it was a beautiful sunny day. There wasn't a cloud in the sky. Sun was shining. And I thought to myself, *"This fella doesn't know what he's talking about."* Oh yes he did! The minute they opened the door of the plane and I walked down the steps, because there was no gangway thing, good lord! It was about three o'clock, four o'clock in the afternoon. The temperature was already minus something, two or three. It was cold and I hadn't brought anything to wear to compensate for the cold.

The people I'd gone to see met me outside this small airport. As I say, at the time... They may have a new one now. They met me outside this small airport. They roll up in this great big black Russian, because don't forget it was part of the Soviet Union, and the Russians had gone home no more than about 18 months before. I went with them in this great big black Russian, 20 year old it must have been, limousine-type thing. I'd booked into a hotel in the middle of Riga which had the imaginative name of the Riga Hotel. They took me to the Riga Hotel and I was just looking at the car as we were driving. What he was doing as he drove was obvious. Supplies were tight, of things like fuel.

What we did, we got up to about 40, 50 miles an hour on the way in to the city and as soon as we got to 45, 50 miles an hour, he threw the car into neutral and then glided along for heaven knows how long, until we got down to about 20, almost crawling pace, and then he'd put it back into gear and we got up to 40-odd again, and we kept repeating this exercise all the way into the middle of Riga. Anyway, he dropped me off at the hotel indicating there was no point coming in because he couldn't help me with the English, and when I went in the people spoke perfectly good English on the reception, and he would see me the following morning.

The following morning comes round, I had breakfast on my own in the restaurant. There was nobody else in the restaurant, only me!! My driver came back the next morning, and I noticed another thing about the car. In those days all cars had radio aerials. He didn't have an aerial. He had a twisted wire coat hanger stuck where the aerial would normally have been, but it appeared to work because the radio worked, in Latvian of course. Heaven knows what they were talking about, but nonetheless it worked. We went through the procedure again of getting up to 40 and then gliding along, coasting along, and doing all this until we eventually got to a huge factory. Bearing in mind this used to be part of the Soviet Union. This factory was where a lot of lighting was made for use in the Soviet Union.

So, we pull up at the gates and the gates were, oh they were decrepit. They were rusty. They were a mess. There was nobody on the gates. He had to get out to open the gate. There were no workers. I couldn't see anybody. We went through the gate into this huge area, and the first thing I noticed was all over the place, left, right and centre, were cats. Yes, I said cats. But these weren't ordinary cats. These were wild cats who simply lived, fed, and bred inside this factory compound. I was told when we got into the factory, by the interpreter who came, who was a woman, a very nice lady, not to go anywhere near the cats because they would bite.

We go into the building. We get in the lift and it chugs up to about the third floor and I meet Jānis. Jānis was the gaffer of the factory. He was the Latvian. He'd taken over. He was in charge. In the middle of his office, which was a big office, was a big table and round the table sat Jānis at the head, a man who was described to me as the sales manager, a man who was described to me as the engineer, the translator and me. Bearing in mind, they've all got their overcoats on because there's no heating in the building and I haven't, and I'm freezing. I am really cold. It's the only meeting I've ever had in my life where what we did was to walk round the table talking to one another to try and keep warm. We kept walking round and round the table. Couldn't ring him up, you know, from here because at that time, you know like the UK has an international code of 44, France is 33 et cetera, et cetera. Latvia had got its own internal phone system but there was no means of ringing from abroad, except, and this is how we used to contact him, we used to ring him up on a radio phone which diverted through Sweden to Latvia, a most strange situation. He sounded as if he was the captain of the Titanic two minutes before it hit the iceberg every time we spoke to him.

Anyway, we're having this meeting and we're all walking around and around and around, and the sales manager said something. I didn't know what he said, but it was translated, and it turned out that he'd said, *"Why don't we go into the city?"* and go to an apartment block that he knew, *"Go into this apartment block, get in the lift, go up to such and such floor."* He'd got the key to some apartment, some flat, and there was heating in the apartment or flat.

# Chapter Seven

There was heating in the apartment, a few chairs, very, very basic, nothing much, and I suppose a bedroom and a kitchen. Turned out that this was the place that when the Russians came to inspect the factory to see that everything was being done properly, they were probably KGB men I suppose, I don't know, never met one so I can't identify one, they were put up in this apartment in the centre of Riga, just off the centre of Riga, and for their entertainment apparently, according to my translator, a lady by the way, certain other ladies were introduced into their company during every evening. We'll carry on from that because you don't want to know about that. I'm sure you do want to know about that, but that's all I know.

We're sitting there and it is warmer. Considerably warmer. Well, anything was warmer than Jānis's office. That is an absolute fact. We're sitting there and we're talking, we're negotiating, we're talking, we're negotiating, and then the translator says, *"Jānis says it's time for lunch."* Well, over the previous fifteen or twenty minutes, the sales manager had disappeared from the scene into what I took to be the kitchen, and all I could hear intermittently after was chop, chop, chop, chop, chop. Chop, chop, chop, chop, chop. This chopping noise carried on for ages, and then eventually Jānis decides it's lunch time and we're going to stop and we're going to have lunch.

Now, I thought he meant we were going out to some sort of café, restaurant, McDonald's. I don't know whether they've got McDonald's, I've no idea. But no. Out comes the sales manager from the kitchen with three enormous great plates of cucumber sandwiches, hence the chopping. So we all got a share of cucumber. If you didn't like cucumber it was a bit of bad luck you were having. We got a mugful of... Hmm, how can one describe it politely? I think we'll call it black Russian tea, but it was hot. We had the tea, and we sat down. The bread was that awful black, browney, dark coloured stuff that you see on old movies, you know? Wasn't very tasty. Nothing about it was tasty. But when you're hungry enough, you'll eat almost anything.

We did a deal. We did a deal which in actual fact meant that that factory over there, the name of which escapes me, was going to supply us, and he did supply by sea. They came across to Immingham, I think was the docks that they came into, and then they were delivered to the firm I was working for at the time, and they were all actually intended for, a roundabout way of going about things, this was. They were all intended for the French market. They were going into a French supermarket store that I had come across many, many years ago and who wanted to buy what you would call bulbs which correctly in the trade are called lamps. Bulbs come from Holland and come up in the spring. Lamps are sold and put in people's houses. Not today they're not. You're not allowed to use tungsten lamps. So, we bought 60 watts, 100 watts and we bought the candle version of the same, in 25, 40, and 60 watt if my memory serves me rightly. Then when we got them to our place, we responded to the orders from France, put them onto our transport, our own wagon, and our wagon took the lot out to a delivery address in Paris and came back.

I don't know whether our friend Jānis ever found out where they were going, and it doesn't really matter, but he always got paid for them so I don't see why he should bother. But after three visits, he told me that they'd run out of money, and could we help. Well, I mean, you know, you're not likely to be thinking of putting your hand in your pocket to help out an ex-Soviet Union factory that's run out of money and wants to supply you. You're not sure, and you're miles off being sure, for certain, if you're actually ever going to see anything for your money in the rest of your days, so of course no was the answer. We didn't go any further. We found another supplier and carried on from there. But that was Latvia. I can't say much more about it. Cold in the winter, warm in the summer, and well, we did some business, but not a lot. Didn't enjoy myself very much there. It wasn't an appealing sort of place, and I doubt if it is now. Move on to somewhere else.

# Chapter Eight

One final thing about Latvia that I'd missed out earlier was I'd said that there were two people round the table, the walking table, during the negotiation, a translator and an engineer. I felt very sorry for one and not so sorry for the other.

The engineer was an ethnic Russian. He was of Russian nationality and had been put in there... Well, his parents, I found out later, his parents had been put into Latvia after the war when he was only a teenager, or maybe a little bit younger than that. Grown up, and of course in countries like Latvia which were within the Soviet Union, everybody, all the children, the Latvian children, had to learn to speak Russian, but he, as a Russian and a citizen of the Soviet Union, didn't have to learn to speak Latvian. There was a marked difference between the two communities, and of course there was a bit of detestation as time went by, by the Latvians of the Russians. The ones of Russian nationality, parentage.

Now this engineer, when the Russians went back to the Soviet Union, when the Soviet Union was collapsing and Latvia was made, as Lithuania was, and Estonia was, and very many other countries, all became suddenly independent, this chap was left behind with his family in Latvia. Bear in mind, he didn't speak Latvian. He only spoke Russian. He wasn't liked by the community, and I felt very sorry for him because it was of no fault of his own. He was a very clever engineer and he'd done well for the business. At least Jānis who ran the factory had the common sense to keep him on and to keep him as the chief engineer, because without him I don't think, well, I don't think the business would have been quite what it was. It wasn't much then, but it would have been even worse without him. He was, in fact, stateless. Wanted by nobody, least of all by the country he had grown up in.

The other one was the woman, the translator. Now, she was exactly the opposite in many ways. She was Latvian by birth, but she had grown up under the Soviet regime, and spoke Russian, as they all did. She was a clever woman, been to university. All this came from her. This isn't me making it up or creating it or assuming it. It all came from her, because I think she was just looking for somebody to talk to. You'll find out why in a minute. She jumped on the bandwagon, I suppose, of her knowledge and worked for the Russians as a translator and various other things, I'm not sure what, in Latvia.

She told me she had lived in a very fine apartment, all mod cons as we would say. Everything provided free by the Soviet government. She ate well, she went to the theatre, she did what she wanted. She was certainly head and shoulders above the average Latvian, and the average Latvian of course didn't really take to her very kindly. She told me that she used to go to Moscow once a month. They flew her over there and she used to go over and talk about various factories that she was translating for and what have you, and reporting back as to how their performance was going on. Suddenly for her, the Soviet Union ends and a Latvian regime, speaking Latvian, kicking all things Russian out of sight, like the engineer. I remember being told that he had no passport, either Latvian or Russian. The Russians didn't want him because he was just a bind and a nuisance and a load on their backs, and the Latvians didn't want him because they hated the sight of him.

Now, this woman, who was the translator as I say for me, she lost everything with the Soviet demise. She was living in a bit of a flat similar I believe to the one where we had the delightful cucumber sandwiches. She seemed quite at home in that sort of place. But, very bitter about the way that the Russians had deserted her when they'd gone back home at the end of their many, many years, decades of control. They didn't want to know her. The Latvians, well, she had very few Latvian friends because they'd deserted her because of her loyalty to the Russians, for whom there was detestation, a hatred, a dislike, use whatever word you like.

He, I felt sorry for. He suffered through circumstances. Her, no. She'd ridden on the back of her abilities to speak Russian and Latvian, and she'd got a good job, and she'd had a good time. She had had a good life under the Russians. She couldn't grumble too much when the people that she had oppressed, which were her own people, said "*We don't want to know you*", when things changed, and my word did they change. She couldn't really grumble too much, and I had little or no sympathy for her.

On the last day that I ever spent in Riga, this was in the summer. This was a lovely Sunday summer day. I was flying home on the Monday. There are only so many flights a week. It isn't a daily flight to Gatwick, or I think it's Heathrow now, but there isn't a daily flight. Baltic Airlines it was called. I decided that I'd come out of the Riga Hotel and very bravely, for me, have a wander around Riga, see what I could see. Well, there wasn't much to see at all really, and I eventually ended up in a park, sitting on a park bench, just taking it all in and observing I suppose is the word that you could use. Lots of local people with their children, having a nice time. I noticed in the corner there was sort of a monument, an old monument. I don't know who it was to because the statue had been pulled down. It might have been some sort of Soviet thing that they'd destroyed since their departure. But, the base of the monument area, which was quite large, was still there.

Suddenly, out of nowhere, out of the corner of the park, suddenly arrived a bunch of lads, oh I don't know, age group 18 – 23, 24, black shirts. Now, I'd heard of all this sort of thing, but I'd never seen anything like it, never really believed it existed. And there they were, dressed from head to foot in black, wearing some sort of swastika armband. It wasn't a swastika, but it was something which is obviously intended to be similar, and they were obviously extreme right wing. They were there and they were armed, and they suddenly turned up, one of them had got a microphone, or one of those loud hailer things, and he proceeded to tell us all how he was going to put the world to right in the next ten minutes. But, more importantly, I looked round the local people, whose attitude had changed from having a real nice day out to one of definite fear, definite fear of these men, these young men. They hadn't come in there to sell ice-cream and be friendly to folks. They were there to attempt to impose their views and the people in the park were too frightened to wander away, so they had to sit through it.

It went on for about half an hour, this tirade of nonsense from this lad, and these others were stood around him, military positions, all armed. Whether there was a bullet down the spout I don't really know, but I wasn't really wanting to find out, and I thought the best thing to do was to copy the Latvians and sit there and mind my own business and hope that eventually, and it did happen, that they would go. After about half hour, 45 minutes, I don't know, seemed like an age to me, and they wandered off, presumably to go somewhere else to give another soapbox-type speech. But the people in Latvia were... The people of Riga were in obvious fear of these gangs, and it makes you wonder, really, when you look back now and you think of it, did they ever achieve anything or were they, because of the advent of a democratic society, did they just simply wane, fall away, disappear and are probably now very well respected. Probably the local chemist or something. But that was the middle of Riga.

The following day was the day to come back home. Now, I told you about Riga, that it's not got the biggest airport in the world. This was, I thought, a very amusing situation. I think I said there were three gates. I was wrong. When I went back, I found out that this Riga airport had got two gates. Two gates. You imagine an airport with two gates. Even the little airport not so far from me at Humberside I think has got about six. But this had got two. I went to get onto the flight, went through and was just sitting around, and actually there was a door just to my right which had got *"One"* on it and two or three yard to the left, there was another door, a gate, with the number two on it.

Well, the London flight was going from number one, so I kept my eyes on the sign above number one, and it makes you wonder why these officials who have this authority do these things. They changed the gate from one to two. So suddenly, the sign above gate one said nothing, and the dead sign above gate two suddenly said *"London Gatwick."* No explanation given. The plane didn't move one inch, because it was the other side and we could quite clearly see it. Not the faintest idea, and I never will have, why they bothered to change the gate number. You know what they say about officialdom gone mad? I think that was a minor example of officialdom going insane. Anyway, we got on the plane, flew off and landed in London.

By the way, just on the topic of flights, if you are reading this and you are anticipating loads of scary times darting around the skies of the world, I'm afraid I'm going to be rather boring to you. I only ever had one funny moment, disturbing moment, strange moment. The rest of the time were absolutely conventional, boring flights, nothing happened, except a bit of turbulence, but you can't do much about that, and I haven't got any sort of, *"We were escorted in by Russian jets, or Chinese jets, or whatever,"* stories to tell you.

The only one I can tell you which did put fear of God up me to be honest with you, and the only other bloke on the plane, I think, who saw it. I was in China… We'll come to China much later because it's far too big a thing, but this happened in China. I was flying down from a city called Ningbo. Now, Ningbo is five times the size of Birmingham and nobody in Britain has ever heard of it apart from one or two loons like me who have actually been to it 40 or 50 times.

I went once and I took a customer with me from Folkestone, a man from Kent. I don't know if he's a Kentish man or a man from Kent. There is a difference isn't there? Something to do with the River Medway. I'm sure people will write to me and tell me what the difference is. I can look it up for myself I suppose. I took Graham, Graham Allen his name is, with me, and we went to Ningbo and we did our business, and on the way back we get back to Ningbo airport, which is a very nice, modern airport, reasonably-sized place, but very simple to get through. Much more simple than most airports.

Fascinating thing, you know, about Chinese security. You know when you're here in the UK, or any other country that I've ever been to, to be honest with you? You know when you go through this gateway thing and it beeps and all the rest of it if you're carrying a Kalashnikov or whatever they're called, or you've got a ten-bob piece in your pocket, I don't know, that you should have put into the tray? When you go out the other side, if you've beeped, you're frisked by a person with a wand... Can't think of a better word. Wand-type instrument from head to foot, up and down. Everywhere. Now, here, a man frisks a man, and a woman frisks a woman. In China, they don't have that rule at all. It's the first one to you who frisks you, and I have been frisked by some of the ugliest women in China that you can possibly imagine. Don't think it is anything of a sexy or exciting experience. It is an absolutely awful, dreadful, embarrassing experience. None of them ever found anything that's of any use to them, and I've been waived through. Not with a smile, good God, smiles cost money in China. No, straight through.

Anyway, Graham and I get through this particular day and we go in the lounge and we get our free, what's it called, can of 7-Up or something like that. We're told we just wait for the plane to be announced it's going to leave in half an hour. The plane took off. We're on this Hong Kong-based airline, called Dragon Air, and we've got a two, two and a quarter hour flight down what in China is called the east coast route. That's the Beijing, Shanghai, Hangzhou, Ningbo, Wenzhou flights all going down to Hong Kong, and they all follow the same route. There's only one trouble with that. If there's any delays to one flight, there's delays to all the rest of them. We sat on the plane, I would think, 45 minutes before we were given eventual clearance to taxi out to the end of the runway and to take off.

Off we go, and we've been up there an hour, 30,000 foot, above the clouds, sun's shining, the lot. People are reading newspapers, the English language newspapers which are provided as well as the Chinese of course. I think we were the only two foreigners on the flight. We were certainly the only two Brits, that is a fact. And Graham and I just happened to be glancing out of one of the windows to our right, when suddenly coming from our starboard side of the airline, was another Airbus, zooming straight, almost straight towards us. Well, that suddenly zoomed upwards and we dived down to the port side. Nobody at all, other than Graham and I, batted an eyelid. Nobody saw it.

It was definitely, and should have been put down as, a near miss, because by gum it was a near miss. We weren't very far apart, and at the speed that they're doing up there, we were very grateful to get on and get out of it. We carried on. Nobody seemed to notice. Nobody said a word. Carried on and landed in Hong Kong, and that was that. But I remember it to this day, and I know full well that Graham does. That was the only... And for the amount of flying that I did, I was lucky. That was the only incident-type thing that occurred in the whole of my flying experiences.

I must say that the timing of flights in China is appalling. They give a time, but it seems to just go when it wants. Whenever there's a slot, you get in it and off you go. Most of the pilots seem to resemble Biggles, if you remember Biggles as a cartoon character, and also a character in books, which I used to read as a kid. They all look like Second World War, Biggles-type pilots.

They all looked alike. Apart from Dragon Air; where Dragon Air was completely piloted, if that's the word (if there's such a word in the English language) by Brits, New Zealanders or Australians.

While we're on that topic, let me just tell you one quickie. I'm on my own this time, doing the same flight, Ningbo to Hong Kong, and it was just after (sorry to bring up cricket again), just after England had won the test series to retain the Ashes, or to win the Ashes, can't remember which, against Australia. I get on the plane, not thinking about cricket, just thinking about getting down to Hong Kong, the restaurant I was going to for a nice meal that night. We're flying along and the pilot came on and I can only assume he was talking to me and nobody else because I was, as far as I could see, the only non-Chinese or Hong Kongese, I don't know. He just gave the up to date report, we were at 30,000 and what have you feet, we were now flying over Wenzhou or somewhere, and we'll be landing in Hong Kong in about an hour and a quarter.

I beckoned the purser lady to me and I said, *"Excuse me, the pilot who's just been speaking, is he Australian by any chance?"* and she said, *"Yes, why?"* I said, *"Oh no, no particular reason."* Bearing in mind England had just beaten Australia and won the Ashes. I said, *"You wouldn't happen to have a piece of paper would you? Just a small piece."* *"Yes."* She went off and brought me back a little piece of paper, and I had a pen in my pocket. I mean, a salesman without a pen is useless. I had a pen, and I wrote on the piece of paper, *"Can we play you every time?"* folded it up and said to the purser, *"Would you mind giving that to the pilot? The one who made the announcement please."* And she said, *"Yes,"* and she looked at me rather quizzically, but no matter, she did it. I saw her... I mean in those days the security wasn't like it is now. I saw her open the door, tap him on the shoulder and give him this piece of paper, which he opened and read, and she came back. Nothing else happened and I thought, *"Well, he's a busy man. He's got to get this damn thing on the ground in Hong Kong. He's got a lot on his mind."*

About half an hour later, she came back with a piece of paper from the pilot. She said, *"Captain whatever his name was has sent you this."* *"Thank you very much."* I opened the piece of paper and as true as I am sat here riding this bike, he'd written the word, *"Bollocks,"* on it. I'm sorry to use such language, but that's what he'd written. When I got off the plane, I expected him to be there meeting and wanting to have another crack at me or something, but no, he just stuck in his cabin up the front and I never saw him ever again.

Oh, one other time up there as well, on the same route... I could write a book about this route. About half an hour from landing, I decided, *"Oh, I think I'll go to the toilet,"* because when you get down to Hong Kong airport, oh, anybody who's been, well any of these big international airports, it's heaving with people and I've got a briefcase and I'm very, very concerned with the briefcase about going into a gents' toilet, putting it down, somebody rushing in, snatching it, grabbing it and, well, off they go with a lot of my valuables including my passport.

This particular time, I went to the loo and it was locked. I thought, *"I'll hang on a second. It might not be long that I have to wait,"* and it wasn't. It was only a moment or so and the door opened and it was the First Officer, the co-pilot, whatever you call them, I don't know what the official term is. He came out, and he was a western lad, and he said something like to me, *"Sorry to have kept you waiting."* It became quite obvious immediately from the way he spoke to me that he was a Lancastrian. You know, you could just see him saying, *"Over there..."* You could just see him saying that. Or hear him saying that. Of course, rather than miss out on a good little story, a good little tale, a good little something or other, I said to him, *"Oh you're from the north of England then obviously."* *"Yes,"* he said, *"And where are you from?"* and I told him. And I said *"And you are from where?"* and he said, *"Bo-lton."* I know it's difficult to put an accent on a piece of paper, but he said, *"Bo-lton."* And I know I shouldn't have done this, but you know, when you're a devil, and I am a bit of a devil at times, you can't resist it can you? And I said, *"Do you know, I never knew they let Lancs fly aeroplanes,"* and disappeared into the toilet. I never saw him again either. But, decent airline, Dragon Air; only flies round the south of China.

But, yes. I'm afraid those are about my only airline stories that I can think of right now, or want to tell, and certainly the one of the near miss is the only daredevil one that I've got. The rest of them are extremely boring journeys with not much to talk about and not much to say and not much to relate to you.

# Chapter Nine

Having finished the story of Latvia, instead of having a change, let's stay in Eastern Europe. And this was a place called Slovakia. I could finish – start and finish the story quite simply by saying, never ever again and full stop. But what happened was so bizarre, so weird and so strange, I think it's worth relating to you.

There is a very, very large lighting factory in Slovakia in a town called Senica. I'm sorry about the pronunciation, but it's as good as you're going to get from me. And I wanted to have a word with them about maybe becoming their agent in the UK, if they hadn't already got somebody or if they didn't believe in agents or whatever. Anyway, I got in touch with them and they asked me to go across to Senica. Well, I had planned a visit to a supplier not so far from Lyon in France. Then I was going across into Southern Germany, across the Bodensee or Lake Constance, I think it is. I think the French call it that – and then come home. But I looked at the map and thought, *"Whoa, from there, I could drive through Austria and the next country is Slovakia."* And so that's exactly what I did. And what I decided to do, because I wasn't too sure on the monetary side, I decided to ask the people in Senica to book me a couple of nights at a hotel, which they did. There was only one hotel in the town, so I didn't have much choice. Pretty basic it was, but nonetheless it was clean and that was all right.

I wasn't sure about the monetary system. I didn't know whether it was euros only or whether you had to get Slovakian money. It turned out at the time, they were taking both and thereby starts my downfall. What I did, because I wasn't sure about whether they were taking credit cards, you never know with some of these smaller countries, these ex-Soviet countries. You just don't know. So what I decided to do was to take quite a few pounds, maybe 700 or 800 euros and when I got to the Slovakian border with Austria, I went into the bureau de change and changed... I think it was, yes I'm sure it was, £15 worth of euros into Slovakian currency. Now, I only got £15 because I was assured that everywhere I went they would take euros.

I drove on through pretty miserable countryside really, nothing to talk about, nothing to shout home about, nothing to tell you about. And eventually came to Bratislava, the capital, which is very near the Austrian and Hungarian borders. There I joined a motorway heading north-west and eventually came up at an exit which said Senica and drove into Senica. Found the hotel without much trouble because it wasn't a very big town. I booked into the hotel, rang the man who was my contact and he came round the following morning and picked me up and we drove in his car, leaving my car at the hotel. Nothing much happened in the business negotiations. It turned out that... it was a bit of a waste of time, to be honest with you. But nonetheless you get that in sales. You can't win 'em all. It happens. Some you win, some you lose and this one was a loser.

So after two nights, the next morning, I get up. I paid the bill with a credit card. So I've got all this money in my pocket. Keep coming back to this topic. There are all these pounds and euros in my pocket. I hadn't spent a penny in cash. Paid the bill with a credit card and set off driving back towards Bratislava and hence I was going to go on into Austria and home. To be honest what I was doing, I was leaving on a Thursday to get the Friday night ferry from Rotterdam to Hull for the sole purposes of getting back to Barnsley to watch Barnsley play Brentford on the Saturday afternoon. As the story unwinds, you will find that I never had the delights of seeing the glorious 0-0 draw that was played out at Oakwell because I wasn't even in the UK, let alone get back to Barnsley. I got back on to the motorway and was heading off down towards Bratislava and then when I got on the outskirts my intention was to take the sign towards Vienna and just keep going until eventually I would stay somewhere overnight and the next day head on and get onto the ship and that was that.

About ten or so miles from Bratislava, I saw a sign for a service station coming up and I thought, *"Mm, I've got 15 quid's worth of Slovakian notes in my pocket which are absolutely useless to me and I don't really want to be bothering about messing around changing them when I get back. I'll pull up. I don't really need any fuel, but I'm sure I can squeeze 15 quid's worth in and*

*that'll get rid of the Slovakian money and I'll carry on."*
So I pulled in. Very modern, very new, very posh. Sold
absolutely everything. You didn't serve yourself. A
little old fellow came rushing out and I showed him the
15 quid's worth of whatever they were called and I said,
*"Just use... fill it up,"* and he understood enough to do
that. So while he's putting this £15 worth of petrol in, I
went into the service station just for a wander round,
see whether they'd got any sandwiches or anything like
that. Just something to eat which I could stop at a layby
somewhere and eat and what have you. And I did that
and he came in and he told his boss man behind the
counter that he'd finished how much he'd put in and
I went to pay the man behind the counter. Took out the
wallet with not much care really or attention as to what
I was doing and he could quite clearly see that I in
Slovakian terms had got a small fortune in my pocket.
I paid him the Slovakian money. Actually the bloke had
overdone it a little bit, so I had to give him a few euros,
which was even another step towards my downfall
because he saw that I'd got several... almost a thousand
euros and I had to give him another 20 or so just to get
the bill right. Got back in the car, set off.

I'd been going only perhaps 15 minutes when I got on to
the motorway to go towards Vienna and I'm tootling
along, nice afternoon, not a care in the world really,
apart from the normal ones that a businessman has
about his company and what have you. And all of a
sudden on my inside, because obviously they drive on
the right-hand side there, on my inside a little old
banged out something or other came racing up, two
lads in it and sounding their hooter at me to attract my

attention. I looked to the left and I saw these two and one was quite clearly trying to indicate to me from the hand gestures that he was making, that I had a flat tyre. Well I had no inclination of a flat tyre, because you know when you're driving along and you've got a flat tyre, the damn car starts to bump, bump, bump, bump, bump, all along and you have to pull up, but I hadn't had any bumping sensation. That's the limit of my car mechanical knowledge, by the way – bump, bump, bump and we've got a flat tyre. I thought, *"I don't know where it is because I haven't got any problem. The car's running perfectly normally for me."* But you know what it is, you always believe what people indicate to you.

So I pulled up onto the hard shoulder and he pulled up or they pulled up, the two of them just in front of me, a few yards, five/six yards in front of me. Came to my window, which I'd wound down, and he said... he indicated quite clearly there was something wrong with one of the tyres. So I thought, *"Oh I'm going to have to change the tyre."* So I got out and he indicated to come with me and look at the back rear driver's side tyre.

Well he's got me down on my hands and knees looking at this tyre; this perfectly healthy, normal, nothing wrong with it tyre, and I'm thinking I don't know what I'm looking at, but I can't speak to him because he didn't speak any English or he didn't let on that he did. I don't know whether he did or he didn't. And his pal, his friend, who I hadn't taken much notice of, went round to the other side of the rear of the car and when I'm on the floor looking at this perfectly good tyre, I can suddenly hear a hissing sound. And that's when the alarm bells started to ring. It had become quite obvious to me within seconds that our friend at the other side had got a knife. He'd punctured my other tyre. He came round to my side of this car. I stood up with his colleague. They put the knife to my throat/face, whatever you want to say and said, *"Watch and wallet or knife. You've got the alternative."* This was quite... they didn't say it in English, but it was quite obvious, the alternatives.

So I thought, well, you know, hmm, discretion is by far the better part of valour, so I gave him my watch and I will tell you this truthfully, I have never to this day worn a watch. I have always had the attitude that if somebody's going to pinch one, they've pinched one already and they're not going to pinch another, and I have never had a watch on my wrist to this day. And of course I put my hand in my back pocket and gave them the wallet and they knew full well that there was a load of money in there. The good tyre was then knifed as well, meaning that both rear tyres were flat and I was lumbered. They ran off, got in their little car and sped away over the hill. I rang my office. I had a hands-free unit in the car. I rang my office in Barnsley, told them to get in touch with the factory in Senica and tell them what had happened, tell them to get some help to me – the police or something, I don't know, and I would wait there and see what happened.

Well, over the next hour, four police cars turned up, each with one officer in, just one officer. Four police cars each with one officer turned up to see whether

I was alive, kicking or dead. Nobody spoke any English. I didn't speak any Slovakian and gradually one by one just leaving one at the end, they all disappeared. Eventually, about another hour later, the people I knew from the factory where I'd left the hotel that morning, arrived and they were very apologetic and very sorry and very sad and all the rest of it, and they had been told... they'd bought two tyres and they'd put them in the back of their car and they changed over my two flat tyres there and then on the hard shoulder, on the spot with the policeman watching. The policeman then insisted that we go into Bratislava to his local station and make a statement about what had occurred. I wasn't too bothered. I just thought I want to go home personally. But there again, I had no credit cards, I had no money, I had nothing. And they said to me, *"Go in there. We'll come with you. Make a statement. We'll all go back to Senica..."* where we started from at the beginning of the day, *"...and tomorrow we'll give you some money,"* which was 500 quid, which was very kind of them, *"...and we're very ashamed that this has happened in our country."*

Well, I've not been in many police stations in my time, I'm very pleased to say, but of all the ones that I have been in, this is the tattiest place I've ever seen. It was awful, absolutely awful. And there was a guy there sat with an old typewriter, something like my mother used to use when she worked for my dad in Leeds in the middle 50s. And I'm telling the Slovakian factory people the story. They're telling a policeman in Slovakian. He's typing it all out with one finger and the clock's going round and round and round and it's getting very late in the day. I'm hungry, I've had nothing to eat and all the rest of it. And eventually we get out into the two cars and I've got to follow them in the dark back to Senica. Well they wanted something to eat, so we had to pull in to a McDonald's. We went into a McDonald's, I remember that. We had something to eat in McDonald's. I think they call it food, but I think it's a rather loose name personally. And we drove back to Senica.

Now, when we got back to the hotel in Senica which I'd left that morning, the look on the face of the boss man who was still on duty had to be seen to be believed. He must have thought that I loved his hotel so much, I couldn't bear to go home and I'd come back for another session, not quite the situation but nonetheless there I was. They said, *"We'll see you in the morning."* Fine.

Morning comes along and I'm sitting in the hotel having my breakfast. I remember vividly – two boiled eggs and some soldiers. Even at my age I was eating the soldiers. And my mobile rang with an unknown number. Mm – and I was rather doubtful in view of what had happened the day before about answering this, but anyway I did. And a voice said to me – a man's voice said to me, *"Is that Mr Burrows?"* and I said, *"Yes, how can I help you?"* And he said, *"Well my name's Perry."* I'll never forget his name. *"My name's Perry and I work for the British Embassy in Bratislava and it's come to our attention through the Bratislava police that you were almost assaulted yesterday, but definitely robbed."* And I said, *"Yes, that's quite true Mr Perry."* He said, *"Well we're just ringing up to see that you're all right because you never know in this world what might happen."* And I thought, *"Oh that's cheered me up no end."* He said, *"You do know, it was only a couple of weeks ago since that fellow in…"* He mentioned a town in Lancashire, *"…had his head chopped off by…"* I thought, *"Oh good God, please don't keep cheering me up so much Mr Perry."*

And he said, *"Well anyway, I'm glad that you're all right and I'll ring you roughly this time tomorrow, just to make sure that you are progressing on your way back to Barnsley."* Well I'm still waiting for that 'this time tomorrow' call. It may be coming at any minute, I'm not sure. It's only about 18 years ago. Anyway, he never did ring back. And I paid the hotel again and the people at the factory came back to make sure I was safe and to shake hands and wave me bye-bye and wish me good luck on my way home and say, *"We look forward to seeing you again."* And I thought, *"Well I wouldn't look forward to it so much because I've made my mind up that I am not coming back here ever,"* and I never did go back.

This time I followed my same tracks as I'd done the day before. Went past the same petrol station, not buying any more petrol and drove off. And with my 500 quid in my pocket in euros that is, the equivalent of, and I'd arranged with my assistant in Barnsley to book me a room at Frankfurt Airport, the Novotel. No particular reason, except the fact that I know I was driving past it and therefore… because I'd seen it on the way out and so therefore to save time that evening, I'd know exactly where I was going to.

So I re-traced my steps, got back to Frankfurt, parked my car, went to the reception and of course because I hadn't got a credit card or anything like that, even though I told them the story of what had happened, they were having none of it. They just said, *"Right, you've got a room. It's so many..."* Well, I don't know, say 120 euros for the night. And they held out their hands and I had to give them 120 euros. The restaurant was closed. I said, *"Can I order something on room service from the room?"* *"Yes of course you can."* So I went up to the room, looked at the room service menu. Ordered something. I know it began with tomato soup because, well there wasn't anything much particularly appetising I fancied. So I think I had tomato soup and some sort of beef something or other. But they wouldn't bring it in the room when they came up to my room with the food, until I'd paid them again because obviously I hadn't got a credit card and they'd been told not to leave any food with me until I paid. So I paid and I ate it and I got up the next morning, had my breakfast, got in the car, drove on to Amsterdam, which was quite a hefty drive and got on the Saturday night ferry, by which time I already knew that the epic at Oakwell had ended 0-0 and came across to Hull. And then I drove home.

I can't say too much about Slovakia because that's the only experience, except don't go to Senica. If anybody tells you you've got a flat tyre, oh no you haven't, just ignore them and keep going.

A few months later, I'm at home one afternoon and Royal Mail had been and there was a card telling me to hurry myself down to Barnsley sorting office because there was something of extreme importance for me waiting there. So off I go, parked up opposite the sorting office, when I shouldn't have done, but I thought, *"Oh to hell with it."* And I went into the sorting office with my little card and the bloke came back with an A4 size envelope – a flat envelope. And I looked at it and the postcode was Bratislava. And I thought, *"Oh they've got my money back. They've got my wallet. They've found out about…"* I got in the car, I opened the envelope and I looked inside and all it was, they'd sent me a translation of what he'd typed with one finger, but this time in English. I felt so reassured at receiving that. It was so reassuring and gave you confidence to carry on the following day.

# Chapter Ten

I've never really seen the great attraction of Spain as a holiday place. On the occasions that I've, of course, been to Spain, it's been to Barcelona and to, more often than not, Madrid. And I always found that flying in, particularly when you're coming in to land, over all that brown, barren land, which has been scorched by the never-ending sunshine, that's got an appeal to many, but not to me. So Spain has never been a place that attracts me an awful lot. But I had a brief encounter into Spain, and I say brief because I only got about a mile in, if that, into Spain on this occasion.

It was my intention to go to a lighting-come-security exhibition in Madrid one year and to take with me two things. One was a brand new product which we had recently designed which was an outdoor infrared detector, which if, as I've said before, the inside one was ugly, this was even uglier, but there again it wasn't my doing. And the other thing to take with me was our managing director, a man called Tony Stewart. Now Tony has been a friend of mine now for too many years to remember, but I suppose it's in excess of 40. I remember the day I met him and I remember a great deal about him. And on this particular occasion he decided to come with me to Madrid. But we decided we didn't want to fly. We wanted to go somewhere differently.

So what we did, we drove down to Dover and we took the ferry to Calais and then the train to Paris and then we were going to go – Tony had read about this train somewhere – take this overnight sleeper to Madrid. And we wanted to go on this because the purported conditions on the train were excellent and the restaurant was even better. Well, we got onto the ferry at Dover without anything going amiss, but as we got out into the middle of the Channel, the fog started to descend towards the French side. And by the time we got near to France, as we hoped we were, we couldn't see... you couldn't see if you went out on deck, your hand in front of your face. It was an absolute pea-souper.

It took me back to wartime movies of Jack Hawkins and John Mills running around in a sweater and a pair of cut-off wellington boots shouting, *"All men overboard,"* or whatever they shout when it's time to ditch the ship when it's been torpedoed. And I'll swear the first time that we knew we actually got to France was when we hit the harbour wall, with a gentle bump at Calais. Well they bussed us from Calais to the – those without cars – they bussed us from the docks at Calais to Calais-Ville, that's the railway station in Calais and then we got on a train. No TGV high-speed trains in those days. We got on a train which took us down into the Gare du Nord in Paris.

Now on the ferry, because there wasn't a lot to see, we'd had a fair bit to drink. I think that's probably an understatement – a fair bit to drink – but we weren't driving. We weren't bothered. We were just going down to Paris, so it was another train and we piled onto this other train and we sat in these two seats. Everything had been arranged by a travel agent, even the seat numbers. And we sat, not next to one another literally, but next to one another with the aisle in-between us. And off we went down to the Gare du Nord, the north station in Paris. Every so often as we're going down at a not particularly great speed, 50, 60, 70 at the very best, a young lady came up and down the corridor in-between us pushing a trolley.

Now, with it being France, it was a bit difficult to get through to Tony that France was different to us. They didn't speak the same language for a start. But my French is more than passable. It's quite good actually. I've even been mistaken for a Belgian, which when you're British, is quite a compliment. This young lady was going up and down with this trolley at regular intervals and from what I could gather, from what I could see, there was one per carriage. So you got passed up and down quite often – very often. And she was carrying the ham sandwiches which they love in their baguettes and their ham and their cheese baguette sandwiches and their tuna sandwiches and all the rest of it. Cans of Coca-Cola and other soft drinks.

We weren't at that stage very much into the soft drink category. We were into whatever alcoholic came out of a bottle. We weren't going to tackle French beer, not that it really mattered to me because I don't like beer of any description, to be honest with you. So we were onto the wine. And she kept coming down and as she passed on each occasion, well more often than not, held out the glass and had yet another drink of some sort of red plonk that they were flogging on SNCF. That's the French for British Railways. Société Nationale des Chemins de Fer is actually the translation of it, but I won't be big-headed by saying that.

And Tony, he'd had a few. He won't like me to say so today, when he reads this, but my word, he'd had a few. And I was carrying, fortunately, all the money. I was carrying all the Francs and I was thinking to myself, as best I could, that I'd got to keep reasonably sober. Not overly sober – no point in that. We'd still got one devil of a long way to go to get to Madrid. But one thing that had escaped Tony became clear when we got about half an hour from Paris, when the young lady came round for the last time, and after the last time pouring the drinks, she asked for the money. Now this surprised my erstwhile managing director somewhat, who, when I paid the girl quite a considerable amount of Francs actually, he thought it was for free. Well, there's not much for free in this world and there certainly isn't the drinks on French railways. We get down to the north station, waddle down the platform, go to the taxi rank. I'd been many a time to Paris on business. I knew exactly where everything was. Get in a taxi. We asked for the Gare Saint-Lazare. Now Saint-Lazare is the station which takes trains down to the south-west and of course Madrid is basically going overnight south-west of Paris and it's a fair, old journey.

Got into the station, a very, very, very big, very impressive Victorian-type building, but the one thing that was missing and missing in their droves was passengers. I couldn't understand why there seemed to be so few people in this massive railway station. That was until I looked at the list of trains that they'd put on the sign that's above your head. And I looked at the ticket which we'd already had issued to us in the UK and looked at the train number and the train number was up there and the destination was next to it, Madrid, and the word next to that was 'grève'. Now I'd had a few to drink, but as I said my French isn't bad. And I knew enough to know – well not enough to know, I knew damn well, that grève means strike and I thought, "Oh. Oh dear, oh dear, oh dear. This is a disaster in the making." Now Tony was left in the middle of the station. I'd gone to look at this thing because I had to go a bit nearer to be able to read it and I left him about 20 yards behind me.

And I can see him to this day. He had his suitcase and he was sitting on his suitcase in the middle of the hallway of the Saint-Lazare station. And I've got the unenviable task of going back to him to tell him that the train that we are wanting to catch in a couple of hours' time… there was no great rush by the way in all this… was, from what I could make out, not going because there was a strike. But before I went and told him and made him topple off his seat on his suitcase, I went into the information office just to make sure. And it was fully explained to me, that it wasn't the French on strike, just for a change, it wasn't the French who were on strike, it was the Spanish railways that were on strike.

So the train wasn't leaving tonight. It was going to go at seven o'clock in the morning because by the time we got down to the border, the Spanish would be back at work, the strike would be over and whoopee, we could carry on to Madrid albeit arriving a little on the late side. But since the exhibition went on the whole week, it didn't really matter and we'd got open tickets to come back.

Problem. We need somewhere to stay, to put our head, just to get through the night to come back to the same railway station the following morning for about quarter to seven-ish. Go outside, taxi rank. Plenty of taxis. Got in a taxi. Said to the driver in my very best French, "*We have a problem. We need a hotel room.*" He said, "*You've got another problem.*" "*Oh yeah, what might that be?*" He said, "*Well this week's the European Union Annual Farmers' Conference and Convention,*" and you can imagine how many farmers there are in the European Union. And it was the glorious club that we've just left, by the way. "*And I think you'll find it won't be easy for me to find you a room.*" Well you'd think a place the size of Paris with the number of hotels they've got there, that can't be right. But then when you shake your head a bit and come out of the drunken stupor that you're almost in, you think, well this fellow does this for a living and he should know what he's talking about. We might well be struggling. I don't know. He says we will.

Well he turned out to be one of the most helpful taxi drivers I've ever met anywhere in the world. He ran us all over Paris within reasonable distance of the Saint-Lazare station because we'd got to think of tomorrow morning. Left us in the cab while he went into the hotel, "*Have you got a room for...?*" We said one room which we can just share – we don't care – will do. And he kept coming back out with, *"I'm sorry, I'm sorry, I'm sorry."* And this went on and we must have been running around for about, I should think, an hour and a half because it wasn't difficult for him to find hotels, it was difficult for him to find a room.

And eventually he said to us, *"Well I'm sorry, but I can't think of where else I can go, unless I go to the really upmarket, expensive hotels that I wouldn't have thought that you were wanting to pay that amount for, for one night. But it's the only places I can think to go."* Well there is a big hotel in Paris called George V. And he said, *"Well I think we might be able to get you into there, but the cost is going to be about 120 quid apiece."* Not 120 quid a room, £120 apiece in Francs, as it was in those days. And I said, *"Well look, we've got to find somewhere. Just go and see."* And he went to the George V and he came back out and he said, *"Yeah, they've got a room – a double room and they'll charge you so much..."* and it was a hell of a lot of money." He said, *"But at least it's a room and you can still get a meal if you want one because they serve until midnight in their restaurant, or midnight and beyond."*

So we went in there. We had a meal. We went in the room. The room was absolutely splendid. The cost was splendid as well, if you happened to be them and not us. And we spent the night there. We got up early the next morning. We'd now sobered up. And at about quarter past six we're climbing into another taxi and we're off to the Saint-Lazare station. They were true to their word. Looked up at the board. The train was there.

They honoured the ticket from yesterday. We go on. We sit in the seats which were allocated by number and we sit down. The train sets off and we're due to get down to Madrid at a certain time, late afternoon, early evening.

We set off and after about an hour, an hour and a half or so, the guard comes round checking the tickets. He looked at the two tickets and punched a hole in them, as they used to do in those days, and I said to him, *"There's no problem with the strike in…?"* *"Oh no, no, no, no, no. Everything's back to normal. You'll be fine. The train's going all the way to Madrid."* This happened about three or four more times as we trundled our way southward through France. We'd got more holes in the ticket than you can absolutely think about. It was only when we got to within about half an hour of the Spanish border that the last ticket man came round and he looked at our tickets and he said, *"Where are you going? The ticket says Madrid."* *"Well yeah, that's where we're going. We've been told that the train's going all the way to Madrid. The strike's over."* *"Oh well…"* he says, *"…I'm awfully sorry, but they've called another wildcat strike and the train's just going across the border to the first town in Spain,"* which actually is just a few hundred yards in Spain. It's called Irun. *"And we're stopping there and everybody's off. The train is not going to Madrid and I don't know when the strike will be over for you to carry on with your journey."*

Oh God! So I've got all this to explain to him, Tony, in English. The train gently pulls through the last station in France, which I think is… is it Biarritz? I think it might well be. I stand to be corrected there. And we pull into... it wasn't a mile. We pulled very gently into this railway station with a big sign up with Irun. That's like the best pronunciation I can imagine. I-R-U-N. Now the difference between France and this part of what is, of course, Basque country in Spain and of course at that time, there was an awful lot of bother going on. I know there was a big independence movement. There were a lot of murders. It was reminiscent of the IRA and what have you over in Northern Ireland. And we pulled into Irun, got off and we almost stepped into another world. It was tatty, it was old. It hadn't had a coat of paint since Harold Wilson was prime minister. Oh dear, oh dear, what a mess. And there we are stuck. Nobody spoke a word of English. But I did notice, if you looked through the hallway, if you can call it a hallway, of the station, I noticed a police station. At least I know what police is in Spanish. And I noticed a police station, not very far, 100 yards to 150 yards down the road on the right-hand side. And I said, *"Come on, let's walk down there and let's see if there's anybody in there who speaks any English."*

Well we did and as we walked through the gate, we got the shock of our lives because everybody was armed to the teeth with sub-machine guns and God knows what. And they looked at us in complete bemusement and some, not inconsiderable suspicion, particularly a woman who obviously looked at us and thought we looked British and spoke to us in, not bad English, sufficiently good English for us to understand. And she said they were sorry but they had to be careful because they didn't know who was going to come bursting through the gates. I explained the situation. She said, *"We've been told to tell everybody who might ask that that train's going back to Paris at ten o'clock tonight."* I said, *"Well it's only about half past one, 12..."* about one o'clock I think it was. She said, *"Well, what I think you might do, there is a flight."* And I looked round. I said, *"This town's got an airport?"* *"Well an airport would be an exaggerated word,"* she said. *"No, not an airport, no. It's got an airfield. And a little something or other takes off from there with about 20 passengers and flies down to Madrid every afternoon and there's one today, a bit later. I suggest you get in a taxi and go and see if they've got any seats for the two of you. I doubt it very much because everybody who wants to go to Madrid will have already booked, but you can try. They may have had cancellations."*

So we get down to the airfield. It's not far. It's only a little tatty little country place. We go into the car park and we said to the taxi driver, *"Hang on, just wait there."* And we went into the terminal building and I start to splutter a bit in French and thinking, *"Oh I don't know."* And this bloke at the other side of the ticket counter, to my utter and complete amazement, in the best Oxbridge English you have heard for an awful long time, told us that the plane was full, but if we wished, he would put us onto the reserve list at numbers 13 and 14 and if we wanted to come back at whatever time it flew, we could see what the situation was, but he thought it was a waste of time because there were only about 14 seats on the plane and they were already booked up and there were already 12 before us on the reserve list. So I thought, well this is a waste of time. And I said to this ticket man who spoke all this very, very good English, *"What do you suggest?"* He said, *"Well I suggest you go and get a damn good meal, go back to the railway station and go back to Paris and go home. That's the only thing I can suggest to you."*

So he went with us to the taxi and he said to the taxi driver in Spanish or Basque; it could have been Basque, I don't know, I wouldn't know the difference if you paid me, to take us to a restaurant. And he says, *"Oh he knows a very good restaurant. It's up in the hills a bit, towards the Pyrenees, but it's up in the hills, but it's very, very good and they open all the day round. So although when you get there, there won't be many people there, if any, they will do you a meal."* Thanked him very much for his kindness. Complimented him on his English, which was better than mine and off we go. I never did ask him why he spoke such good English, but never mind. Perhaps I'll nip back and see if he's still alive.

We started to climb up and up and up and up and my mind sort of started to float towards Basque country problems, headlines in the paper, 'British businessmen found dead in Basque village' and oh... God love us. My memories were quite good in my mind of 'British businessman found dead at side of road in Slovakia'. Now it was 'British businessmen found dead in Basque country'. He took us to this place, which was quite nice from the outside and we went in and there was actually absolutely nobody inside in terms of a customer, but there were four staff. And the staff were the boss - who was a huge great Basque Spaniard fellow with a great big moustache – a huge moustache. He looked like an RAF Battle of Britain pilot. There was his wife, who looked... well there must have been an uglier woman in Basque country, but I can't imagine what she must have looked like. And then they had between them two very beautiful daughters. How these two ugly so-and-sos had managed to produce these two beautiful girls, I'm not quite sure, but anyway that's not the reason that we were there. We were there for a meal. We told the taxi driver to come back at something like six o'clock because the train was going at ten and I wanted to leave nothing; nothing at risk about getting on the train to go back northwards and back towards home.

Anyway, we go in and we get a meal and it was very, very good, very, very nice. The only drawback was that the boss man, he of the big moustache, didn't trust us an awful lot. You could see he didn't trust us an awful lot. And he seemed to walk around with a great big butcher's meat cleaver most of the time. And more headlines came to mind of 'British businessmen found with cleaver in forehead'. But I think he thought that we'd come chasing up the girls. Well the thought was grand, but the idea was bloody ridiculous to be quite frank with you and fraught with so many problems, that you could forget it.

Anyway, we get through the meal and we've still got about an hour and a half, an hour and a quarter before the taxi was due back. And we had a few to drink. We'd seemed to have spent the whole of this trip doing nothing much more than drinking. And Tony said to me, *"Go to the suitcase, your suitcase and get out the sample of this thing that we're supposed to be taking to this security exhibition in Madrid."* I enquired why and he said, *"Because we're going to try and sell it to him, to at least probably get the meal for nothing."* Now sometimes in this world you hear some crazy suggestions that you know haven't got a lot of chance of working, but I can't think of anything before or since dafter than what he suggested. He blames me for this, by the way, to this day. He says it was my idea. Well I'm writing the book and I can promise you, it was his idea.

So I go and the suitcase is near the exit door and I think they thought I was going to make a run for it because he of the big moustache began to walk towards me, cleaver in hand, and I said, *"No, no, no, no, I'm not going. I'm just going to fetch something."* He didn't understand me, but when I came back he was quite content. And I had in my hand this, black-coloured it was, this sample, infrared detector for use externally, which would have been actually fine for him in the winter evenings to trigger outdoor lighting, so he could see if there was any bother outside. And that's fine if he was buying one from a local electrician who was going to fit it. But to try and sell one of these things to anybody at any time is a bit... it's hard work, to put it that way, and he couldn't understand what on earth it was. And I handed the detector over to Tony and he said, *"Well you're the sales director, you sell it."* I said, *"It was your idea. You sell it."* And he beckoned the bloke towards him.

He didn't like the beckoning bit. That was very unpopular. Out came the cleaver again. And he beckoned him towards him. And I shall never forget the next three words which came from his mouth. The British have a habit of believing that if you put an 'O' after every word of English, then foreigners understand you. Now, it's not true. And the next three words which were uttered were, *"Automatico lighto-switcho."* Well I don't know what *'Automatic lighto-switcho'* means to you, but it doesn't mean a great deal in Basque, or Spanish, I can promise you. And this guy looked at us and thought, *"Hello, they haven't paid yet. Is this some sort of con to get out of paying?"* Well, as luck would have it, before any more conversation could take place, the taxi driver came. He came an hour early. He'd got the times mixed up, but it didn't matter. I thought it was most opportune that he was there.

We paid the bill in French Francs. They took both because of their proximity to the border. And we got back in the taxi and set off to ride back down the 20 miles, I suppose or more or less it might have been, until we arrive at the railway station. We've plenty of time. We only need to crawl down. When we came out the weather had changed a bit and it was... the sun was shining, but it was also raining. You know those days where you get sunshine and rain at the same time. Now, I can always remember from being a kid, being a young lad, when my father was alive, so it's before I was... it was 12 or before. My dad, who was from the south, used to use an expression which always puzzled me, but because he was my father and in those days you believed what your father said and you did what you were told, he used to say, *"Oh it's a monkey's birthday again."* Now I never asked my dad; I never said, *"Well, what do you mean monkey's birthday?"* He always referred to a day when the sun shone and the rain came at the same time as a 'monkey's birthday'.

Now, I went through life, right up until a couple of years ago, using this expression to various people, who thought I was mad and didn't understand it. And I always used to explain that it was something my father used to say. And after I'd retired, I don't know, we were having this type of weather one day and I decided to look in Google for 'monkey's birthday'. And do you know, a monkey's birthday is to older meteorologists, if that's the word, if I can pronounce it, is the correct expression to describe exactly what my father had said, mostly used in Somerset and Dorset. And my father came from neither. He came from Essex, but maybe it had spread across the south of England. Maybe the monkey used to pop around and maybe he was quite a travelling lad. But that's what it is – a monkey's birthday. And if you don't believe me, I suggest you look it up and you'll find I'm telling the truth. This is not a joke. Well, it is a joke, but it is the truth – a monkey's birthday.

Anyway, going back to Basque country, we get down to the railway station, we get on the train. Nothing eventful happened. We got back to Paris. We changed over to the train to Calais. We kept off the drink and stuck on the tea and coffee all the way back up to Calais and we crossed over again uneventfully over to Dover where my car was in the car park; in the multi-storey car park. That was safe and well and we drove home. And we were extremely tired when we got home. We'd done all that from leaving Yorkshire to getting back to Yorkshire. We'd spent a fortune, got into a Spanish railway strike, not got anywhere near Madrid where we were wanting to go. The sensor was still in the suitcase where it was when I packed it before I left home and we were back at home. So a good time was had by all, but an extremely expensive time was had by all.

I went many more times to Spain on business, but I never had anything quite so... hmm, what's the word? Odd? Happening again as the, what I've come to call, the monkey birthday adventure.

# Chapter Eleven

Spain's never been a place I've greatly taken to. I know flying into Madrid for business over a very parched – when you're coming into land – a very parched and very brown countryside, doesn't look anything like as attractive as this country does. But we hadn't done any business there for – well, forever, I think. I don't think we'd ever done any business there. And I'd been to an exhibition in London where I'd picked up on a couple of business cards left to me and I decided to go and do a joint visit in Madrid. Got to Madrid, was met at the airport by a man who I recognised and remembered from the exhibition in London, a gentleman who would be... hmm, probably in his 70s, I would think, early 70s. And a very nice gentleman. Very well dressed, lovely car. Everything about him was correct in the business sense. We drove into Madrid. We went to his premises. Hmm, and it became quite obvious really from very early, that he wasn't going to be the man for us. What he stocked and what he did, had no bearing upon what we did. I think he was looking, quite justifiably, to branch out into other things. But I'm afraid those other things weren't us. I just couldn't see it happening. Within an hour of starting the negotiation or the talk, I just couldn't see it happening.

That evening, he was very kind and he said he would take me out for a meal. And he came and picked me up at the hotel somewhere in Madrid. I can't remember; it's too long ago now. And we get in the car and we go to a typical Madrid backstreet place, where the food was, I'm being reliably informed, was absolutely excellent and where many dignitaries, in Spain, in Madrid in particular came to visit. He told me that it was a place that Spanish royalty – the minor Spanish royals, not that I even knew the major Spanish royals, but the minor Spanish royals came quite often. And perhaps more importantly in his eyes, it was where a lot of Real Madrid footballers came to eat with their wives.

We went up some stairs and upstairs was a typical, typical, typical continental-style restaurant. Small tables, wooden chairs, all packed very tightly and closely together. And we ordered a drink, an aperitif and he said to me, *"The menu here is purely and simply in Spanish. I take it you won't understand much of it, and anyway, I want to choose for you the very, very best."* Very kind of him, very kind indeed. He didn't turn out to be so kind, for reasons that will follow. And he started off by choosing a soup for me. He said, *"Do you like soup?"* and I said, *"Yes, I do like soup."* And he ordered what was on the menu. I looked and it was gazpacho tomato soup. Well I'm very keen on tomato soup of any type. Now not being so very familiar with Spain and what have you and Spanish food, I thought gazpacho may well be a brand. It didn't turn out to be like that at all. And it came and I imagined it was going to be a hot tomato soup. Put my spoon into the bowl. Took a mouthful... Now I don't like olive oil for the very simple reason that olive oil doesn't like me and we won't go any further into that except I'll leave it to your own imagination. And it was basically olive oil with some tomato puree inside it to make it look red and tomato-ish. And from the first mouthful I was thinking I'm going to pay for this, not in cash, but in another way. I managed to get down about two-thirds of it and I just couldn't manage any more. It just wasn't my taste whatsoever.

The main course was lamb. I can remember it was lamb. Nothing else on the plate, just lamb chops. It's the way they do things over there. And a dessert followed by cheese, which is again the way that they do it. And all along we had a bottle of wine. He took me back to my hotel. We discussed a little further in the lobby and I think we both came to, what was quite obviously the obvious conclusion, that neither company was made for one another. It wasn't a marriage made in heaven, shall we say. He smiled, I smiled, we shook hands and we never, ever quite frankly met again.

I was going a couple of weeks later... the appointment had already been made to see a possible agent in Stirling, north of the border. And between the dinner in Madrid and the – it might have been ten days, but it was quite a while – appointment in Stirling, I had had a terrible time. I couldn't go far from the house. It was awful. I could not shake off this gazpacho stuff. But I decided that I really ought to try and do my best to see this man in Stirling because he had pursued us for some considerable time with a view to becoming our Scottish agent. And I decided I would drive to Doncaster because I thought I could probably get as far as Doncaster without a disaster, get on the train to Edinburgh or Glasgow – it's not really important – and stand up all the way. And you can gather where I stood up and what the door was opposite me. The guard, every time he went round checking on tickets and what have you, and there were plenty of seats, seemed to think that I was some sort of standing-room only lunatic and kept saying, *"Well you can go and sit down. You've got a seat. You've got a seat."* And I nodded and smiled and never... I was a much younger man in those days. Never took it into my mind to tell him the real reason I was standing where I was standing.

The meeting in Stirling was interrupted on frequent occasions, but the main in Stirling proved to be a good man, knew his way round the Scottish electrical wholesale trade, and we decided that he would become our agent and work on a commission basis, which is a quite normal thing to do for an agent. I promised him we would get him literature and we dealt with him, I should think, for two or three years until – oh, I don't know, the mutual admiration society between us wore a bit thin and he just decided that he would move on to pastures green.

I came back from seeing him and I got back into Edinburgh or Glasgow and I got on the train down to Doncaster. I'd left my car in Doncaster. And again it was a standing up job all the way. And I stood up all the way down to Doncaster for a fear of any eventuality and eventually got down to Doncaster, got in my car and got home and, you know, I woke up the following morning and the bug had gone. The bug, if it was a bug, had gone, but it took me two weeks of rather unpleasant discomfort to get rid of it. And all I can say is that every time I go anywhere and I see on a menu 'gazpacho' I avoid it like the proverbial plague.

While I was also in Madrid, and before the plague of gazpacho struck me down, I went to see a man who I'd also met at the exhibition at Olympia. Now this was a different kettle of fish altogether. He was in the security industry and had a market for our security products, although his main business or his other business was supplying hotels and huge office blocks and whatever with very, very large TV aerials, circular TV aerial-type things, like massive Sky aerials that you see on houses today, which they shoved on the top of the hotel and picked up Radio Tokyo. Why the devil they wanted that, I'm not quite sure, but they managed it. And that was his major business, but he wanted to get into something a little bit different. He had a little interest in security; did a couple of security lights and we thought in London that this was going to be a reasonable idea. He came to pick me up in his car from the hotel, the morning after the gazpacho incident and we went to Corazón de María No. 5. I'll always remember that. What my pronunciation is like, I'm not quite sure. But that's where we went. I'd had not much of a breakfast, just a smallish breakfast. Last night was weighing on me a little bit that I should be careful. And we got there at, I should think, about half past nine.

Now when you're abroad, the one thing you must remember is that abroad ain't here. Abroad is not here.

Different culture, different habits, different most things. And we just sat down and we talked and he never offered me a tea or a coffee, which of course here you would do as an obligation. But we talked and he decided he'd like to take on some of our products and sell them exclusively in Spain from his Madrid office. He may have an office somewhere else. I'm not sure. I thought that yes, it was a good idea that he sell for us, but I thought the exclusivity was a bit much because Spain is a very large country. It hasn't the population of ours, but it's most definitely a much, much bigger country.

Anyway, we agreed to carry on and go forward. His name was Don Eduardo... Don, I think is some sort of title. Don Eduardo Tur Borja. And Eduardo... we became on very, very familiar Christian name terms over the years, Eduardo turned out to be one of the nicest men that I ever met in business in my life. I would have trusted him with everything and with anything. And we struck up a friendship that carried on for many, many years until I moved away from the particular trade, more back to lighting and lighting only, and lighting was in no way his field. And sad to say our relationship waned in the sense of contact. I used occasionally to send him an email asking as to his wellbeing, but like most things of that nature, they die a death within a certain while. And I stopped emailing him and he... well it wouldn't be email in those days; it would be faxing, I suppose.

I stopped contacting him, he stopped contacting me and it's some considerable time now since I heard of him, although I did look on the internet and the business is still there. And he's still at Corazón de María. Now whether he is still alive, I don't know because his son, who I knew as a very young man, a teenager, is I believe running the business now. And Eduardo, would need to be in his late 80s, I would think, to be still with us, but a nicer man I've never met. A gentleman. Actually once he came to our premises over here and he was absolutely splendid and insisted upon meeting all the directors and all the staff and everybody took him immediately to their hearts and liked him intensely. I hope he's still with us. I don't like to write to the son because Eduardo may have passed away and I don't want to reap up old sorrows. But that man, Eduardo Tur Borja was definitely the gentleman of all gentlemen and I wish that he's still alive. And if the world was full of Eduardo's there would never be a problem anywhere.

# Chapter Twelve

On the topic of nice men, I, again at this exhibition; it was very useful, this exhibition at Olympia. I don't know whether it still exists, I really don't, but I met a man from Aachen in Germany. And he was most keen to become our lighting distributor. There were German competitors of course, but he wasn't in with any of those and they wouldn't let him in because they'd got their own arrangements made. And he wanted a quality alternative. By the time I met him the products were very, very good, very, very high in their quality and good in their performance and we had very few failures. So the next time I was in that part of the world, I'd taken my car across and decided to call and see him. He gave me the address and we agreed a date and a time.

Now I got there a little early. They of course, a bit like the French, all locked up for lunch and 'back in two hours' it said in the window in German. I knew what 'stunde' meant, it means hour in German. And two is two, whichever way you look at it. So I parked my car. A quiet street, no yellow lines. Well I don't know if there were yellow lines in those days or whatever colour lines they had in Germany, but I parked my car. And I noticed on the corner was a bar-cum-cafeteria/restaurant-type place, a bit like a German 'Little Chef', if you know what I mean. And so I thought, well I'll walk up here and I'll have something to eat and kill an hour and he should be back very shortly after that.

And I went up to this restaurant place and no English; they didn't speak any English and I spoke no German, but I understand enough what was written up on the board of today's specials. I understood enough to be able to order something. And I think I ordered... well I know I ordered two or three gigantic... well long sausages, along with sauerkraut, which I'd never tried prior to that and I've never tried it after. A glass of beer or what they call beer, what I call lager, something else that I don't take to much... well I can't remember the last time I had any. I think it's drinking for drinking's sake personally. And I sat in there and we tried to pick a conversation – a few words. Football obviously is easy and things like that. They like football, I like football. Aachen's got a football team. Barnsley have got a football team. I'd heard of Aachen.

They hadn't heard of Barnsley – no surprise in that. And we parted about an hour, an hour and a quarter later when I saw a big Mercedes drive up to the shop, open the gates at the side and drive down into the yard at the back. I took it that that was him coming back from his lunch and I wasn't far wrong. And I gave him 15 minutes or so just to settle in after coming back lunch. The salesman's training never left me. Don't just burst in straight, two minutes after somebody's had a meal or been out. They've got to listen to answerphones and all the rest of it, look at faxes and what have you and they don't want you on the doorstep immediately.

Eventually I went in and there was him and his wife and two or three staff and they were all very affable and kind and very nice people. How old? Well he'd be a man of – must have been again 70. I based this upon a story he told me, which I'm going to relate to you. It's not a long story, but it's not a pleasant one, not particularly. In actual fact, he was quite a leading light, if you'll pardon the pun, in the German lighting business because at the Hanover Fair, which is an exhibition that used to be held every year in Hanover, which included lighting – lighting has now moved to Frankfurt because lighting has become such a big deal, there was a sort of a tower block thing about four or five storeys high and major electrical companies used to rent that like a demonstration area out and nobody else was... it was only for lighting. It was only for them and he had a very large area there because in the years to come I visited him at Hanover and talked to him.

Now, the first time I met him properly was in his office in Aachen and we hit it off and he wanted to carry on from the conversation in London. He liked what he saw and he did a bit of business with us over the years. But what I remember about him, I think most, was after we'd finished sort of talking about products and what have you, he turned a little bit to his personal situation, about having a wife and kiddies and what have you. And he said, *"You know, I'm lucky to be alive."* And I said, *"Oh yeah, why is that?"* because you don't like to bring up the war, but the war was the reason. Towards the end of the war, we did a tremendous blitz on the city of Dresden where we killed thousands of people in the one night. I'm not asking for sympathy for them. They killed millions of people over a six-year period and perhaps you could say that it was just the good lord getting his own back on them. The day or two after the Dresden raid, he told me, despite the attempts of the Nazi party to hide, shield, keep under wraps what had happened in Dresden and the sign that everything was crumbling and they were getting to the end of the war and they were going to lose, it had all got out. An event like that could not be kept quiet. And the RAF decided to leaflet bomb; drop a load of leaflets on two more cities in Germany that they regarded to be of tactical importance. Don't ask me; I've no idea. I'm not a military man and never wanted to be and never will be. But he told me that we dropped a leaflet in Germany and the headline to the leaflet, which was a chilling one to anybody who picked it up, was 'Aachen und Essen, wir haben sie nicht vergessen' which translated means 'Aachen and Essen, we haven't forgotten you'. Or I suppose a little bit more crudely put, we would say 'Aachen and Essen, it's your turn next'. And that meant that the people of Aachen and Essen, which are not near to one another; they're cities that are a long way apart, were on tenterhooks waiting for a Dresden-type attack.

Now they didn't get a Dresden-style attack, but they got one very, very heavy bombing raid in which a lot of people, thousands of people or more were killed in Aachen and he remembered it as if it were yesterday. He graphically described the events of seeing people screaming on fire running through the streets of Aachen. It must have been the most dreadful thing for people to a) experience and of course b) look at. He'd no detestation of us, the British because it would have shown in his attitude towards me. He had no detestation of the British whatsoever for this. His detestation was of the man who led Germany at the time, the party and the man who led Germany at the time. He blamed them entirely for what occurred. And he didn't blame us at all and he was very pleasant with me and so was his wife. And business was done and we became friends. Again he would be a man who I'm sure will have passed on now, but he had family and unfortunately the name of his company and the man escapes me. But a bizarre and awful story. Followed up slightly by... well no not slightly, very much by, a few years later there was a lighting exhibition in Essen and I decided I was going to this.

Now this Aachen and Essen business, I'd completely forgotten about all this at the time. And I went to stay in a place called Wuppertal. Now anybody who hasn't been to Wuppertal hasn't seen the ugliest thing that God ever created. They have trains in Wuppertal. Tal is valley. Wupper may be a river, I don't know and it doesn't really matter, but Wuppertal is a long, far-stretching group of towns all jointly called Wuppertal. East Wuppertal, West Wuppertal, North Wuppertal, South and lots of other place names, all commencing with the name Wuppertal. And as I said they have buses, they have cars, they have trains, but they have – and Hitler built this – they have an overhead tramway, an overhead tramway. Well of course they used at the time the best technology available and it looks just like something out of a Lego kit waddling its way down the valley from one end to the other with carriages on the top taking you from one part of the city maybe 20 miles at least to the other end of the city. The other thing about it which is unusual is the awful noise it makes.

I arrived there at night and I went somewhere nearby to where I'd booked somewhere to stay and I went into the city for a meal. And because it was dark, I hadn't seen this overhead railway contraption and it was only when I was getting out of the taxi to walk down... he had to leave me at the end of the street because it was a one-way street... to walk down the street to the restaurant, that I heard this absolutely thunderingly loud... it was like being in the middle of a thunderstorm – noise, but not far above my head. And you got the immediate feeling that you were about to witness the end of the world. And then I looked up and I saw this thing and nobody else was taking a blind bit of notice of it other than me. So I thought, well it must be... well I looked and it was quite obvious what it was. But it's one of the ugliest things I've ever seen. Whether it's still there or not, I do now know, but I've never seen anything like it, nor would want to. It was awful.

The next morning, I went to the local railway station to get a train into Essen to go to the exhibition. I also recall two young lads – they were only school boys, ten or 12 years old, coming up to me on the platform. And I'd seen a train pull up with Dusseldorf on the front and a few minutes before these two lads came up to me, I saw this train with Dusseldorf marked on it, pull out of the railway station, presumably on its way to Dusseldorf. And these two lads came up to me and didn't know where I came from of course, and I made out from what they were saying to me was, *"Has the Dusseldorf train gone?"* And I said to them, *"Well I'm English, but the train that you can see in the far distance is the Dusseldorf train, so I'm sorry, it's gone."* They grasped what I was saying, but the giggling and the humour that followed from these two boys was something I will always remember because it must have been the first time, maybe the only time that they had ever spoken to a foreigner. And they thought that it was quite amazing, that there was a foreigner in their town. I couldn't quite grasp the amusement at the time, but I grasp it more now.

I went to Essen. I had a look round the exhibition. It was a very, very good exhibition. It was a very, very high quality exhibition and the products on display were, to put it mildly, expensive. They were out of our league and I don't think anybody in that building would have been interested in taking on our products. But you live and you learn. Came back to the railway station. There was a newsagents and I looked on there for a British newspaper, saw the Daily Express, I think as the only one and that was a couple of days out of date, but nonetheless, I bought it for something to read on the train back to Wuppertal. Anybody who knows me is quite aware and will tell you that the sight of me buying and reading the Daily Express is a rare commodity indeed. I don't agree with much it says, except for the date on the front, and even then I only believe that when I've checked it.

Being serious, I got on this train, a little local train like they are running around here – Leeds to Barnsley, Leeds to Sheffield, et cetera, et cetera. And I sat there and I put my briefcase on the rack above me and began to read the newspaper. And I'd sat opposite two old ladies, must have been, oh, I don't know, well into their 70s, if not 80 and it's the only time in all my travels that I have ever, that I've been aware of, ever come across an anti-British reaction from a passenger on a plane, on a train or anything, a passer-by, anybody at an exhibition. It doesn't matter. It's the only time it's ever occurred to me or ever happened to me. And it only happened with one word. The two old ladies that noticed me, noticed the newspaper I was reading. We're in Essen bear in mind and bear in mind 'Aachen und Essen, wir haben sie nicht vergessen', this was the other half of the Aachen and Essen. Essen's quite a big city, by the way. And I remember one of these old ladies saying one word to the other.

That word was 'British' - and they got up and they left to find seats in another part of the train. At first it puzzled me and then my mind took me back to the story I'd heard in Aachen and I realised that to some people the activities of the war were still very much alive and kicking with them at the forefront of their minds and they didn't like us for what we had done. Maybe they were right. Maybe they were wrong. This is not a book entitled '*Who was to blame for the war? Please discuss*'. I don't want to go into it and I won't. But it's the only time that my nationality has ever caused me any sort of embarrassment. Nobody else took any notice of me, so I gather I was okay. I felt rather sad about it. To be honest I felt very sad about it.

# Chapter Thirteen

I think that's enough of the misery. I left Wuppertal to get a train to somewhere because I was going to see a potential customer in Liechtenstein. Not many people have been to Liechtenstein. I doubt whether there's a great deal of business done between this country and Liechtenstein and my visit to that lovely little place didn't improve the situation by one penny. It was nice, it was pleasant, the guy was smashing, but he wanted to buy three of this and five of that and we weren't into this type of thing.

I got a train down to a part of Germany. There's no railways in Liechtenstein, or there weren't at the time. And I got a train down to somewhere not so far away, but over the German border. Got off the train, walked down the platform, walked out the front. There's a man waiting for me with my name held up on a card. We got in his car and we set off towards Liechtenstein. He explained that to get to Liechtenstein from where we were entailed crossing over a little bit of Austria and then we go Germany, a little bit of Austria and then into Liechtenstein and Switzerland was only a cock's stride away as well.

I recall getting in the car and in my pocket – I don't know why it was in my pocket, but it was – I had a large bar. I've always had this fear of foreign food ever since Gazpacho day. And in my pocket I had a large bar of Cadbury's Daily Milk chocolate, you know the ones with the dark blue wrapper. Well the dark blue wrapper greatly resembled in colour and the chocolate bar in size, a British passport of those days because we didn't have these red, European things or burgundy European things that we have now. We had a dark blue UK passport. But I also had this great big bar of chocolate in my pocket. We drove a few... I don't know, ten miles, in southern Germany. Where would we be? South-west Germany somewhere and there were the signs saying that... Sorry, it must have been the Swiss border. Yeah, it must have been the Swiss border.

Anyway, there was a sign for the customs which were coming up in Switzerland in one mile or one kilometre and he said, "You'll need your passport." Well I'm always in it for a laugh and to see what you can get away with and they weren't really... I saw cars just driving through and holding passports out of windows and nobody got stopped. And we were only going into Liechtenstein. And I don't know whether Liechtenstein's even got... I know it hadn't got an army. It must have some sort of customs officials and police force. And as we approached the border, he got his passport or some sort of identity card that got him through into Liechtenstein. And as we got up to the border post, I thought, "Go on, be a devil. See what happens." I turned the back of the Cadbury's pack around so the word Cadbury's was facing me and not outward and waved the Dairy Milk bar at the customs official, who promptly saluted me and waved me through. Obviously he had a great regard for the British. Either that or he liked Cadbury's chocolate. I'm not quite sure which. I like to think that it's the British that he had a regard for. It's the only time I've ever crossed a border using a bar of chocolate as a passport, but believe me, it worked. The capital of Liechtenstein is called Vaduz, a small town, very pretty, population of about 4,000/5,000 maybe today and not much else really. A very small country. We had a meal that evening. It became obvious that the visit was one I could have done without. Time I could have spent better elsewhere, but you win some, you lose some.

The next morning I wanted to go back to this railway station to carry on my journey, but this man, who was a very nice man, a perfect gentleman, insisted or wanted to insist that we go in a cable car up a mountain because he said when you get to the top of the mountain, there's a rather unique feature and that feature is that, by taking a stride in either direction, you can go from Liechtenstein to Germany to Switzerland and back to Liechtenstein. A nice little sales gimmick, a nice little tourist attraction. But I was neither there for gimmicks nor attractions; I was there to earn a living. And apart from anything else, I'm terrified of heights and of cable cars and despite his – oh, desperate attempts to get me into this cable car, I am keeping my feet on the ground and I ain't going up there at any price.

I remember when my father was alive, we were in Switzerland, I think, with my mother and this is when I must have got the fear of heights from, I think, my mum because we did a similar thing there. My dad wanted to go up this mountain and of course my dad being my dad, he always got his way and we went up this mountain. And my mother was absolutely terrified and she did a good job of frightening me as well. And what she did to occupy the time while we went up the... was that she watched a fly walk up a man's trouser leg – on the outside, I hasten to add – and that was how she concentrated her mind until we shuddered to a stop which frightened the life out of her, I remember, had a look round and came back down. Never seen a woman more pleased to have both feet on terra firma than my mother that day and me too. She really had frightened me.

Just briefly running away from where we are geographically, I've had that fear ever since. I have stood frozen at the bottom... frozen in the sense of not being able move, frozen at the bottom of the Eiffel Tower, frozen at the bottom of what they call the 'orange peel tower' in Shanghai and somehow was induced and went up the Blackpool Tower. I don't know how or who got me up there, but they did. But my word was I glad to get down. But it's never bothered me in aeroplanes at 30,000/35,000 feet. I suppose it's because you've got something solid under your feet that you don't have the same sort of fear. Up there, I don't know, there's just something about it that I can't tolerate.

I'll tell you a little strange, if maybe a little amusing thing. I was once in London on business and I'd been to see somebody in central London-ish and there was a tube station across the street and the line, I was going out onto the Northern Line out to see somebody at a place called Kingsway, I think it is. It doesn't matter. And I went into the tube station, bought my ticket and as is their want in some London tube stations, there was an extremely steep, long escalator and the darn thing had broken. It wasn't working, which meant that I'd got to walk down it and I froze at the top. I couldn't do it. I couldn't get down the escalator.

So I went out into the street. I had to go back out into the street. Got in a taxi and this is absolutely true, asked him to take me a couple of stops up the Northern Line to a station where there was no escalator and we were all on the flat. And that's true, I did that and then I went to Kingsway. I never told the bloke at Kingsway. I didn't want to shame myself. But the only thing I can remember really much of Liechtenstein was heights, the desire to go up there and how pretty it was. It's not big enough for a holiday because you'd pass through, you'd see it all in a day. But a lovely place nonetheless.

# Chapter Fourteen

The first time I went to the Hanover Fair – well, I think every time I went to the Hanover Fair, I always took my car. I used to go to Hull, cross to Rotterdam, drive through Holland into Germany and then go so far towards Hanover before finding somewhere – a hotel with a restaurant, stay the night and then carry on the next day. The first time I did this, I pulled off at a town called Bochum and went off the motorway sort of driving towards the town centre. I hadn't gone very far and I saw a sign for a Novotel on my left-hand side. Went in to the industrial estate and there I found a theatre, the Novotel and to my great delight Bochum FC's football ground. Never on the two or three occasions that I stayed in Bochum was there a home game, but I always managed to ask for a room in the hotel where I could see from the window out onto the ground just in case there was a game and I could watch it from the room.

The next morning, same routine every time. Drive up to Hanover, about another two hours, but on their motorways which closely resemble racetracks because there seems to be no law whatsoever, no rules whatsoever concerning speed or safety. They just roar along, whereas we tend to be... we think we drive fast, but; oh no we don't, oh no we don't. We are very well-behaved on the roads by comparison to the Germans. And I drove into Hanover on a Sunday. The exhibition began on the Monday. Now the common thing to do was to book a B & B or something like, which was in actual fact living with a family and you could do this through an address in London where each year they offered such a service. And the first time I went, I got an address for the week or five days or something like that and I found it pretty easily – a quiet area, nice old Victorian stone-type house, pulled the car up outside, no great problems, no parking restrictions; knocked on the door and a man came to the door who spoke English with a very strong American accent. It turned out that he had worked in America, California for many, many years and his wife had been with him and his wife and he was now working back in Germany; a very big house, but they let out rooms at the Hanover Fair to people like me.

Now, I was meeting up in Hanover with a Chinese bunch who were unpredictable to say the least, unruly and downright rude, to say the most, at times. When I got into this house and I put my suitcase in the hall, the man of the house, who would be, I don't know, he'd be in his middle 30s; his wife would be two or three years younger and I noticed that they had a very, very young baby. This man said to me... he called me Chris and I called him whatever his name was, Johan and he said, *"Can you help me?"* I said, *"With what?"* *"The Chinese won't behave. They arrived yesterday. They please themselves. They gave me the names of three or four Chinese who were supposed to be stopping in a single room just to keep the cost down, but they've been here two nights now it's never been the same four on the two nights. And they all smoke. My wife and I don't smoke and one of the prime reasons why we don't permit anybody to smoke is the baby. But I have told them that if they want to smoke, they can go out into the back garden."* Now I knew these Chinese only too well and I thought... I couldn't believe it. He had got no chance whatsoever of getting these people to do as he wished. They would please themselves.

The Chinese please themselves. I promise you. They literally please themselves. *"Will you speak to them Chris? Will you have a word with them? Can you be a controlling influence on them? Can you do anything about it? We can't keep having the baby breathing in all this nicotine stuff, nor us. And you don't smoke either?"* I said, *"No I don't smoke. Where are they now?"* *"Oh, they've gone out into the city. I don't know whether they'll be back later. They'll have gone looking for a Chinese restaurant where they'll spend hours,"* but there's nothing untypical about that. The Chinese when abroad look for Chinese restaurants. They don't accept the menu that you and I would see. They just say to the Chinese owner, *"I want to eat what you eat,"* which is real Chinese food, not the stuff that people go out and buy every day. I waited for them to come in, but when I went to bed they still weren't there and I didn't hear them come in.

The next morning, I got up, went down for breakfast. He'd gone to work and there was his wife there. Well, his wife was a very attractive girl and she was walking around in a pair of knickers and a top and nothing else. I thought, *"Well this is not going to encourage the Chinese to behave because they will think that because she's dressed like that, they can please themselves what they do."* I had my breakfast. It was an excellent breakfast that they put on – absolutely excellent. All cold meats and jams and bread of various types, and butter. It was excellent. But by the time it got to the time we'd designated that we should be going down to the fair, because I'd got to drive there of course and I'd got to park and everything else and you can imagine the traffic on the first morning, it was absolutely horrendous – no sign of any Chinese.

So eventually I just decided to go on my own. Parked up eventually. Walked across to the fair. Used my pass to get in, which the Chinese had arranged previously, and eventually found the stand, which they, over the weekend must have put up. There wasn't much on the stand. It was a pretty awful thing. And as per all exhibitions that I've ever been to where there is quite a considerable Chinese content in the way of exhibitors, they all go in the same hall. Now this is because the Chinese lighting association pays for them to go and pays for the flights, which is always a Chinese airline, direct to the nearest airport. So when I get there, all the stands were Chinese. I knew one or two of the people and we spoke just briefly, but none of the three or four who I was expecting from the company that I was associated with. They turned up eventually, I don't know, an hour and a half after the exhibition had opened. Not a care in the world. I got the impression that they weren't bothered about being there. They'd gone for nothing and they'd just gone to enjoy themselves and weren't really bothered about selling very much because of the exhibition, because they were already selling a load of stuff all over the world.

And in the evening we all got in my car. It was a bit of a squash actually, but we all got in my car and we went back to the digs, shall we call it, only to find the most irate German that you could possibly wish to meet, greeting us all at his front door. Now, he took me on one side because of his command of English and said to me, *"They've ignored me again. They were all smoking this morning in the room prior to going down to the exhibition. I have told them explicitly there is no smoking allowed in this house. Can you please try and stop it?"* The lead one amongst them, who spoke the greatest amount of English, was a lad who used the English name Timothy and I'd known him for several years and he was Jack the lad – pleased himself, did as he wanted, took no notice of anybody, least of all me. But I told him what the man had said and that he had threatened that if they didn't behave, he'd turn them out, but I could stay. So I determined that at nights they could go out looking for their Chinese restaurants and I would go out looking for a German, a western French, something recognisable as food to me and we would just spend time together at the exhibition.

Every night when I got back to the digs with them, there was another complaint from the German owner. Last night it was a different four to the night before, except that Timothy was the common denominator and I'm telling him, *"You cannot come to somebody else's country, somebody else's house, ignore and flout the rules of the house and hope to get away with it."* And he said, *"Oh yes, we'll do as we're told. We'll behave."* Well I knew it was all rubbish. I knew it was all lies. I knew they wouldn't do it.

And we got round to the end of the week and it was the last night, the Friday of the exhibition and we were all staying there and then they were going to the airport on the Saturday morning and I was making my way home in my car. On the Friday night I went out for a meal and a drink and something else – which I'll come to later – with an Irish customer of mine and they did whatever they were doing. We never ate once together and we never ate a breakfast, never. Whether they had any breakfast, I don't know. They had this awful habit, these Chinese, at exhibitions, of not eating any of the local food. At every exhibition that I've been to where they've been, there is a man who comes around with an order pad in the middle of the morning and takes a Chinese food order off them. He then brings it back and they sit there, customers walking past them, customers who are too polite to stop and ask for prices et cetera because they see the staff on the stand eating. Get it through to them, get them to understand? An absolute impossibility. Why? a) Because they're Chinese, and b) because every other Chinese is doing exactly the same. So they just left it to me to speak to anybody that came onto the stand during their lunch hour. They didn't go anywhere. They just sat at the back of the stand.

Anyway the last night I went out with my friend from Dublin and came back. It was the last night and it didn't matter; there was no rush in the morning. I'd got to get back to Rotterdam for the Sunday. I'd decided to stop on the way back as well. I wasn't going to break my neck on these German roads, which I didn't trust. I had a key. They'd given me a key to the front door and I walked up the path, put the key in the door, opened the door and there in front of me was our German house owner who had grabbed hold of Timothy by the lapels of his jacket and was threatening to knock him into the middle of next week. And he said to him, and I will never forget this, *"If you weren't going home tomorrow, you would be certainly leaving here tomorrow."* I said something along the lines of, *"What have they been doing?"* *"Oh, you can guess. Smoking again. They've totally ignored me the whole week. You can come anytime you like Chris in the future, but these people will never come again. They will never come to my house."* I said to Timothy, *"Aren't you in any way ashamed of what you've done? You've flouted the rules of the house. You've ignored the man and you haven't got the decency to apologise."* And he just looked at me as much as to say 'I couldn't care less. We're all going home tomorrow, so what the hell?' Yeah.

So tomorrow came along and exactly that happened. And even on the last day, we didn't have breakfast together. I was in my car and gone before they even came downstairs. It never struck them as odd that I was up and away either to the exhibition or to go home. They just seemed to be there just for a bit of fun. But that was our German friend who spoke very good English who'd absolutely had enough.

The next year, I did exactly the same thing. Crossed to Holland, Bochum, stopped the night, no football match unfortunately, on but to a different place. I thought, *"Oh no, I daren't stay at the same place. I daren't. He'll think I'm bringing..."* And I went to another house which was very, very nice. Nice people again. And their son was away at university and they'd converted the attic into a flat for him so he could live in it without bothering mum and dad. And so I lived in that for five nights. I hardly ever saw mum and dad in the five nights because they were both working. They were up and gone so early in the morning. But similar to the year before, the breakfast they left was excellent. But this time we had some Chinese who I didn't know, but they were behaving in the same way as the previous lot from the previous year.

And the man who owned the house on the second year, he reported their behaviour to the exhibition centre and to the Chinese people in charge of the Chinese stands. Just to be bloody-minded, the Chinese then reported him to the people who organised the Hanover Fair for the poor breakfast that was on display and was available. Now if that's a poor breakfast, then I've never had a good one. The breakfast was superb. They did it just for damned bloody-mindedness. There is no other way to describe it than that. And thankfully I was glad that they were nothing to do with me and he couldn't associate me with them.

One fascinating thing about that was it was a very good television in the flat for the son who was away at university and one night I got a takeaway and brought it into the house and I always remember, I watched the European Cup Final on the telly, which was a nice way of spending an evening. I don't know who was playing in it because it was two foreign sides. I can't remember who it was. But nonetheless I enjoyed that night and I enjoyed being away from the Chinese. They are not an easy lot to deal with. I'm coming on to China in a big way later in the book, but they, I can promise you, are a very, very difficult lot to deal with.

On the next year, which I think was the last year of lighting being at the Hanover Fair, these same people, Timothy and his gang were all there and we were supposed to be staying until Friday night when it finished and then we were going on... they were staying in Europe a bit with me because they wanted to go to see a potential customer in Belgium, which is of course not too far a drive down through Holland and what have you. And so I had them for longer. But on the Thursday, me thinking we were leaving on the Saturday morning, on the Thursday they announced that they weren't bothering to stay for the last day of the exhibition. It was a waste of time. It was a waste of time because they'd done no work. That's why it was a waste of time. They'd done no work whatsoever.

They'd left it all to me. I'd got loads of business cards and I'd got loads of contact for them. But they knew I needed them for the Chinese end of my business, so they did nothing. They simply left it to me to handle. So on the Friday... and the exhibition didn't finish until Friday teatime... on the Friday we were driving, they wanted to go to Amsterdam. Now I know why they wanted to go to Amsterdam and any man who's been to Amsterdam knows the theory about why they wanted to go to Amsterdam. They wanted to see what they couldn't see in China. Now we get towards the outskirts of Amsterdam. It didn't take an awful long time, but we'd nowhere to stay. I'd been ringing all week trying to find a hotel room, but finding two hotel rooms for the number of people we had was proving impossible. Everywhere around was no, no, no, no, no. We got to the outskirts of Amsterdam and we came to a small town and I saw a tourist office. I went in this tourist office and I asked a man could he recommend, could he phone through, could he get me a couple of rooms, one for me and one for the gang outside in an Amsterdam hotel. And he said to me, *"I have turned away dozens of people today asking the same request. It is, this week, the annual tulip festival in Amsterdam. It is full of flower growers from all over northern Europe,"* but mainly Holland. *"The hotels are packed, absolutely packed."* But they wouldn't have it, the Chinese. I said, *"There is absolutely no point me driving now into Amsterdam because there is nowhere to stay and we will find nowhere to stay."* But they insisted and we did. I went for a meal and I don't know where they went, but I'll have a fair guess. They'll have gone to a club.

We met up again about 11 o'clock at night and we have nowhere to stay. But not the following day; that was a Sunday, on the Monday were due in Belgium to meet somebody. So I said to them, even though it was 11 o'clock at night, *"Look, let's drive down to southern Holland and the further away we get from Amsterdam, the more chance we'll have of finding a hotel."* And

I drove at that time of night something akin to 60 miles, stopping everywhere, little towns everywhere, *"No, no, no."* These tulip people were absolutely everywhere. Until eventually we came across a hotel, which was a good 60 miles away. It wasn't any more than 20 or 30 miles from the Belgian frontier, to be honest. And I managed to find a hotel – a nice one – with a couple of rooms.

The next day was Sunday and that was a problem. You see here, it wouldn't be a bad idea to go to the coast, a seaside town and have a walk round, have lunch, have another bit of a walk round and then tootle off to this small town in Belgium. I've forgotten its name. I was driving a van, a big people-carrier-type thing that we'd hired for the occasion and when we got to this seaside town where you've got the front and the beach and the weather was reasonable, I was actually quite tired. I was very tired and I said to them, *"Look, I am going to sit here in the car. I'm going to have 40 winks. You have a wander round. Get an ice-cream. Just do what people do at the seaside. And come back in a couple or three hours and we'll set off for Belgium."* 20 minutes later when I've just dropped off, there's a knock on the window – they're back. 20 minutes and they are back. I said, *"What can you possibly have seen in 20 minutes?"* *"We bored. We want go lunch."* *"Oh"*. Now at that time a lot of restaurants in Holland used to close on a Sunday, but they weren't bothered about any restaurant; they wanted a Chinese restaurant – surprise, surprise. I was driving down this road to go back out towards the motorway to go down to Belgium and on the right-hand side was a big building set back in its own grounds and it was called the 'Ying Tong' or something, Chinese restaurant. *"In here."* I said, *"Yes in here, but can't you see what it says on the gate. Closed in all languages. Closed. Fermé. Closed. They're not open on a Sunday." "They open for us."* Fair enough. So we drive in. We're the only car bar one in the car park. I took the other one to be the owner's. And we drove in, I parked the car, I sat in the car. I thought, *"Well, I ain't wasting my time knocking on the door."* And anyway if they're Chinese, it's not English they want to speak; it's Mandarin. They knocked on the door. They chatted to the owner.

The owner relented. They waved to me and the four of us sat in an empty restaurant eating a Chinese meal which he had prepared simply because they were Chinese. And then they turned to me and said, *"You pay because we haven't got any money,"* because at that time, a year or two ago, not everybody, particularly the Chinese, had credit cards. So I paid the cash. And we went back to the car; the van. Got back in the van, got back on the motorway and drove, I don't know, an hour and a half and we were in this small town in Belgium, where again we went looking for somewhere to stay. No problem in Belgium. We got somewhere on the Sunday, easily on the Sunday night. The first place I went to, I think. And that was the Chinese in Hanover and in Holland.

Just a small aside from this, Timothy who was my major contact there at the time – not for long; I branched out further than him, but nonetheless for a few more years, he was the major man I dealt with. He ended up stealing from me $7,000, which I've never seen to this day and the older one who was there who owed me, oh I don't know, something like $4,000 or $5,000 commission on some jobs, gave me in China a cheque drawn on a Hong Kong bank and when I got to Hong Kong the bank said, *"The cupboard is bare."* Now, I never saw the $7,000 and I've never heard from Timothy since. I don't know where he disappeared to. He can't be more than his mid-40s now. The other one who gave me the bounced cheque, he died of lung cancer. He was a very, very, very heavy smoker and it came as no surprise to me when I heard that he had passed away.

The Belgian trip was a complete and utter waste of time. They were in actual fact a lighting manufacturer themselves in Belgium and they didn't like the look of anything that we had from China. I took them to a railway station where there was a train back to Amsterdam and they flew home from there. And I've never been as glad to see the back of a bunch as I was to see the back of them.

# Chapter Fifteen

I suppose it's about time I mentioned our cousins across the water. I've only been twice to America. Once for pleasure; a holiday with my wife. Thoroughly enjoyed it, would recommend it to anybody. I'll tell you about that another time. The time for business was not so enjoyable and I wouldn't recommend it to anybody.

We – the '*we*' being me and the man who was managing director of the company I worked for at the time – flew from Heathrow by Air India from a gate which was tremendously well covered for security. At that time they were having a lot of bother in India and a lot of people being killed and they were concerned about the safety of their aeroplanes. But nonetheless we booked it and we went, and because I'm writing this to you now, proves that we got there and back safely. Just as a matter of interest, the next gate to the Air India gate was, of course El Al, the flight to Jerusalem or Tel Aviv, I can't remember which. I suppose that was there for very much the same sort of reasons.

When we got to Kennedy Airport in New York, we then had a transfer to another airport in the area called Newark. Now any resemblance between the very, very nice town in Nottinghamshire called Newark and this dreadful dump that is Newark is purely coincidental and purely name. But we were told it was the second most poor city in America. Well, if it was the second most poor, I certainly wouldn't like to stay at the poorest. We only allowed an hour and a half between flights and I told the chap who'd done the booking we would never get across. We were arriving at roughly rush-hour in the evening and I remember the flight on from Newark to Dallas, Fort Worth because Fort Worth and Dallas share the same airport in Texas, I remember it being only an hour and a half later than we had arrived. We came out of the airport in America, jumped in a taxi, said to the taxi driver what we wanted and he said, *"It's impossible. At this time of day with the traffic congestion as it will be, there is no way I can get you across to Newark to book into that flight."* The only thing I remember about the journey in the taxi was we went through the Abraham Lincoln or the Lincoln Tunnel named after Abraham Lincoln, I suppose, towards Newark.

We got to Newark round about six o'clock, about the same time as the flight was due to leave and I said to the chap that I was with, *"Well there isn't much point getting out of the taxi. We might as well find a hotel and see what we can do in the morning because the gate will be locked."* But of course, he was the sort of fella that knew absolutely everything and thought that the whole world would move for him. Well of course it doesn't and it didn't. Exactly what I'd forecast happened. We went into the airport, we went to the gate. They told us the gates were locked, the aeroplane was currently taxiing down to the end of the runway.

*"Come back tomorrow morning and we'll honour the tickets on a flight about seven o'clock the next morning."* This meant we'd got to go back into the airport building and try and find some way of getting a hotel. Now in America they have a telephone-type system where if they've got, say for example, 20 or so hotels in the area, not far from the airport, they list them and rather than having to dial the number, which of course you don't know, you press a button and that button immediately dials the hotel.

Well I started at the top and nothing happened and I got down to about the sixth or seventh one which was the… oh what do they call that? It was a well-known American… Johnson, that's the name, a well-known American hotel. I think it's Howard Johnson, but I wouldn't be sure… hotel group. These were the first ones to answer to phone and they said, *"Yes, we have a room."* We'd gone all that way business class to share a room rather than get two rooms, but nonetheless, we did as he said. There were two Terminals at this airport and we'll say we were in one. And they said on the phone to us, *"Go to Terminal 2 on the over-ground railway-type thing and wait for us inside the door, the glass doors. Do not go outside. It is not safe to be outside. Do not go outside."* Well if ever a warning was justified, this was it. They said, *"Our driver will turn up in about quarter of an hour, 20 minutes in a people-carrier-type thing. He'll let you in to the vehicle, lock you in and if he's anything like his normal self, he'll want to have a cigarette and then when he's had the cigarette he'll drive you to our hotel."*

All that occurred. We stayed inside of the glass perimeter window. He came in. He introduced himself. We got in the car. He locked the doors. He went for a cigarette. He came back and he set off driving towards this Johnson hotel. It wasn't far – 15 minutes or so. But when we were pulling off the main road towards it, it was fortified like a prison. It had massive, great walls round it with barbed wire on the top. And I said to the man that I was with, *"I thought I'd booked a hotel. We seem to have booked the local nick."* Anyway, obviously it gave the game away that Newark was a pretty... we'd been told it was the second poorest borough in the country and this hotel only proved what we'd been told.

We went in, we checked in and they gave us a room and they gave us a menu. They said, *"Do you want to eat tonight here?"* We said, *"Well yeah, we might as well do because we've got to be up early in the morning,"* because the flight out to Dallas tomorrow morning... they were honouring our tickets, by the way. In other words, there must have been plenty of room on the flight the following morning. We went into our room and they gave us a menu which we could look at and then go down to the restaurant. When you see American films on the telly, you hear all these... well I do anyway, all these unpronounceable foods that they all seem to be eating and it really is ridiculous that I don't recognise at least 70% of what they're talking about. But when we looked at this, this was nothing better, probably worse, nothing better than a Little Chef. It was anything with chips.

So I said, *"Well we're only here the night. Come on."* And after having a shower, we went down to this restaurant. The staff didn't speak much English and there were an awful lot of Spanish/Americans who obviously speak Spanish. But we pointed to what we wanted on the menu and it came and it was something and chips, but it filled a hole; filled a space and we went back to the room, spent the night there. Got a morning call, went and had a bit of breakfast, which wasn't something and chips, and we got back in the people-carrier-type thing and he took us back to the number 2 Terminal, dropping us off as near to the door as he could possible get. Short of mounting the pavement, that's how near we were to the door. And we went in and it turned out he'd taken us to the wrong Terminal. It didn't matter. There was time aplenty.

So we had to get this overhead thing back to Terminal 1. And it ran at regular intervals. There was no driver. It just went backwards and forwards, backwards and forwards all day long, I suppose. And we were the first two in and it filled up. It waited until there were about 10 or 12 in, then obviously somebody somewhere pressed a button and the thing set off. And I thought, well me being me, *"I'll test them out on a bit of British humour, see if they understand."* And I said out loud to the man who was with me, *"I tell you what, you drive, I'll take the fares. You drive, I'll take the fares."* Now they all looked at me as much as if I was speaking Swahili, except for one man who thought about it, realised what I'd said and laughed. And I thought, *"Good grief, one of them has got a sense of humour."* The rest hadn't. We get over to the other Terminal. As I've said earlier in the book, I'm afraid I can't report any dodgy flights. It was a perfectly normal flight.

We get to Dallas Fort Worth. We get in a taxi because we didn't know where on earth this place was. We were going to The Holiday Inn. We'd booked The Holiday Inn from the UK thinking The Holiday Inn had got a good name, can't be bad. You are definitely joking about it can't be bad. The taxi took us. He got to The Holiday Inn. He pulled off the road, up through the gates, up a slope and dropped us off. And every time we were ever dropped off anywhere, it was always as near to the door as he could possibly get. They gave us the room keys and menu to look at. Well the menu in Dallas Holiday Inn was only marginally better than the menu at the Howard Johnson in Newark.

Now I noticed as we'd driven down the road just about 150/200 yards short of the gate, there was one of these diners that they all seem to think so much of. So I said to my mate, *"I tell you what, never mind this. We've no hurry in the morning. It's not like the hurry we had this morning. We'll go down to this diner and it's only a couple of hundred yards at the very most, we'll walk it."* Now there's a four-letter word that means something different in America. We walked it, uneventfully. Went in – not many in. A third full at the very best. And we said, *"A table for two."* They looked at us with the accent as if we'd come from Mars. We sat down.

We of course had... we're in Texas now, so we had the obligatory steak after having something like a soup. And then I'd seen that the one thing they had got a whole variety of... I'd never heard of such names and I've never seen such variety and I'm a great lover – and my wife will tell you – I'm a great lover of ice-cream. And they had everything, but I'm really only partial to vanilla or strawberry and maybe lemon sorbet if I'm pushed. I ordered the ice-cream which came and it was okay, but while we were sitting there eating I did also notice that every time anybody came in to the car park, again this habit of the driver getting as close to the door as possible. I watched one man who'd got his wife and two children. He came so near to the door he might as well have come in with the car. He dropped the kids and the wife off and then he had to go and park the car in the proper car park. And they were all looking rather worried about all this until he safely got into the building.

We finished the ice-cream. I asked for a tea. I might as well have asked for a pint of Barnsley Bitter, to be quite frank with you. There was no tea, so I had to settle for coffee. I don't like coffee, I'll be absolutely honest with you, of any variety, of any nature anywhere. So I had to have a coffee because he was having a coffee, the guy I was with. And we came out. We paid and we came out and we walked it – again this word walk – walked it back to The Holiday Inn. It was only a couple of hundred yards, up the drive, in the door and just inside the door there was a big coloured gentleman who was in a fancy uniform and quite clearly was the boss porter we would call him. Doorman. I'm trying to think what word the Americans use and spell wrongly. But I can't think of one for the moment. But they spell everything wrongly. It's ridiculous.

We said good evening to him and he spoke back to us and he said... I can't do the accent because I'm writing the book. He said, *"Where have you two boys been?"* Boys! Which was very kind of him. *"Where have you two boys been?"* The lad I was with was younger than me, much younger than me, but I was no boy. *"Where have you two boys been?"* So we replied that we'd been down to the diner. *"Hmm,"* says he. *"And how did you boys get to the diner?"* *"We walked it."* And he almost had a fit. *"You went out of this, our grounds and you walked it down the road?"* *"Yeah. We walked it and we've walked it back, believe it or not,"* thinking that he thought that we weren't physically fit enough to do this 400 yard round-trip. He said, *"You're lucky to be alive or at least you're lucky to still have your watch and your money and whatever on you."* And I felt like saying, *"Well actually my watch is in Slovakia, so if they can go and get that back for me, I'd be very grateful."* And he said, *"If any of the brothers..."* he called them brothers, *"If any of the brothers had seen you two white boys walking down the street, they would have taken that as being an affront. This is a coloured area."* Oh, thinks I. We were a bit lucky here then there were no lads knocking about.

The next morning he's still on duty. *"Where are you two boys walking to today?"* he said with a smile on his face. *"Oh well, we're not walking today because we don't know where it is. We want to go to the exhibition centre. There's a lighting exhibition."* He said, *"Yes I know. Everybody knows there is, but there's nobody else bar you two as far as I know in this hotel that's got a ticket to go there."* He said, *"You see the big, yellow bus..."* You know, on the American movies you always see... I've come to the conclusion the Americans have got a surfeit of yellow paint because every bus, every taxi is painted yellow. I've yet to work out why and I've quite frankly yet to be so bothered about it to ask why. And outside there was a yellow, single-decker... I never saw a double-decker bus in America. There was a single-decker yellow bus with... Well, he was a brother; this was a sister who was driving this thing. And we go to get on board and she says, *"Are you going down the exhibition centre?"* *"Yeah, we're the two that's come from the other side of the world to look at your lighting."* *"Right."* And she puts it in gear because, as he'd said, there were only us two that expressed any interest in going to this exhibition. And she drives down the hotel drive to the gate.

Now one thing I'd noticed the night before – well we'd both noticed the night before, was opposite the main gate was... since this book I'm hoping is going to be read by ladies as well as gentlemen, I'd better be careful how I describe it... was an adult theatre, shall we say. We'd picked all the best places to stay as you can tell. An adult theatre and naughty video shop, which of course my friend and I had no intention of visiting, and if you believe that, you'll believe anything. It was purely and simply because we didn't have the time. And this woman said about the only humorous thing I've ever heard an American say. Because she'd heard us just sort of saying, *"Look at that place over there,"* and she just turned round because obviously she was waiting for traffic to go past to pull out and she said, *"That's the Dallas City Library."* And I thought that was quite amusing, the 'Dallas City Library'. And I said, *"Oh yes, why do you call it that?"* *"Well..."* she said,

*"...just for the simple reason that there's more people go in there than go in the Dallas City Library."* I thought very good, very good, very good. It's the only funny thing I've ever heard an American say. It came across rather well.

Anyway, long story short, she pulls out and we go about a mile or a mile and a quarter and there's this great, big exhibition centre. We pull up, we get out and we have two tickets which we've already pre-registered in the UK via the American Embassy, I think it was. Not the new one, not the new, ugly-looking thing, but a proper embassy which they had before, and we went in. And there was an old-ish fella on the desk. Well he was into his 70s, well into his 70s and he looked at our address and all we'd put down was the name of the company Yorkshire UK. We hadn't given the full address because I'd said, *"Don't give them the full address. Just put down the name of the company, put Yorkshire and put UK. That'll do."* And this old boy, who picked up these two passes to get us made two more passes to fasten to our jackets, a great beam came on his face, a beam as wide as the Dartford Tunnel, but a damn sight cheaper. And he said, *"It's absolutely wonderful that you have come all this way to see our exhibition."* I said, *"Well that's quite all right. It's a lighting exhibition. We're in lighting. You've got lighting to sell. We've come to look. Do you know the UK?"*

It turned out that, at his age, he was a man who'd been a soldier in the Second World War and he'd been on the D-Day landings so he was lucky to be alive. And of course that meant that he'd lived and was stationed somewhere – as they used to say – in Southern England. But he'd heard of Yorkshire. Well I obviously think that everybody's heard of Yorkshire. If you haven't heard of Yorkshire, then you're past hope, aren't you? Anyway, he said, *"Well I hope you enjoy yourselves boys."* It was nice to keep being called 'boys' because I was by no means a boy.

So we went in to the exhibition and decided, well where are we going to go? Where do you go? Which stand do you go to first? And we walked around and people kept talking to us and looking on the badge and I could see that a great many of them had no idea what UK meant. And one fella said to us – and I remember this vividly – *"What state is the UK in?"* and I said, *"It's in a right bloody state with this Tory government."* That's given my politics away. My friend was a true-blue conservative. I think he's the only one in Leeds, but there again, somebody has to be the lone ranger. And I'm afraid, it didn't get us anywhere because he thought, as you can tell from what I've said, that the UK was part of a state in America, which just goes to show that you lot that don't know where Bawtry and Wetherby are, aren't the only ones that should buy an AA book. We wandered around. We saw not much that we liked. Believe it or not, British lighting is years in advance of American. And apart from a few outdoor lanterns which were cheap, I'm afraid we weren't doing very well here. We weren't doing very well at all.

It gets round to lunchtime and there was a thing pointing to a café where we went and it was one of these places where you walked round with a trolley, pick up the sandwich and the bun or whatever you want and then at the end there's drinks, which were... well looking at what everybody was having, they were nearly all having Coca-Cola. And I watched these people and every single one of them, without question, was getting about 80% ice and 20% liquid and paying the full price for it. Now without mentioning where I come from again, this sort of attitude doesn't go down well here. I'd have gone for 20% ice and 80% liquid, but of course that wasn't the American way.

It gets to be my turn and I got one of those great big red tumbler things that a certain cola company do and I said to him... I handed it... one of those and he starts with this scoop thing to fill it up with ice and I just said, *"Excuse me..."* I don't think he'd ever heard the words 'excuse me' in his life in America. And he turned round to me and he looked at me and I said, *"I don't want any ice."* *"But everybody has ice."* I said, *"I don't want any ice. I want a cola. I don't want any ice."* And if looks could kill, he would have killed me on the spot because they were obviously selling ten pence worth of coke – that's given the game away – ten pence worth of coke or 10% of coke or whatever percentage it was and the balance was just frozen blooming water – ice! And he didn't like it when somebody said, *"I don't want any ice."* I said, *"No, I'll pay you..."* 50 cents or whatever it was, *"...but I want a full mug of liquid."* And he did it because he'd no choice because that's what the price list said, but he didn't like me.

We had a sit down, chatted with one or two people who were bemused and bewildered and... I'm not saying bothered, but that we'd come all this way. And we met a man on a stand who rejoiced in the name, as some Americans do, of Randy. Now when they say their first name is Randy, it always makes me smile. It's all down the same lane as the adult theatre just down the road. I cannot understand why they abbreviate a perfectly good name – presumably they're called Randolph, I don't know – to Randy. And Randy was a giant of a man. I'm big enough, but Randy would have made two of me – and a bit more. But he was a nice man or a nice guy, they would call it. Well, so would we these days, but not me. I don't use words like 'guy' as far as I'm aware or as rarely as possible. I don't know what he was selling. Oh, he was the cheap lantern man, that's right. He was the cheap lantern man where we did have an interest. And he said, *"Well if you're interested, shall we have a meal tonight?"* I said, *"Well not at The Holiday Inn, I hope."* *"Oh no, no, no, no. You're in Texas. Tonight you go to a steakhouse,"* because of course Texas is very famous for its beef. And we got in a taxi.

We went to the address that he stipulated and when we went inside, again getting out about two foot from the blooming door, we went inside and there he is occupying the best part of two seats by a table. Round comes the menu. I had a look at it and I just could not believe the size of the steaks that were on offer. The smallest steak on offer – and I kid you not – was called a ladies' steak and that was 14oz of red meat – a ladies' steak. Well 14oz is a lot more than I would normally eat of steak, but we both ordered a ladies' steak because it's the most we could get down us, I think. Randy had a 25oz something or other steak, two jacket potatoes in that silver paper and loads of vegetables. We had one steak, one potato and some vegetables to share. A bit of a dessert; mine was an ice-cream – well I like ice-cream. They didn't do tea, so I got another cup of coffee. We didn't have wine or anything like that. Randy wasn't into his wine. He was into his massive steaks. And we talked a bit of business and we said we would have a look at his catalogue when we got home and more than likely place him an order. We did place him an order actually. Two or three, I think, but I wouldn't like to be sure of that. He got in a taxi. He got us a taxi and he told them to take us back to The Holiday Inn and that was it.

On the way back, we stopped. The taxi driver just pulled up and stopped without any instigation from us, without any request from us. He just stopped. And we wondered why. And we sat there for about 25 seconds wondering why we were here and why we'd stopped because there wasn't much traffic. And then he realised that we didn't know where we were. So he told us, and he had stopped the car at the spot – the exact spot – where John Kennedy was assassinated. And I tell you for nothing, that the area from where the man shot him to the area where we were sitting looks an awful lot greater on the TV film because apparently television has a habit of exaggerating sizes and distances. Coming to the point absolutely, you couldn't see how a man who was anything remotely competent with a gun, and I mean all the American love guns, could miss him. And of course, he didn't miss him, and of course the world changed on that one moment. We only stayed a couple of seconds more and he took us back to the hotel and the next day we got up and we got another taxi. We didn't stay another night. We didn't go to the exhibition again. I phoned the two airlines – the airline back to New York and the airline onto the UK, which was Air India, to see whether they could change our tickets and because we'd booked business class they were very helpful. So we flew back to New York.

Now just as an aside, I was reading only yesterday where there are apparently 11 expressions that we use in Barnsley that identify us as being from Barnsley and one of them is 'it looks black over Bill's mother's'. Another one's 'coil oyle'. Now, 'looking back over Bill's mother's' I think is pretty obvious. I think it shows every sign of 'it's about to rain heavily.' And 'coil oyle' - well it isn't in the AA book, but it's in the same league. We landed at New York just in time before the thunderstorm - of all thunderstorms - started. It wasn't just black over Bill's mother's, you couldn't see Bill's mother's, that's a fact. We went into the Air India lounge and ugh, a couple of hours after we should have taken off, all the passengers are in this here lounge and the rain is still unbelievable, absolutely unbelievable. And they decided, the staff, to fly when it stopped but only fly if a show of hands among us the passengers voted for flying because the runway was darn near underwater.

Well the majority voted and I voted with the majority to fly once it stopped. It stopped about an hour later and then they put us on a bus to take us to the aeroplane. More yellow paint needed. And we got on this bus and it was a single-decker-type thing. I think they put two on. The things you see on the movies, on the films. Now our bus got very full and we were at the end of the queue and the seats were all taken. We go up the steps and the driver's still letting people come on and crush on and we could just about get in all right. But there was a yellow line drawn across the bus and it said '*All passengers must stand beyond this line*'. Now this guy who I was with – and I've used the word 'guy' deliberately here because I think he was picking up American habits all the time we were there.

This man that I'm with decides that it's more comfortable – and he was right in that issue – to stand the other side of the yellow line because there was more room. But rules are there to be obeyed, not to be broken and you'd got to stand the other side, the driver's side if you like, of the yellow line. And he was the sort of man that if he didn't fancy standing the other side of the yellow line, then he wouldn't stand the other side of the yellow line. And the driver turned to him and said, *"You no move, we no go."* And just so he got it quite clearly, he repeated it. *"You no move, we no go."* And he looked at me and I said to him, *"For goodness sake…"* (I won't mention his name). *"Move over the yellow line and stand at the side of me and let's get across to this plane, let's get up in the air and let's get home."* He did, we did and landed in Heathrow and came back north.

For months later Randy was pursuing us for this order which he eventually got and I used to send him messages by fax. There wasn't any emails in those days. And my email about the orders always used to end up with, *"Have you digested the 25oz of steak because I've still got most of the 14oz still with me?"* He never replied because I'm quite positive, again, British humour doesn't travel and he didn't understand what on earth I was talking about. But we got his order. I'm afraid they didn't sell very well because the design, the style, they may have been cheaper, but the style and the design were distinctly not British. And we may have placed a repeat order – I don't recall – eventually. I don't recall.

We never did any more business either way in America. You've got to remember that one difficulty with America is that if… You see, if a voltage is concerned, if the product has a transformer, for example, then you've a problem because they work on 110 and we work on 240. You've also got to remember that the lamp holder inside the fitting in those days… today, well LEDs have taken over, but in those days, the size of the lamp holder, they didn't use the bayonet cap lamp holder, they just used the Edison screw lamp holder which we could manage. We stock the lamps that fitted, but in this country they're called E27; 27 is just the diameter. The American fitting is 26, so the lamp holder is no good for the lamps that we stocked and the Americans had to buy in the right lamp… Oh, it's all a load of nonsense. I won't bore you anymore with it. But they weren't compatible with our system.

Randy, I don't know what happened to him, whether he left the company or not. He came from Chicago, did the lad, which is a long, long way from Dallas. Eventually his faxes stopped. Our orders stopped and I never heard any more of him after. I'll never forget the trip to America. I'll never forget the way things were and I'll never forget the poverty at times we did see and I'll never forget, *"You don't move, we don't go."*

# Chapter Sixteen

Let's have a look at Denmark. The Little Mermaid country. Been there a few times. I think I've been everywhere a few times. I met a man at an exhibition, same exhibition at Olympia, and he was all full of himself and what he could do for us in Denmark and what he couldn't. It all ended up as couldn't, but then again you win some, you lose some.

The story started with me in Madrid, flying... I'd gone to go and see a customer, big customer in Lyon. I had two big customers in Lyon, one a British-owned company, and the other a French-owned organisation. Went to see them two, and we'll come to France at a later time because I love France, and everybody who knows me knows it's true. I've got to then fly from Lyon to Paris, two or three days in Paris, and then fly to Copenhagen, where I'd never been before. I went to the airport in Lyon which was not very big. I think there are a couple of airports in Lyon. This wasn't particularly large.

I got on a plane with a lot of French tourists who had been on holiday in Spain, and I got next to an old lady on the back... I was on the very last seat of the plane. We chatted in French, which was good for me. I don't know if it was very good for her, but it was certainly very good for me. Off we go. Again, an uneventful flight, but beautiful. Beautiful, sunny day, and we went over the Pyrenees and it was a fantastic sight. Something I shall never forget. Carry on another hour or so, maybe less, touchdown in Lyon. I've got a hotel booked, and when I come out, I will get in a taxi and go to the hotel.

Go through the customs, show them my passport, things are a bit different in those days, and went to the carousel, the only carousel for my blue, Cambridge blue it was, coloured suitcase, which was at the beginning of a four week tour around Europe with me and this was only the fourth or fifth day. So I'm stood there with all these French tourists, and the luggage is going round, and round, and round, and you know that sinking feeling you get in the pit of your stomach when you're getting round to the last few cases, there's nothing else coming through the rubber flappy bits at the end, and there ain't no Cambridge blue-coloured suitcase.

We end up with all the French gone and two suitcases… Sorry, one suitcase left. Mine? No. This is a red, a bright red suitcase. No blue case. No blue suitcase to be seen. So, at all airports there's a lost luggage place. I went there, told them the situation, and some bloke said to me, *"It's there. It's going round and round and round."* *"Look, I've told you. I have lost a blue suitcase. That is bright red. How can it be my suitcase?"* *"You go check."* He insisted that I go and check this damn suitcase, which is a total waste of time. It was a totally different design. It was a totally different colour.

It wasn't mine. But it had got a tag on it with a name and address. I could see that from a distance. Now, if you're from Bolton, and you lost a red suitcase years and years ago, I last saw that suitcase in Lyon, because it was a fella from Bolton in Lancashire who owned the suitcase. So where my case had got to, I don't know, and he wouldn't know where his case had got to, but I did know.

So there I am, just with my briefcase, the clothes I stand up in, and thankfully, passport, money, et cetera but no clothes, and I'm at the beginning of a four week tour round Europe. So, there was nothing else for it but to fill in a form declaring it lost and leaving it to them and telling them the name of the hotel that I was staying at, just one night in Lyon when I went to see this UK customer with a couple of hundred French branches the following day. He was very helpful, to be honest, the boss-man there. He took me down to a local bank and with an American Express card that I had at the time, we managed to get me some more euros... Not euros, more Francs, more currency, more Francs than I had on me at the time.

I left him and I got on the TGV, very high speed train up to Paris. I'd told the people at Lyon airport the name of the hotel in Paris. Splendid Étoile it was called, and it's very, very near the Champs-Élysées and the Arc de Triomphe.

The next day I get up there and I have an agent in that northern part of France, a chap called Bob Genier, who became a lifelong friend of mine until he died.

I explained to Bob, because he didn't speak a word of English, but he loved everything British. He was a real Anglophile. Bob is a name in France that doesn't exist. If your name is Robert, you stick with Robert. If you use the name Bob it means you're an Anglophile, and they don't like you dropping the French name Robert.

I told him the full story. We visited the customers as we would normally do, but between, we were riding around in his car and I told him the full story, and he took me to the head office on the Champs-Élysées of Air France. Between us we recounted the story to somebody at Air France, and I don't know whether they didn't believe me or what, I'm not sure, but anyway, they give me 400 Francs, which was about £40. What, in terms of clothes, when you're my build, I was supposed to do with £40, I'm not quite sure. Not quite sure at all. There wasn't much that I could do. I spend a few days with him walking around. I must have been... I had bought a deodorant, so I wasn't smelling that badly. I get to the day when I'm leaving him and I go to Roissy Charles de Gaulle airport, and I fly by Air France up to Copenhagen.

The next day in Copenhagen... As I say, it was a country, never mind a city, a country I'd never been to before, Denmark. Met a man there who was full of himself, but not full of business. There was nothing much to be gleaned from him. He kindly took me for lunch somewhere in Copenhagen. He enquired whether I'd ever seen the Little Mermaid. I said, *"Only on postcards,"* so he took me down to see that, and I was... Well, I was disappointed. I was amazed. I didn't realise it was going to be as small as it is. He was very kind but there was no business. It was quite clear that there was no business from him, even though he was going to try hard if I sent him some samples, which I did in turn do.

I left Copenhagen the same afternoon for a flight to a place, I believe it was Aalborg. Small airport. Arrive in Aalborg, about an hour's flight from Copenhagen. I hadn't got a customer there. I was going to Aalborg because I wanted to go to Gothenburg in Sweden the following day and there was a flight from Aalborg to Gothenburg that suited me. So, I get to Aalborg and I've got no customers. I'm just staying the night in a hotel, back to the airport and up and away the following day. Go to the hotel in a taxi and I thought *"it's bloomin' quiet round here. There's not much doing."* It was a working day, I thought. Not much doing round here. There's nobody about very much. Nobody on the streets.

Went in the hotel, registered, checked in with the young lady who spoke good English and asked what time I could book for dinner, and she said, *"You can't. The restaurant is closed."* *"The restaurant is closed?"* She says, *"Yes. There's only about three guests and you're one of them. Today's a bank holiday in Denmark. Nobody's working."* I thought, *"Oh jolly good. That really... I've got no suitcase, I've got no clothes other than what I stand up in, and the restaurant's not open."* She couldn't think of a restaurant in the town that would be open because to them a bank holiday is a bank holiday. It means it's shut. Everything is shut. Or nearly everything you'll find, as we carry on. I said, *"What about room service?"* *"No, nothing open til morning for breakfast."* She said, *"The only thing I can suggest is that you go out. It's not a very big town. You walk around and you just hope that you'll find that there is something open."*

Well, I did this and I'm walking up this street and down the next street, and there is plenty of restaurants, but they're all closed. There is nobody. There is absolutely nobody. Just a few cars, the odd person on the street, nothing. Virtually nothing. Until I walk down one particular street, and as I'm walking down that street, there was an alleyway to my right, and I looked down the alleyway and there was... Down there was a sign. An illuminated sign. And being the good lighting salesman that I am, I noticed it was lit. So I walk down and I notice that in red it said, *"Restaurant,"* and also over the top there was a red light. Now, I thought no more about it. I was just so pleased to find a restaurant that was open.

I went in. I had to go up some stairs. When I got up the stairs, there was quite a few people in, and there was a bar with a barman. I asked, and he spoke reasonably good English, if they were doing food, and he said, *"Yes. There's a menu on the table. Pick a table and I'll come and take an order off you,"* which he promptly did. He give me ten minutes and I had a steak I remember, and all the things that go with it. It was only when I was eating the steak that I realised that every customer in the restaurant was a man. There were no couples. Well, there might have been some couples, but they certainly weren't men and women. Everybody in the restaurant was a man.

Now, I don't want to be rude and I'm very aware of political correctness and all the rest of it, and I don't care what people's sexual inclinations are. I'm not interested. But, I know what mine are, and I do feel a little discomfort, or I did in those days. I wouldn't today. Things have altered. I felt a little discomfort where I was. I had a dessert, asked him for the bill, paid and went. Hmm. Got back to the hotel. She said, *"Did you find anywhere?"* I said, *"Yes,"* and told her the brief story. The girl smiled. She said, *"Oh I forgot about that. I didn't think you'd want to go there. That's why I didn't tell you about it."* I said, *"Well, I found it."*

Next morning, breakfast, taxi, out to the airport. Get out to the airport. Now we're back to a working day. There's quite a few people in the airport. It's not a big airport, there's only two gates, but there was a big Boeing... Either a Boeing or an Airbus, I can't remember which, and a little Cessna seven seater job. There were two flights on the board. One was Copenhagen and the other one was Gothenburg. I thought to myself, *"I don't need telling which aeroplane of the bigg'un and the littl'un is going to where."* Now, the weather was dreadful. The cloud was very low and it was pouring with rain. They announced the first flight. Most people... Well actually, it was everybody bar two, me and another man. Everybody bar two went and got on the big flight, they just walked across the tarmac and got on the flight to Copenhagen on the big plane, which left my imagination proving itself to be quite right. We were on, me and this other fella, we were on the little Cessna I think they call them. Seven seats it had, anyway. That was going to take us to Gothenburg. Now, I'd never been on a plane this size in my life, and I've got to admit, a little bit of fear and a little bit of concern, and I'd have rather been doing anything than getting on this plane.

I was the first one on of the two of us. The other fella sat down opposite me, because the seats faced one another. It was a peculiar configuration. At the front there was a curtain, and behind the curtain was the pilot and the first officer. The engine started up, and we're ready for off, and the first officer opened the curtain and proceeded to give the two of us the normal spiel, the speech, about, *"Good morning ladies and gentlemen."* There weren't any ladies. *"Welcome to Air whatever it was called."* Air Dane or something I don't know. *"Our flight to Gothenburg will take an hour and twenty minutes. Our flying height will be 7,000 feet,"* which is nothing by comparison to what you're normally flying at, but there again it was only a small aeroplane. What was bothering me is there are a great many mountains between Aalborg and Gothenburg, particularly as you are coming in to land at Gothenburg, and I was writing the obituary of, *"British man dies in plane crash in southern Sweden."* Put that out of your mind, because I tried to put it out of my mind, because it obviously didn't happen.

The chap who was there with me was a young fella, late 20s, and he introduced himself in very good English, and I said to him, *"And what do you do?"* He says, *"I sell biscuits."* *"Biscuits?"* *"Yes, I work for the Oxford Biscuit Company, and my area is Scandinavia plus*

NOT FOR ALL THE TEA IN CHINA

*Iceland."  "Oh, fine.  You'll know your way about then?"  "Yes, yes, yes."*

The first officer, when he'd gone back to his seat, hadn't pulled the curtain back properly, and therefore I could see out of the front window of the plane, what they could see, and what the three of us could see was absolutely nothing except for cloud. We flew at 7,000 feet in pouring rain, bumping around all over the sky to Gothenburg, me just hoping and praying that we wouldn't bump into an unexpected mountain. It wasn't until we got within, I don't know, a couple of hundred feet of the ground that I actually saw the ground.

We landed safely, and I took another flight to Stockholm, which was a bigger plane this time, about the same size plane as I'd seen earlier that morning in Aalborg, again in nothing but cloud and rain. Got down to Stockholm. It was still pouring with rain. I had arranged to see a potential customer down there who did do a bit of work with us over the years but I never went back. I just left him to do Sweden to himself, and flew back.

That night, took a flight... All this is happening in the one day. Took a flight to Oslo. All this is occurring in cloud and rain. I never saw an inch of the ground until we got there. Now, I'd no customer in Oslo, but I had a potential customer in a city called Trondheim. Trondheim is about halfway up the western coast of Norway. There only is one coast isn't there, apart from the southern one? Up the western coast of Norway, and I had decided that there was a train that went up there, and it went up overnight. But because we were so far to the north, it never actually went dark. It was a fascinating journey, winding its way through mountains and hills, and then flat bits and what have you, until we eventually got to Trondheim the next morning, where I was met by the customer, a man who wasn't a customer but became a customer, a very good customer, and he took me round Trondheim for a little look round the place. I'd taken some samples on top of the ones that we'd sent him and he gave me a nice order. He gave us several nice orders as the years went by. I was there a couple of days discussing things with him, talking about the products that we did and the products that we were hoping to do.

It was getting very near to Christmas at this time, and I was going from Trondheim by train to Bergen to catch a flight home to Newcastle. Normally at this time of year, you would see a lot of snow in the Trondheim area, in that part of Norway, but it had remained a little bit mild for a while down at a coastal level. I got on the train, a day time train, down to Bergen, and as we got higher up we started to get into loads and loads of snow. I mean two or three foot deep this snow. Somewhere out in the middle of nowhere was a small town with a railway station, and we stopped to let people get on and off. When we started to carry on down towards Bergen, a man came walking round the train dressed up as Father Christmas. He was giving all, and everybody, a present from Norwegian Railways, which I thought was very kind and I thought it wouldn't be a bad leaf to take out their book and to learn for British Rail. He gave me one, and he asked if I was married and I said *"yes"* and he gave me something for my wife. At that time, I had a step-daughter, and he gave me something... I don't know what it was of course. I've forgotten. They were all wrapped up. He gave me something for the step-daughter, and I brought them back down to Bergen.

When we got to Bergen it was, I don't know, pretty late in the day, about I should think eight o'clock in the evening. I went out to the... The flight was about 9.30/10 o'clock to Newcastle and would take about two and half hours, maybe a bit more because it stopped off in Stavanger, which is a town in Norway. We flew... Again, it was still pouring with rain. Thankfully, not snowing otherwise we could have been completely lumbered. Flew down and this time the airline was Dan-Air. Now, a lot of reps used Dan-Air for flights up into Europe, and particularly northern Europe, and they hadn't got the best safety record, to put it mildly. All the reps, such as me, used to call it Dan-Dare Scareways, which perhaps was unfair, but nonetheless it was a bit of a laugh, a bit of a joke, and they don't exist now so what the hell.

We went up to so and so feet, dropped down again to Stavanger. They fed us and they had some very attractive, very nice air hostesses, and then we took off from Stavanger for about the two-hour flight, maybe a bit more, I can't recall, down to Newcastle. When we got up and away at 30,000 feet, flying down to Newcastle, the girls, who had disappeared mysteriously, suddenly appeared in Santa Claus outfits, somewhat short red skirted Santa Claus outfits, and it was lovely. We were going home for Christmas, all of us, and they were walking up and down singing Christmas Carols to us, and I thought that was very nice, very pleasant, and something which a lot of people could learn from. Landed at Newcastle, thanked them all for what they'd done. It made it a pleasant journey, out of a journey which was... Could have been a bit hairy, but they'd taken that away from us by being so pleasant and nice and kind.

I knew of a train to Leeds, and I'd arranged for my assistant from Barnsley to pick me up at Leeds station at such and such a time, which would be in the early hours. She did very well. She did what I asked her. She turned up in her car and she picked me up off the Newcastle train. The funny thing about Newcastle station was there was a train due at we'll say, I don't know, half past eleven at night, which was going to Leeds and onto wherever and I got there five minutes after it had gone. I thought, *"Oh dear. Now I'm going to have to find somewhere to stay and some means of telling Michelle, that was my assistant, that I'm not on the train."* But, there was another train there, and the guard, or the bloke on the platform, said, *"Where are you going?"* and I said, *"I'm going to Leeds, but I've missed it. I'll have to wait for the morning."* He said, *"No, you won't. That other train there is also going to Leeds because it's the first one back from Leeds in the morning. You'll be able to get on that. They're allowing passengers to pay to go on there."* So I did, and I followed ten minutes behind the main train in another train.

Thankfully, Michelle had added two and two together at the other end in Leeds, found out there was a second train coming down from Newcastle and waited just to see if I was on that, and I was. We went to her car and she drove me home. So, from thinking it might well be a rather belated Christmas arrival, it turned out to be just what I wanted, and I would always thank the people on Dan-Dare, or Dan-Air, for the very pleasant way they treated us, and Norway has always got that little extra special place in my heart, that extra special place, and one day I hope, I'd like to go back. But I'm going in the summer, I'll tell you. I'm going in the summer.

# Chapter Seventeen

Let's go back to Scandinavia for a couple of wee ditties.

I'd been at an exhibition. I've always been an exhibition man. I've always believed that the people that you meet there are going to do you more... Because you're meeting human beings face to face, they're going to do you more good than a million bloomin' adverts, or a million emails, or a million Google responses. Not that any of that existed in those days of course, I'm just referring to now. Met this man down at, it would be Olympia, it would be the security exhibition, and he liked what he saw on our stand and he said that he thought that he could do well for it in Denmark, and he proved to be quite right as the years went by. He sold a lot of stuff for us and we did very well, and it was a very good relationship. I was sorry when I left the company to lose people like him.

So, I have to make my mind up, *"Am I going to Randers? Yes."* So I went to Randers. I got over there through Copenhagen and then a train up to Randers, got a taxi to the hotel, went into the hotel, booked in, had a quick look before I went up in the lift to the room, had a quick look at the menu for the restaurant that night in the hotel. Hmm. Not so good. Not so good at all. Not very good at all. Nothing very appealing to me, so I decided that I'd just go in, have a shower and I would then go back downstairs, go outside the front where I'd seen there was a few taxis hanging about when I'd arrived, in the hope that there would be at least one because that would be enough.

I get in this taxi and go back down into the town. It was only a five or six, seven minute drive, and I went back down into the town. I found somewhere which looked clean, reasonable, looked at the menu, yes, various things I fancied and could eat, so in I went. Had a meal, paid, came out and then the big question was, well, it was only about half past seven at night. In those days I used to eat very early, not nowadays, I don't, but in those days I was... I suppose it was to do with being brought up with my mother and we didn't have dinner, we had tea. We had us teas. Us teas. I thought... I suppose I was doing the same thing on my trails round Europe. It could only have been about 7:15, 7:30 when I came out.

Well, there wasn't much in that hotel apart from a bar and I didn't really fancy going back up there at that time so I decided to have a wander round, a walk round the town, just to see what there was. To be honest, there wasn't much at all apart from the obvious shops that you see, and banks and things like that. But I did catch, out the corner of my eye, a cinema over to my left, down this side street. I thought, *"In for a penny, in for a pound,"* so I went down the side street. Now, I don't know about you but my Danish is not what you'd call red hot and I wasn't too clear of the two offerings that they had on at the same time, what the devil they were both about. So, it was a bit like flipping a coin and, you know, heads was left and tails was right. And I went in and I went to the desk, the pay desk, and paid to go in the one to my right-hand side. I noticed that when I paid and I said I wanted to go in there, the woman at the desk gave me a sort of a wry grin, and a smile and a wink, and I thought, *"Hmm, she's either being extremely friendly, or she knows something I don't."*

Well, it turned out that she wasn't being friendly, she knew something I didn't. I'd pay to go into, and I found within minutes of sitting down, I'd paid to go into and watch a blue movie. There can be no other description to it than that. I thought, *"Well, I've never seen one of these before in my life."* Things were different in those days, you know. We really knew... Even married men in their 30s as I was, or 40 maybe nearly, at the time, I knew so little of life by comparison to what is known... What things people do today. So I sat through about half an hour of this grunting and groaning, and screaming and shouting, and I thought, *"Oh dear, I can't be putting up with this. It's a bit boring really,"* and I came out. I didn't look to my side to see what reaction I got from her, I just kept my gaze straight in front of me, out, end of the street, saw a taxi rank, in it, back to the hotel.

Next day, had my meeting, everything went fine, an order was placed, we had a meal at lunch time. I'd arranged to stay another night. That night I ate in the hotel and the next morning, I'd got a train back down to Copenhagen at about half past twelve I think, round about lunchtime. I paid for the hotel, went outside, got in a taxi and asked to go to the railway station. I went to railway station early because I'd seen when I was down there, these compartment things that you can put a coin in and open up and put your case in, and then go for a wander round and come back quarter of an hour before your train, and go on the platform and off you go. And that was exactly my intent.

Overnight it had turned a bit cold. Well, to be honest with you, it had turned very cold. But never mind, I'd got my overcoat with me this time. It wasn't like Latvia. I decided to have a wander round, but as I was wandering around, the weather turned worse. It went from cold to sleet to sleet and snow, and the wind got up, so I found myself wandering around this Danish town on my own, nothing else to do but look in the shop windows.

Now, at the time, I hadn't been married very long to my second wife, and I saw a lingerie shop, and we're in Denmark. We're in Scandinavia remember. A lot more broad minded than where I was living at the time. I saw one or two things in the window I thought, *"Ooh."* My second wife was an extremely attractive lady. It turned out at the end of it all that she was more than attractive to more than one man and I wasn't alone in her attentions, but we won't go into that because I'm sure, although you'd love to know, I'm not going to tell you. I went in and they spoke to me in Danish. I said, *"I'm sorry, I'm British."* *"Oh, that's no problem, we all speak English because we get quite a few tourists in the summertime. What would you like?"* I said, *"I really don't know. Something for my wife. I've only recently got married and I'm going home, flying home from Oslo back down to Heathrow in a couple of days."* I know Oslo's in another country, I haven't got there yet! *"I'd like to take something back for her."*

As I'm walking around the shop with this woman on my right shoulder, we come up to one of these mannequin-type things that you see in women's shops, and this mannequin was clad in a bright red... Barnsley shirts, that's what appealed to me, you know, the fact it was Barnsley's colours. Bright red, very short, shorty nightdress and a pair of matching... Oh, I'd better give it a proper word. Knickers, we'll call them. They didn't cover a great deal from the looks of it. But only having been recently married, I thought *"Oh,"* you know, *"This'll do. She'll really like this. She'll really think I'm suddenly turning into a sort of a lover of great intent and great passion."* So, I bought it and left. Went to the station, got my suitcase out the little cubbyhole, got on the train, went down to Copenhagen, got on a plane. In those days... At the end, because I'd made a few quid I travelled business class because it's a hell of a sight more comfortable than economy, but in those days everything was economy and as cheap as you could possibly make it.

So, I get on this aeroplane, and there's three seats on either side of the aisle and we've got about a two hour, two and a half hour ride down to Heathrow, and the other two people who were one against the window, one in the middle and I was the aisle seat. I got chatting to them on the journey and they were Americans, and they were going into London, and I think they'd got a few quid. I think they were saving it all on the air fare by travelling economy. I think they could have afforded to travel business. Maybe there wasn't business class. I don't really know. I didn't look.

When we get to Heathrow, the man said to me that he'd never been to the UK before. He didn't understand the money. He didn't know... He was frightened to death of the accent and the language and all the rest of it. He just asked me if I'd... Where was I going, and I said I was going to King's Cross station for a train to Doncaster. *"Where are you going?"* I said, and he said, *"We're staying at The Savoy."* I thought, *"The Savoy? And we're travelling economy. That's a little bit of a contradiction in terms, but never mind. That's his business not mine."* He said, *"Would you do me a favour, because I'm a little bit frightened of stories I've heard about London taxi drivers taking advantage of American tourists by charging the earth for fares?"* I said, *"What do you want me to do?"* He said, *"Well..."* I said, *"I tell you what, you ask for The Savoy. You ask for The Savoy, and then I, when we get to The Savoy... He'll think we're all going to The Savoy. But when we get to The Savoy, I won't get out. I'll say, 'Now, you take me on... You charge these people for this part of the journey, and then I want to go from here to King's Cross.' But he won't know that until we get to The Savoy. Don't tell him and I won't give the game away by speaking loud so he can hear my accent."*

So we come out through all the necessary places where they stamp this and stamp that, and we get the suitcases and we go outside the front. We queue up and we get a taxi. I say, *"Go on then. You say what I've said. You just ask for The Savoy hotel."* So he did, and he and his wife got in, and I followed them in to the taxi with my bag. Now, I sat in the seat with the back to the driver, so my voice was travelling away from him not towards him.

We get to The Savoy, and I'd ask the man who was in charge of the taxi rank at Heathrow how much did he think it would be approximately in those days to go to The Savoy, and he said, *"Savoy from here, about £30."* It'll be about £80 today, but in those days, about £30. I said, *"To go on to King's Cross?"* He said, *"About another £10. It's in inner London and he'll charge you more for it."* I said, *"Fair enough. That'll do. At least I won't... I want to get home."*

So, we get to The Savoy. He stops the car right outside the door. If any of you know The Savoy, you go up a little cul-de-sac affair and then you spin round, come out and carry on. We get to the door. A very posh-looking fella in a fancy suit and a top hat opens the door. This greatly impressed the Americans. They asked the man, the taxi driver, *"How much?"* and I tell you quite honestly, the taxi driver... I couldn't see the meter because I'd got my back to it, and the Americans didn't understand what they were looking at, or where to look for, to look at the meter. He said, *"£100."* £100! Can you believe it? And I just said to the Americans, *"You get out the taxi,"* and I got out as well and I said, in the broadest possible Yorkshire accent I could drag up, *"It's not any more than £30, and I'm*

*going to King's Cross station. They're giving you £30,
and I'm giving you whatever the balance is. I've been
told that that'll be no more than about £10."*

Now, the taxi driver felt absolutely robbed by this
because he didn't realise that one of the three of his
passengers was not an American, and he was very, very,
very distraught and annoyed. So much so that when
they gave him the £30 and I said to him, *"That's all
you're getting so don't start shouting and bawling
because that's all you're getting,"* he decided that he
would make a remark about where I came from, and a
remark about my parentage. Well, he got one right and
one wrong.

Yes, I'm from Yorkshire, which is something that he
said with an old English adjective before it, but the
other wrong he got wrong, because I can assure you,
and I'm looking actually at a picture as I speak to
you now, as I do the book, I'm looking at a picture of
my mother and father's wedding day in 1941, or 2, or
whenever it was. The first bit, Yorkshire, yes. The
other bit which began with B, no, and I can prove it.
We go off to the King's Cross station. I just stuffed him
a £10 note on his passenger seat, didn't say thank you,
didn't say goodbye, just went, and he muttered and
grumbled and whatever. *"You can please yourself.
You've got £40. You've done very well out of it, and
I'm off."* I get onto the train, get in a taxi, I couldn't be
bothered with messing around with buses, it was all
taking too long, because there is not a train from
Doncaster to Barnsley. I couldn't be bothered. I just got
in a taxi outside and he ran me home.

All along of course, I'm guarding my suitcase as if I've got the crown jewels inside it. I thought, to a certain extent, I had got the crown jewels inside it. I certainly thought I'd got the gateway to several nights of enjoyment, I'll be polite, and I couldn't wait to go upstairs with the suitcase and my then wife followed me because she wanted to get hold of all, as women do, *"I'll take all the mucky washing off you."* So, I go upstairs. She follows me upstairs. I open the suitcase and I say, *"Before you take the dirty washing, there's a present for you."* Before looking at the present, she was all over me, kissing and thanking me and what a wonderful, nice man I was, how pleased she was that she'd married me, and all this other rubbish, as it turned out in the years to come.

And, then she opened it, and there was this bright red, little mini-nightdress plus knickers. I visibly saw her face sink, although she didn't say anything. She put it in the drawer and the next time I saw that or them was several years later when she decided that she was going to run off with somebody else and I had to go, when she opened the drawer and chucked it at me, and said, *"who did I think she was, some sort of bloody tart?"* Nothing had been further from my thoughts. But she threw it at me.

I don't know what happened to it. I've no idea. I had in actual fact arranged, as soon as she'd told me she was... We were going to part, I'd arranged to rent a house in another part of Barnsley, and I only ever saw her once after that, and the only other time I spoke to her was when she rang me to tell me the dog had died, which

I was more sad about that than anything because I thought the world of the poor little fella. Maybe she gave him the nightdress to play with. I don't know. Maybe she dressed him up in it. I don't know. But it was most certainly not, and it never led to, a night to remember.

# Chapter Eighteen

During my wanderings around the world, I've seen one or two unpleasant sights, a lot of funny sights, but only one sight that I would quite honestly say to you stood out as being something out of the ordinary, something quite different, something quite excellent. I'm hesitating about using the word magnificent, but maybe for the people involved, it was. I can't be sure. This was in Taiwan, a place I only ever went to once. Everybody, when you see these programmes on the television and they're cracking jokes, they talk about Taiwan and people buying rubbish from Taiwan. Well, let me assure you from the word go. Taiwan does not supply rubbish. Taiwan is not cheap. It's more expensive than here, and I most certainly couldn't afford to live there.

They have a funny relationship in Taiwan of course, because Taiwan isn't very far off the Chinese coast. It's about an hour, an hour and fifteen minute flight from Hong Kong to Taipei, the capital. But, the two governments, and of course the Chinese don't recognise the Taiwanese government as a government. But, nonetheless, they don't invade it and take it over, which they could do in a minute, because they are somewhat concerned at the reaction and possible actions of the rest of the world, particularly the Americans. So, they shout and they bawl at one another across the straits. It's all quite amusing at times just to read in the paper such absolute garbage and nonsense that they both talk about one another.

I used to have an agent there who, what he did for us was to find a factory making a certain electronic product. His name was Kevin, I think, his English name. He did a very good job for us at finding this particular product. What he made at it, I do not know. What I do know is we made a lot of money at it. I've talked earlier about going Air India to New York. I tell you quite honestly that the profits from the product that he sourced for us were the reason we could afford to go to Dallas. We paid for all that out of what we were making out of the Taiwan deal. So I thought once, at least once, I should go, when I'm in China, when I'm in Hong Kong, and get a flight out to Taiwan and meet him, which I did. He took me to the factory where they were supplying this electronic product, and wasn't much of a place actually. It wasn't much at all. It wasn't somewhere that you would willingly buy from in the sense of rush inside on your own volition, and think, *"Ooh, this is just the spot for me."* No, no, no, by no means. By no means. But, who was I to complain? The quality of what we'd bought from them had been excellent. The return rate was well under half a percent, which for products from the Far East was brilliant. We were absolutely delighted. The business side of it was fine.

I decided to stay in this hotel which he'd arranged for me for a couple of nights, because we went to a couple of other factories that he'd arranged visits to where he was also an agent. Nothing ever came from any of them. On the second day, which might have been a Sunday, I'm not sure, he said, *"I want you to come with me and I want to show you something."*

Now, the history of Taiwan, or Formosa as it was formerly called, was all linked to the revolution in China in the late 40s. The communist leader who won the revolution and it's still the same lot in power today, although of course he's died, was Mao Zedong, and the nationalist leader, who we would call I suppose the western-biased leader was Chiang Kai-shek. These two men were daggers drawn for years, and years, and years. There was lots of lives lost, lots of fighting, and eventually, Mao Zedong and his communist hordes won the day, and Chiang Kai-shek fled over the straits to what was then Formosa, which is now Taiwan, and they've barked at one another and growled at one another ever since.

This particular day, he said, *"I want you to come with me to a park in the centre of Taipei."* It was a nice day, sunny day, and we went into this park… He'd parked his car, we went into this park and we walked not so far, but towards the centre of the park, and I saw a large edifice which was a statue of a man round which there was a giant square. Either side of the square, facing one another, two soldiers. Not in uniforms like we have with the busby and the red coats and all the rest of it. Not in old-fashioned, traditional uniforms, but in modern-day military uniforms. These two lads are standing facing one another, either side of this square.

They stand there for two hours I was told and then they change the guard, and what he wanted me to see, Kevin, was the changing of the guard. That these two soldiers could stand there two hours without moving was, well, nothing less than absolutely wonderful, and the effort that must have gone into it was fantastic.

At the end of the two hour period, although I wasn't there the whole two hours, maybe about 35-40 minutes I was watching these two lads stand there, in the bottom right-hand corner of the square, comes some sort of what we might call a regimental sergeant major. Forgive me, any ex-army people if I'm wrong, because I know nothing about the military. We'll call him a regimental sergeant major. He was definitely the boss, let's put it that way. Behind him walked two more soldiers. This was the change of the guard, these two who were on duty were to be changed for these two who were arriving. The performance, and I mean performance in a nice way, in a polite way, in a proper way, that they gave to change the guard was, well, it had to be seen to be believed. They were carrying modern day rifles with bayonets on the end, and they were throwing these things up in the air, I don't know, two or three times their own personal height and catching them when they came down.

Eventually, after having done this a few times, these two walked to all four sides of the square where people were watching from behind nothing more than a rope. Today's security would never have allowed this. I was stood against the rope. I'd been there early. I was first in front of the... I could touch the rope. I was touching the rope. They came… One of these two came marching straight towards me. He marched into the middle of the square, turned to his left and he marched straight toward me, twirling this rifle with bayonet fixed for all he was worth. One mistake and anybody who would get it would be dead or could very easily be dead, and he walked straight toward me. I will never forget he must have got within how far? 18 inches of me, no further. 18 inches of me. And I'm a big lad. And he looked straight through me. His expression never changed. He never indicated that he was there. I did nothing. He did nothing. I didn't stare at him. He just stared straight through me, and then he turned to his left, and the one at the other side did the same thing and they marched with the sergeant major off into the far corner and out of sight. I bet they needed to have a damned good sit down, if not sleep, and a drink and something to eat, because what they had just done and what I had just witnessed was one of the things that I will never forget.

I've never met anybody else in my life who has ever seen the changing of the guard at the Chiang Kai-shek mausoleum in Taipei, but I honestly suggest to you that if you are ever there, and if I assume that they still do it, and Chiang Kai-shek was treated like a God, then I suggest that you whatever you don't do in Taiwan, one thing that you do do is to witness the changing of the guard at the mausoleum in the middle of Taipei. They talk about a night to remember. This was a day to remember, most certainly. And yes, they were magnificent. I'll give it the word. They were magnificent.

# Chapter Nineteen

I only ever went to Russia twice. Once was on holiday. I always remember coming back on Bonfire Night because at the time I was married to a lady with a step-daughter and the step-daughter was left with the neighbour next door, but we'd got to get back for the bonfire. But the story that I'm going to recount is nowt to do with Guy Fawkes, who was a Yorkshireman by the way, but absolutely to do with going to Moscow, to the light show, which they, in my opinion rather stupidly, hold in the winter. Now, anybody who's been to Moscow will know that the winter, which starts about, I don't know, middle of October right through to the end of March, is, well, decidedly cold. It absolutely is unbelievably cold. The wind that they have there when it's cold is what my dad always called a 'lazy' wind. It doesn't go round you, it goes straight through you.

This particular time I decided that for once... I'd seen so much advertising over the years of the Moscow light show. I thought I'd go to Moscow and see what there was in terms of a Russian lighting industry. It turns out that actually there is very little in the sense of a Russian lighting industry. Not from what I saw anyway.

There wasn't a flight from the north of England direct to Moscow. We had to go the wrong way to go the right way. We had to go to Munich to then fly up to Moscow, so it took quite a lot longer to get there than it really ought to do. I recall when we landed at... There's probably five or six airports scattered around Moscow. I recall when we landed at this particular airport, when we came down the steps... Again, there was none of this arm thing and keep you in the warm. It was bitterly cold. When we came down the steps, there was just a way to walk to the Terminal building, and this walkway was lined on both sides by armed... I assume they were armed. Armed soldiers. Why they chose to put armed soldiers against a flight that was coming in from Munich, carrying businesspeople predominantly, I really don't know, but I didn't feel like asking.

We'd arranged over here with the Aeroflot organisation to be picked up by a people-carrier-type thing, or a car, we didn't know what we were going to get, but something, at the airport, which would take us in to the hotel, which we'd again booked over here. There were two of us; my assistant and myself. We go to the desk after we've gone through the immigration, we go to the desk for transport, cars, or whatever it said over the top, exactly where we'd been told to go, we followed all the instructions I'd got from my travel agent, and we went to this desk and this woman who spoke... She looked like a Russian shotput champion, quite frankly, from the Olympic Games. She seemed lacking completely any interest in what we wanted, but nonetheless had to stand up for a moment just to come to the desk to talk to us.

I told her my name, I gave her the passport. They can read, because the Visa which you have to get to go into

Russia, is done in their alphabet, so they can read your name as they would write it, and your name as we would write it. I've still got that Visa thing upstairs in the house now. No, she couldn't find anything for me. Not a thing. Not a thing. So I said, *"Look, it's all been booked. Here's the paperwork. It's all been done,"* but that didn't seem to impress her a great deal. It really didn't impress her at all. She couldn't, quite frankly, have cared tuppence. But what she had decided she was going to do was she would believe me that we'd paid and she just said, *"Go and sit over there,"* on a bench. It was just a bench. It wasn't a proper seat. We both went and sat on this bench, and the floor was swimming in water. The winter was a bit late in arriving that year, and when we got there they were getting quite heavy rain.

# Chapter Twenty

A continuation of the Russian situation…

The airport was absolutely awash with water from the torrential rain that was coming down, and they did nothing to clean it up, to sweep it out. It was absolutely appalling. It was a disgrace. Anyway, this woman sent for what you can only describe as a people-carrier thing. Something which carried about seven. We clambered in, put our luggage in. The driver did nothing at all to help us, nothing at all. Off we set in the pouring rain to the address of a hotel which I'd given him, which we had written down in Russian. He was a maniac. A complete and utter maniac when it came to driving. We were everywhere, all over the road. I'm not quite sure now to this day whether the Russians drive on the right or the left. He seemed to drive in the middle. Eventually, after lots of oohs and aahs, and *"Aagh!"* and whatever, we got there.

The hotel was an old… It didn't say hotel outside it. There was nothing to identify it as a hotel. He had to assure us, *"Yes, this is the place. Yes, this right. This right. This right."* We went in, and when we went in there was a desk with a porter and all the rest of it which confirmed to us that we were at the right spot.

This fella asked who we were, in very good English actually, and we booked in, and we had a meal, and the next morning came around, and I asked him could he get a taxi to take us to the exhibition centre? Now, although I had been to Moscow before, I never had need to use a taxi, and I found out that the Russians don't have many taxis, not at all. Most of them are just people who haven't got jobs who let out their private car to me and you for an hour or two, a day, or whatever. In other words, they park up near the hotel and the lad from the hotel goes to the first one and says, *"These two people want to go to the exhibition centre. Will you take them?"* Well, of course he will. He took us to the exhibition centre and we paid him, and made it clear to him, because he spoke a bit of English, would he please come back, because it was freezing, honestly, absolutely freezing, would he please come back at about four o'clock? Now I said at the time, which goes to show what a pundit I am, *"That'll be the last we see of him. We'll have to find somebody similar to him when we come out."*

We went to the exhibition. Very few Russian stands, which is what we were looking for, anything that they might have there that we haven't got here, or anybody who might be prepared to make something at a good price for us that we would need here. No. No interest in us whatsoever. Their own domestic market was all they seemed to be bothered about, or countries in Eastern Europe which they had supplied in the past. Most of the stands that we knew were occupied by the self-same Chinese that I was visiting on my visits to China. I met lots and lots of friends and acquaintances who were simply there to attack the Russian market, who were amazed to see me because they couldn't work out why I'd gone. And after I'd had some sort of disgusting sort of lunch, I couldn't make sure myself why I'd gone. It gets round to about quarter to four and we wander back through the door that we'd come in to where our taxi should be at the gate, not expecting to see him, but there he was, as large as life. Good lad, he's here. Good lad. Put us in the car, drove us back to the hotel. Went to the room and...

We were in separate rooms. Went to the room and I got a phone call from my mobile, thinking it was coming in from the office, but when I looked it was coming in from a customer in Doncaster, a lad called Mark Jackson. Now, Mark and I have always had a good relationship, but a funny love/hate relationship if you like. Sport wise, football-wise, I'm a Barnsley fanatic. I know I'm mad. I don't need telling. Please forget it. The telling bit. Mark supports Sheffield Wednesday, although he comes from Doncaster. Now, that's the unforgivable sin to support Sheffield Wednesday if you're a Barnsley supporter, because they nine times out of ten get the better of us. Mark always liked and enjoyed ten minutes of pulling my leg.

But here he is on the phone and I can't imagine he's ringing about Sheffield Wednesday when I'm in Moscow, although does he know I'm in Moscow? Yes, he did know I was in Moscow. Why? Because he's in Moscow too! I said, *"You're in Moscow?"* *"Yes, I'm staying at the Novotel and I think it's just down the road from where I'm told you're staying. My people have told me..."* My people at the hotel he meant, *"... Have told me that your hotel is within walking distance."* I said, *"In this weather, good luck to you. Why do you want to..?"* *"Well, I want to walk round because I thought we know one another well, let's have dinner together in your hotel."* I thought, *"Here we go. Not only do I lose at football every time I see him, but I'm going to lose out of my wallet now because he's going to want it all putting down on my room,"* which he did. I've not forgotten Mark. I've not forgotten, when you're reading this, if you read it. I've not forgotten. One of these days I'll send you the invoice.

We had a meal which was passable. It wasn't bad at all actually. During the meal, and this is something else I've never forgotten either, I said to him, *"There's not much at this exhibition, do you think?"* and he said, *"No. I didn't expect there to be really."* I said, *"Well, if you didn't expect there to be, why are you here?"* *"Oh,"* he said, *"That's simple. My boss,"* and we won't disclose his name, *"My boss has sent me here because he knows you're here, and he wants to see what you find and hope that I find it too."* So, I said, *"Well, have you found anything yet?"* And he said, *"No. Have you?"* And I said, *"No,"* and I was being absolutely truthful. A friend of mine says I only lie when I need to. *"No."* He said, *"But you're going tomorrow, aren't you?"* I said, *"Well, I'm sorry, but you're not going to find much tomorrow, because we've just decided before you got here that we are not wasting another day of our lives wandering around an absolutely dreadful exhibition looking at stands from China which we already know, or stands from Eastern Europe which we don't want to know, or the odd stand from Russia which doesn't want to know us."* I said, *"I'm sorry, but you can tell your boss that one day was quite enough and that's it. We're not going."* We had a meal. We got to the dessert. They came round with the dessert menu. I picked something, my assistant picked something, and Mark picked something else.

The most expensive item on that menu, dessert menu, was mixed berries. Mixed berries. They were the most expensive item. I suppose getting hold of mixed berries in Moscow in November is a little difficult, if not impossible. They must be imported. It was quite obvious that anything imported into Moscow, into Russia, was expensive. They were more expensive than anything else on the menu. Mark went his way back to the Novotel or wherever it was he was staying. It was Mercure I think on reflection. Back to his hotel and we went to bed. Got up in the morning and met for breakfast. The manager of the hotel was in having his breakfast at the same time at a table for two with his assistant. We'd noticed that these two were very close just when passing. They were eating all the mixed berries for free, because obviously nobody had bought them because they were too expensive. The alternative was throwing them away, so one of the perks of the job was to get the mixed berries for breakfast, which is what they did.

We go to the porter fella, young man, and say, *"Is the same driver available for today?"* *"You go exhibit?"* I went, *"No, no, no. We're not going to the exhibition. We just want to... We would like him, if he can, to drive us round the sights of Moscow." "I'll go and see if he's there."* He came back. Tootling up, driving up behind him came this big old, black... A bit like that thing in Latvia with the coat handle for the radio aerial. Bit like the same vehicle. He came up with it and instructions were given, *"Take them round. Just show them what there is to show them."* There is a lot to see in Moscow. But when it's -15 or whatever, it's not pleasant. It's distinctly unpleasant.

First place he took us was the nearest, which I knew was only just a minute away, and that was Red Square. Now, I'd been to Red Square before when I came on holiday, but Red Square is certainly worth more than one visit. He pulled up and he said, *"Red Square. See you fifteen minutes."* And I thought, *"I'm paying the bill. I'll decide how long we stay in Red Square, not you. I'll decide."* Or *"We will decide."* He was exaggerating with fifteen minutes. After about eight or nine minutes of wandering around in Red Square, looking at Lenin's tomb and all the rest of it, quite frankly we were absolutely frozen, and fifteen minutes became ten. Within ten minutes, we were opening the car doors and getting in. Thankfully, it had a heater inside it, which worked. Very noisy but it worked, which was all that mattered, and we thawed out.

If I had a pound for every cathedral that he took us to over the next three or four hours, I think I'd be a very rich man. Got fed up of being taken to the cathedrals, which were all extremely beautiful, all quite small by what we would call a cathedral, like York Minster. Very small. Out we got, we had a walk round, and it was the same things every time. This is the Russian Orthodox Church I imagine that we were looking at. He then took us to a place where there were a lot of nuns. We bought something, I can't remember what it was. It might have been postcards, I can't recall. We bought something in there, not much, just a few pence, and we went off again.

He took us then to where the Winter Olympics had been staged in Moscow and he took us to the end where the ski jump, where you set off for the ski jump, go down the slope and then off you go, you do the Eddie Edwards bit. Eddie the Eagle bit. We got out of the car because there were quite a lot of stalls. No customers because it was so cold. But men were there with little old vehicles they'd driven up in, stalls which were basically trestle tables on legs and the only thing I could see was these Russian dolls, you know the things that you put one inside the other, inside the other, inside the other and you can go on forever, depending on how big the last one is, or the first one. This was just a few days, maybe a week, after England had played Russia at football in a qualifying cup for something. Either the World Cup or the European Cup, and we'd lost. As soon as these fellas found out that we were English, they took great delight in quite obviously mocking us for the defeat. We knew they were talking about football because they got a piece of paper and wrote the score on a piece of paper. I, at least, knew what they were referring to. I think my assistant bought a Russian doll, I can't be sure.

We got back in the car and we were taken then to another very outstanding sight, which was the tomb, or mausoleum I think is perhaps a better word, for the dead of the Second World War, but of course only the Russian dead. That was quite touching. There was, for the weather, still a lot of people there. Everybody who died was named somewhere on a pillar of stone or whatever, or on a slab of concrete that you were walking across. Everybody who'd died was named.

Then off we go to the, what I think, if I remember rightly, was called the White House. Now, this has got nothing to do with Donald Trump or any other previous occupants. As I understand it, the President of Russia, Putin as we have now, lives in The Kremlin, but the Prime Minister of Russia lives in another building called The White House, which is obviously a white house. Quite impressive. He showed us that.

Then he said, *"One final place to show you before I take you back to the hotel,"* and he took us to the British Embassy, which was very impressive. It showed me where we were spending our money in Russia. Outside were two Russian soldiers guarding the gate for if anybody, the Prime Minister of the day in the UK, said anything rude about Russia, if there was any sort of arranged march, then they would be there to deter the marchers. Well, that was the end of it. Back to the hotel.

We decided to go out that night for a meal and we asked the porter for a recommendation, and he told us somewhere, wrote it down in Russian, got us some sort of car to take us there, and off we went. We went in, it all looked very nice from the outside, and when we went in, to my utter amazement every single member of staff, whether they be male or female, was wearing green baize, similar to what they put on snooker tables. And to say they looked somewhat ridiculous would be to put it mildly. They looked like a series of walking snooker tables, these people.

We got a drink. I think we had sherry, I don't know. I think that was what we had. The choice was very poor. The choice of the menu was very poor. But what was fascinating was when we sat down for the meal, the waiter came, he understood enough English, the menu was in Russian and English, he took our order and a couple of minutes later, the pair of us were given a banana. Yes, I said a banana. We said, *"We didn't order the banana."* *"No, everybody get banana."* *"Oh."* So, we peeled back the banana and ate the banana.

We'd ordered some sort of soup, and we ate the soup and they took away the bowl. We'd ordered some sort of meat dish as a main dish, but before they brought that, they brought a banana each again. We said, *"Sorry, we haven't ordered... We've had one banana. We don't want two more bananas."* *"Everybody gets a banana."* So now we've had a banana and soup, and we're now eating the second banana. We finish the second banana and they bring the meat dish. We eat the meat dish. It was alright. It was passable. Heaven knows what meat it was, but it was something or other. We ordered some sort of dessert, I don't know what it was. I couldn't possibly tell you. We'll just say it was ice-cream for the sake of arguing. But before the ice-cream came, I'll give you one guess what we got another one of each... a banana.

This means to our table for two, he has now delivered six bananas. We have now eaten three bananas apiece, plus soup, plus the main dish, and the ice-cream to follow. I said to my assistant, *"We are not having tea or coffee because I have a sneaky feeling that we'll get a banana,"* and quite frankly, knowing what they do to you, I just did not want another banana.

We paid, we went to the cloakroom to get our coats and asked if they could ring for a taxi. *"No. We don't ring for taxis. You have to go onto the street and flag down..."* I said, *"But they don't have... There aren't that many taxis." "You just flag down anybody who stops."* Anybody who stops. *"That's where you're going to,"* and he wrote it down in Russian. *"When anybody stops, get in, go there, and pay when you get to the other end."* From going into the restaurant to coming out of the restaurant, to stand at the side of the street trying to flag down anybody that passed, winter had set in and the snow had started. So, we were like Mr Snowman and his wife, although it wasn't my wife, Mr Snowman and his wife, stood outside trying to flag a car down, and they don't half speed, regardless of the road conditions.

It was taking quite a bit of time to get anybody to stop because they'd all got somebody in the car with them. I looked behind me to find there was a queue of Russians stood behind us, obviously believing that we knew something they didn't, because we, from our dress, were not Russians. We were foreigners. We were stood there and there must have been best part of five couples, about ten people. Pleasant enough people, nobody threatening us or anything like that, nobody wanting money Slovakian-style. Eventually a car stopped. We got in. We went back to the hotel.

Next morning, there is snow absolutely everywhere. It looked about three foot deep, I'm sure it wasn't, but it looked it, and we had a flight home. Now, Visas in Russia are given for x number of days, and x number of days only, and today when all the snow was down was our last day of our Visa. We had to leave that day otherwise we were in trouble. It concerned me that with all this snow falling a) getting to the airport, and b) whether the flight would go or not. Well, my assistant, she was many things but brave wasn't one of them.

We got in this car, this same fella came, and he was told that we wanted to go to the airport. Well, we trundle along and the snow is coming down like half-crowns, as they used to say, and we're getting further and further and further away, a lot further in distance than it felt when we came in from the airport. We're assuming we're going back to the same airport, which in fact we were. We got... I don't know how long we'd been travelling. It seemed like forever, but the road conditions were causing most of that. There wasn't an aeroplane on the floor, on the ground, in sight, until we went round this corner and I said, *"Oh, look."* I saw the tail part of several planes all parked up. He knew where he was. He took us to the doorway. He got the bags out.

He was a kind man. He was a nice man. We paid him and in we went.

We went to the check in desk. No reference whatsoever was made to the weather. We went through and we sat in a lounge where there was a huge window and out of the window you could see the airport, the runway, everything. Well, you couldn't see the runway and you couldn't see any grass. You could see nothing. We sat there for quite some time. Nothing took off and nothing landed. I was getting distinctly worried about the length of our Visa and what was going to happen later in the day. I'd no sooner began to think this than a plane did come in and land. Now we were booked with Lufthansa because we were going back Munich, Munich – Manchester. I said that I'll bet that's our plane that they're landing, but whether it will be fit for him to take off, to go back to Munich with us, I don't know and with the safety record of Russian airlines and what have you, Russian airspace, I'm not too sure I wanted it to take off.

But, they announced it. We got on it. They de-iced the wings, which is the third time it's happened to me in my life, and it's a most reassuring job if it's never been done when you've been sat on an aeroplane, the de-icing of wings, because icy wings mean that if you get up there you just fall down like a stone and that's the end of that. The wings have to be de-iced. Took off, we roared away and we'd been going, I don't know, we got up to about cruising height into the sunshine and we were cruising our way off towards Munich. The pilot came on and spoke in German and in English and told us that the airport had closed immediately after we'd taken off and we were the last flight to leave there that day. No matter.

We got to Munich. We landed. We were a bit late. We had to hurry through the airport to get the Manchester flight. We flew to Manchester and came home.

The moral of the story is quite simple. Don't go to Moscow in the winter. It's cold and it is not at all welcoming, and I don't think you'd enjoy yourself very much.

# Chapter Twenty-One

I'd never been to Italy in my life, I don't think, except as a child when my father took me, before I got involved there for business.

I got involved in a rather roundabout fashion. A man in Italy, in a small town, the name of which is not important, but about 20 miles or so east of Milan, contacted me by fax as it would be in those days to say that he was a manufacturer of die-cast aluminium lanterns, and other products. He had seen that we made passive infrared detectors, which attach to these type of light fittings, would we be interested in talking at least about co-operative, jointly, selling a product which he would market? I replied yes, that I thought that we needed to meet to discuss the issue. He came back agreeing and, as fortune would have it, a couple of weeks later, Mr Marinacci was meeting a friend from America for a business meeting in a hotel not so far from Heathrow airport.

I go down, find the hotel, it was quite easy, go into the lobby, there's two men sat at a table. They came towards me, introduced themselves as Marinacci, and the other men who was his right-hand man I came to find out as the years went by, was a red-haired Italian chap who put an awful lot of work and effort into the whole business. As an aside, I don't think I'd ever seen a red-haired Italian, I must be honest, and I don't think I've seen one since, but that's just an aside, a by the way. Marinacci tells me that in about half an hour or so, this fella from America is going to fly in, land at Heathrow, get in a taxi and come to the hotel to meet us. After the meeting, he's returning back to Heathrow to fly onto somewhere else within Europe. All this worked like clockwork. Marinacci had rented a room for the afternoon from the hotel and we went up in the lift, Marinacci, me, the red-haired fella, and another man... This other man who was with him who had introduced himself. He was definitely Italian. The accent was very, very strong, but we spoke English.

We went into the room. It was just two single beds and two armchairs. I sat on one of the beds, Marinacci on the other, his red-headed friend on the other, and the other Italian sat in the other chair. We discussed and chatted and talked for, I don't know, the best part of three hours I suppose. They all smoked. They all smoked incessantly. It was chain-smoking, and I don't smoke at all and never have done. I suppose it must go down as the one and only time I've ever been in a meeting in a smoke-filled room. It was like waiting for Edward G. Robinson or Jimmy Cagney to walk into the room with an old-fashioned sub-machine gun on their arm and blow us all to kingdom come. It was a rather strange sort of meeting. Everything went off well.

This other Italian was a very, very strong-minded man. Apart from being a very, very strong looking and upright and well-built man - it was like meeting one of the Mafia, not that I've ever met anybody from the Mafia, from the best of my knowledge, but I can imagine that that's what they'd look like in reality.

Everything went well. We agreed that we would send samples for them to test. We agreed a price. They were going to make the light fittings over in the Milan area, and they were going to sell them under the Marinacci brand, and then this other guy who was the owner of a much, much bigger company in Italy was going to sell them throughout anywhere in the world where 240 volt was the voltage that was applicable. We agreed that we would meet up again in two or three weeks' time, at the Italian lighting exhibition in Milan. It wasn't my intention at the time to go to this exhibition, but I decided that I would. I took my car, because taking my car enabled me to go to other places, like France, and Germany, and Austria, and anywhere else, Switzerland, when I was on the way to Milan.

I booked a hotel in Milan, not a very auspicious one. Of course, money was a bit different in those days. We were only starting. I was only starting off. I remember taking the car, and I got into Milan, and anybody who's ever driven in Milan will bear me out by saying that a) it's difficult, b) it's badly, badly, very badly signed, and c) the patience of the drivers, the Italians, is not very great. I was somewhere near the hotel from directions given to me by a policeman, and I couldn't find it. I could not find it. I made the cardinal sin of turning the wrong way down a one-way street. Came to some traffic lights and found myself looking at six lanes of traffic facing me, all coming towards me when the lights turned to green. I'd never done a U-turn and sped away as quickly in all my life, because I knew they wouldn't have any patience with me.

Got to the hotel, parked my car. They had a place at the back. Parked my car and went in. This was a Wednesday, because Marinacci had said to me, *"Come on the Thursday. It's the last day I'm at the exhibition. We will then go to the town where my factory is and we will chat more about what is going to, we hope, happen."* The strange thing is, that night I went into that hotel and I had a meal, and that night was the final of the football, European cup. I think Liverpool were playing in it. I'm not sure. But, anyway, it doesn't really matter, that, who was playing. I remember watching that from the television in the hotel bedroom.

The next day I went down to the exhibition, had a wander around and met Marinacci round about lunchtime. What happened next was somewhat surprising, and it set me back a bit, but nonetheless it occurred. I'd only met him on the one occasion, but we'd had several conversations on the phone and we had exchanged faxes. I went up to the stand, and there he was, and he saw me coming, and he stepped off the stand towards me, shook me by the hand and kissed me four times, twice on each cheek. Now, for a local lad from here to be kissed four times, twice on each cheek, by a man he hardly knows, or by any man for that matter, is a little different and a little odd, and a little strange. But never mind. It was well-meant. We chatted and we decided that we would then go back, in our separate vehicles, to the town where he'd booked me into a hotel, and spend the night and have a meal.

Milan has a terrible reputation for fog, bad, thick fog. This particular night was actually no exception. The fog was terrible, and I was outside the gate of the hotel, so near, before I could even see the sign to indicate that I'd got to the right place. I pulled my car up the drive and parked and went in, and thought, *"Well, that'll be that for the night. We'll eat here, because it just isn't worth going out onto the road in such weather."* Marinacci turns up, *"Come on then. We're going to Milan for dinner."* *"What?"* That's a 40 mile round trip on the motorway. I'm saying, *"No, no, no. There is no need to bother."* But the real reason for me saying there's no need to bother was the fog and the way in which they drive over there. And true to what I thought, and what I was concerned about, we set off for Milan, and we absolutely thundered along the motorway. You couldn't see anything. That didn't slow him down, not one iota. We just kept belting along straight into this brick wall of fog and if there'd have been anything there, we would have hit it. We didn't.

We turned off when he realised where we were, and we went into the centre of Milan, and he'd chosen a restaurant. We went into this restaurant which was very well appointed, nice place. Expensive place I imagine as well. He said, *"I'll choose everything. Don't you bother."* Well, he did, and I liked nothing of what he'd chosen, but I had to eat it all. I did, I ate it, just to keep the peace. He'd got his red-headed fella with him all the time, by the way. He said he wanted to put me in the car and just show me a bit of the centre of Milan. Now, I don't know how he intended to do that in all this fog, because I couldn't see anything very much, but it all turned out, in actual fact, it was all a practical joke which he was playing upon me, and which I fell for - hook, line and sinker.

We got somewhere in the middle of Milan, and I get the feeling we were outside a church or somewhere, in a square. Stood on the street, all the way down and on the street corner, were a collection of what I took to be girls, ladies of the night, and he was just... Wasn't wanting to pick anybody up. He was just laughing at my discomfort. Bear in mind, I wasn't very old at the time, and I wasn't really that worldly-wise, and I'd never been and seen anything like this in my life.

We pulled up alongside a girl who was wearing what looked to be a very expensive fur coat, because it was very cold outside. She was completely lacking in interest of all of us in the car. I noticed she was chewing gum. She came up to the window where I was looking out of and he wound the window down. He insisted that we open the window. He had the controls at the front. He wound the window down and this girl came right up to me, opened her coat to show me that she wasn't wearing a great deal underneath it. This, of course, was the big joke that I would fall for this and, *"Oh no, no, no, no, no,"* and I would start making apologies and, *"Please let's go. Thank you very much. No, no, no. Let's be on our way."*

We drive away and we're going back out towards the motorway to go back to the town where the hotel was, and he said, *"Didn't you like the girl?"* I said, *"It's nothing to do with liking her. It's all to do with it's wrong. It's wrong. I'm a married man. It is wrong."* And then they all, these two, start bursting out laughing. She wasn't a girl at all. She was a... What is it? A transvestite. I honestly could not tell the difference. He told me a bit about the history of it, the story of it. These girls stood on street corners in Milan and other cities in Italy and they picked up men, but within a few weeks they were all shipped back... They all came in from Brazil, and they were all shipped back on a plane to Brazil, until they got a ticket to come back again. It was backwards and forwards, backwards and forwards, until they either got fed up or they got some sort of Visa to work in Italy. That was his big, big joke.

The following morning, the fog had gone and I drove up to his factory, which wasn't far away. Again, we had a wander round with the ginger-haired fella, and the ginger-haired fella was obviously explaining last night's adventure to the lads on the shop floor. Now, they were all laughing as well, but this was at a different thing and for a different reason. The infrared sensors that we were selling, or hoping to sell him, to put with his aluminium lanterns, we used to abbreviate the expression passive infrared detector to passive. It just came off the tongue much quicker and much easier.

I heard this guy with the red hair telling the others some story, and the word 'passive' was mentioned on several occasions, and each time he said it, they all laughed. I'm there, but I don't understand of course what's happening and what the joke is. In fairness to them, they did explain the joke to me. The slang word in Italian for a transvestite prostitute is a 'passive', and I was going into the factory there saying, *"I've come to sell you some passives."* So, hence, I was not only a joke for not knowing one, but secondly an even bigger joke for saying I'd come to sell some.

We did a lot of business with Marinacci until he unfortunately died. As with many companies, when the man at the top goes, things are different. It might fold. The man that comes in to take over might be the son who hardly knows you, has his own preferences. Things changed. When Marinacci went, slowly but surely our relationship went.

# Chapter Twenty-Two

Another occasion in Italy, I had been approached by... These infrared sensors were very popular. I'd been approached by a company called Lanzini, and they were in a town called Brescia. That isn't too far from Milan. It's a bit further to the east than to where Marinacci was. They had approached as well. They made similar types of products but they made an awful lot of halogen floodlights which you used to see outside people's garages and forecourts and what have you with an infrared sensor on. They were very popular as a concept.

Mr Lanzini was a perfect gentleman. I think he was the exact opposite to Marinacci. This man was a gentleman. He had a son whose name I forget, and he had a daughter who was called Elizabeth, or whatever the Italian version of Elizabeth is. She was a lovely girl, a very pleasant girl, a very friendly girl. On the two or three occasions that I went over there, and we did some business but not a fantastic amount, nothing along the lines of the Marinacci business, we went out for meals and we chatted about this, that and the other. He had a pretty fair-sized factory. His office block was at one side of a huge forecourt, square, where lorries came in to deliver raw materials and to pick up orders to take away. Underneath, underground, there was a giant basement, I suppose that's the best way you could possibly describe it, with a sloping floor and roller shutter doors into the basement.

One day when I was there, Lanzini was there and so was Elizabeth, and he said, *"We're doing a bit of business now Chris. I'd like to just show you something that I've got in the basement."* We went down the stairs in the building, into the basement below and... I'm not a car man by nature, I have to say that. I have a nice car as things stand now. A car is for getting me from A to B, and when people, salesmen, at dealerships talk about brake horsepower and other such things, I'm afraid it's going straight over the top of my head. I haven't a clue what they're talking about and I've no desire to find out. But there was no doubt that what he showed me in his basement was one of the finest collections of cars I'd ever seen either on the television or in real life. He had all sorts of things.

His pride and joy was... I think it was... You'll have to bear with me if I'm wrong. It was a Lamborghini from the 50s or maybe before, and it was a pale blue powder-type of colour, and it really did look magnificent. It had white wheels and a top that was retractable. It was the sort of thing that, I suppose, never went anywhere. He didn't drive it anywhere, didn't take it anywhere, didn't want to risk any damage to it. Even a non-car man like me had to be honest and admit that it was a beautiful piece of equipment. He had a Rolls Royce. He had this. He had that. He had the other.

Lanzini was one of the old school of business people. He respected what we did. I respected what he did. We did some business together. Not as much as I would have liked. I thought there was more, but he didn't want to take it any further than just sort of playing around with one or two of our lines, and that eventually became that, and the business did die.

One thing I will say, many years later I was at a lighting exhibition in Paris and they had a stand. He wasn't there. I don't know whether he was still alive, but he wasn't there, but Elizabeth was. I was just walking around and I wasn't wanting to be a nuisance and go push myself up and say, *"Hello,"* to her and all the rest of it. I thought she may have forgotten me because it was quite a long time. It must have been fifteen or more years since I'd seen her. I thought she'd maybe forgotten. But she came rushing off the stand, took me back by the arm, took me back on the stand and, *"Chris, Chris, how many years? How many years? Why you not come and see us? We could have done so much more."* I thought to myself, *"Well, it would have been a good idea if you'd have told your dad that. If you'd told your dad that, who knows. You might be Mrs Burrows now, never mind Miss Lanzini,"* because I asked and she wasn't married, and she obviously had a soft spot for me. It was probably the North Sea, but then again, that would have been very unfair. But she was a lovely, lovely girl. I did like her very much indeed. And I liked him as well. They are still going. They are there today. I haven't seen any of them now for 15-20 years, but I always regard it as being one that got away.

# Chapter Twenty-Three

I can't mention France without thinking most fondly of the man who was, without a shadow of the doubt, in the lighting industry over the years, and unfortunately now he has died, but over the years my dearest friend in the business. He was a man who lived on the outskirts of Paris. He was so typically French that he ought to have been wearing a Tricolour instead of a jacket. But, believe it or not, he was one of the biggest Anglophiles amongst Frenchmen I ever met. His name was Bob Genier. His full name of course, in French, would be Robert Genier. One sign of his love of anything British was the fact that he used the Christian name Bob. He's the only Frenchman who I've ever met who was called Robert who used the English abbreviation of Robert, i.e. Bob as preference to Robert. It wasn't the thing to do. All Roberts were Robert, not Bob.

But Bob, well, he was a man who wore British shoes, British clothes. He loved this country. He really did. He loved this country and he loved its people. He loved everything about it, except for two things. One was its language. He could never get his tongue round anything in English. It was good for my French, I admit, but he could never say anything. He could never get his tongue round anything at all in English. The other thing he didn't like particularly about the UK was, unsurprisingly for a Frenchman, the food. I think that's the reason, more than anything else, he didn't come here more often. Bob loved his food. Some people used to think about Bob that he actually lived for his food. He may well have done, I don't know. He rarely came over here except at exhibitions at Olympia. I think he once came up to the factory in Yorkshire. Once, maybe. He flew into Manchester and came on to the factory, to the office. I don't ever recall more than once. It was extremely difficult, this food thing. He just couldn't settle down to a meat and two veg at any price.

Only once do I ever recall pleasing him with a meal in London. There is a restaurant on The Strand called Simpson's. It's next door to The Savoy Hotel. I wasn't staying at The Savoy Hotel. I was staying at a Novotel at Hammersmith. But, I'd promised I'd take him somewhere good, and this is where we went. We went there for the simple reason that Simpson's only sell British food. They do not sell anything Indian, Chinese, Turkish, French, German, you name it they don't sell it. If you want roast beef and Yorkshire pudding, and you want it to be absolutely superb, and the same goes for lamb, and for pork, and for all other things that we eat. They even sell bubble and squeak, believe it or not. Simpson's on The Strand is the place to go.

I took him there 40 years ago it must be now. Maybe not quite that long, but a long time ago, just the once. From the minute you walk in Simpson's on The Strand, you are walking back into a time when this country was great, and we had an empire and all the rest of it. He looked around and his love of everything British was written all over his face, and he really, really thought it was fantastic. But, I could still see that there was that doubt in his mind concerning the food. But, I was wrong to have doubted it this particular time, because what he had, he thoroughly enjoyed, he must have enjoyed, because the only thing he left on the place was the pattern. I regret in years to come we didn't meet in London more often, just at exhibitions, and that we never, ever went back to that particular restaurant.

He was an agent in France and he could sell... He was an agent for various companies. I know he represented a Belgian company as well as us, but I think most of his income came out of my business. He had the ability to get us into places that I would never ever in a lifetime have dreamt of... Well, approaching, yes, but being successful with, never.

One of them was a firm called Oceanic. Oceanic is Philips-owned, so effectively we were getting in to Philips, and supplying electronics to Philips, for them to put into their product. They did a burglar alarm kit and they put two sensors into the kit. The design of the sensor was theirs. It was a much better looking fitting than ours, but the electronics that went in were the same. We just sent the electronics in the tens of thousands over to this place in France, over in Paris, and they fitted them in to their sensors, put the sensors in the box. Oceanic used to have shops under the name of Oceanic all over France, and maybe other countries as well, I don't know. Other French-speaking countries. I don't know. Like Belgium. Like Luxembourg. I don't know.

But we sold tens, hundreds of thousands of these circuit boards to Oceanic, and Bob got a commission on all the sales. It was only in later years that I found out that in actual fact what was happening was... And this was Bob's business, not mine. If he was getting £1, he gave 50 pence to the fella from Oceanic. The guy from Oceanic, the buyer, was a little bit less than honest, shall we say? But everybody was happy. There was no great criminal activity going on, and we were all very, very happy with the business that we did.

But, Philips are Philips, and although we thought that selling them, say, 20,000 pieces a month was fantastic, and it was, to me, seriously fantastic, they had budgeted for sales of, shall we say, 40,000 a month after a year or two. We'll say two years. When, after two years, we were only up to 20,000, which we thought was wonderful, I'm afraid they didn't think it was wonderful. They didn't think much to it at all. They thought it was a poor show and we were out as quick as we were in. They decided they were no longer going to do the burglar alarm kit and if they didn't have the burglar alarm kit, they didn't need the sensors, and if they didn't need the sensors they didn't need our electronics. So out we went.

Of course, Philips weren't his only customer. In France, there's a very big retail chain called Galeries Lafayette, and Galeries Lafayette, one of their major places in Paris I believe, if my memory serves me rightly is very, very near the Louvre museum where the Mona Lisa is. Now, there's a sight you want to see if you haven't seen it. The Mona Lisa. That's just a little free tip for you. We used to sell various products, nothing like the Oceanic numbers, but nonetheless it wasn't bad, to Galeries Lafayette, and Bob was the man who called. It all transpired again that the buyer was getting a cut, but there again, why worry. Everybody was happy.

I always smiled at the name of the buyer. His name was Monsieur Rat. I can't imagine many people in this country wanting to be called Mr Rat. But Rat is a perfectly common surname in France. Monsieur Rat spent a lot of money. I met him a few times when I was over there but there was no point me interfering. Bob had got it in his back pocket. He knew what was going on. He'd got the business. He'd known this fella for years, and years, and years through selling other things, so I left it alone. I left it to Bob and he did a very good job out of it. I don't know when that ended, because I think that probably was our fault. We stopped manufacturing the sensors. When we stopped manufacturing the sensors, I think they stopped buying from us. It was a sad day. I didn't agree with the decision. But, you have to live with some, and you have to accept the word of the people who pay the bills.

Bob was a wonderful man. I've been out with him for meals where when you look round at what other people eat, you could swear that Bob had eaten as much as all the others put together. I recall going once with my wife, we had lunch somewhere because he wouldn't miss lunch. He had breakfast before he left home, and he had a big lunch and a big dinner, and he did it every day. We went somewhere one day. We went into a hotel, and they... He knew where all the restaurants were. He didn't need telling where to find a restaurant. He knew where they all were.

A typical thing in France in some of these hotels is that they have an island-type thing, a round thing, in the middle of the floor of the restaurant where the desserts are all on display. We'd had the first course. We'd had the main course. My wife didn't want a dessert, but he did. I knew he would. It was a knocking bet that he would. Knocking bet's a Yorkshire expression, I'm afraid. I'm sorry. That goes along with Wetherby and Bawtry for you. It was an absolute knocking bet that he would want a dessert. I say *"a"* dessert because when we stopped counting, he'd had five. Because you could go up and down to this dessert trolley-type thing, it wasn't a trolley, but it was a big circular thing, as many times as you wanted, and you didn't pay any more for going twice, three times, or whatever. I know I gave up count when we got to five. Honestly, he'd had five lots of desserts and we just... I'd had one, maybe two, I don't know, I may be lying. My wife had none at all. We just couldn't not believe where he, as my mother would have said, where he was shovelling it all. But he was shovelling it somewhere. He knew how to enjoy life did Bob, and enjoy it he did!

His wife was a lovely woman, Irene. They lived in a beautiful apartment to the north of Paris, and they rented it. The French aren't like us. They're not a great property-owning nation. They'll settle for rental. He rented this apartment, and inside it was absolutely beautiful. Once, Audrey and myself were invited to an evening meal, a dinner, there, and it was fantastic, the meal, and the interior of the apartment was gorgeous. Externally, it was a bit like going to Del Boy's place. We got a bit scared when we pulled the car up. *"Oh good grief, what on earth is this?"* but when you'd got up in the lift and knocked on the door, and when they let you in, what a different world. What a different world!

As I said, she was called Irene. She was his wife. She was Italian, and at the end of the day, they retired to Italy. She was a school teacher. When she decided to retire she stayed on a few years in France. I don't know how she came to meet Bob, or get married. We never went into that. I've never gone very much for asking other people details of personal involvement. A few years after she'd retired, and I'd left where I was working. I wasn't doing the same as what we'd been doing, and the products that we'd got weren't exactly what he was looking for. I think he'd made a few bob, if you'll pardon the pun. She decided to go back to Italy, to her parents, who were still alive, and retire and he went with her.

I have never, unfortunately spoken to him since. But I'm afraid now he has passed on. I never saw him again. He was up in the hills, up near the Alps, the foothills of the Alps, somewhere in Italy, up in the north there. I never saw him ever again. He'd done more for my business than any other person that ever drew a wage, got a commission out of it, ever did. As I've said before, I admired him, I liked him, and Bob, I thank you. I thank you from the bottom of my heart.

# Chapter Twenty-Four

When I first went to France, before I'd met Bob, I managed to get an introduction to a very nice man, I always remember him, he was the boss man, from a purchasing point of view, for an organisation on the Rue de Londres, London Street, in Paris. He smoked a big pipe and he spoke no English, so again it was good for my French, and he was in charge of the purchasing of a big, big French buying group for electrical distributors, electrical importers. He was interested in our products, and he asked me to go across to see him, which I did. I thought that if you followed the British way of doing things, then the idea was to convince the top man that yours was the product that he wanted, and then he, having agreed with you that yours was the product that they were going to stock and sell would speak to the managers of all the branches throughout France as and when they had regional meetings. The idea then would be that there would be a regional order placed and goods would be filtered through the branches in the region. That's the way, roughly, we would have done it here. Not quite the way that they do it.

Over there, you have to meet the man they call 'the decider'. Each region had a decider man. I went to see this organisation's boss, and he said, *"I want you to come back another time. Now, there's about 25 men going to come to a meeting here. We have a big boardroom. They will be the 25 deciders for the 25 regions that we have in France where we split our branches up. I want you to tell them, to stand up in front of them and tell them why they should be buying your product."* Now, my French isn't bad, but to speak to 25 of them from all different parts of the country, the different accents and different attitudes and certainly different outlooks towards the English, did cause me quite a bit of trepidation. I didn't know what on earth to expect.

We arranged this meeting for whenever, set a date and whatever. I decided to go back, and I knew I'd got to stand up in this room and I'd got to talk these people into buying our goods. I decided to take with me somebody who worked for me. Not because he spoke any French, but because I'd done a flip chart-type thing and he could flip the pages over, and if I wanted a sample he could hand me the sample, et cetera, et cetera, and if I wanted to talk to him prior or after, he was somebody to express my fears and delights to.

So the two of us get there and we stayed in a hotel, Hotel Roi, it's French for King. The King Hotel. Now, I'd stayed there a couple of times before when I'd been in Paris trying to do some business, and it was not expensive, it was clean. All there was was a breakfast room, you had to go out for an evening meal, but there was a couple of decent restaurants within a matter of a couple of hundred yards or less. There always is in Paris. You've only got to open your eyes and you're there.

So we set off that morning from Hotel Roi to go to the Rue de Londres to meet this French buying organisation and their 25 regional deciders. Directors, we would have probably called them. Well, the palms of my hands were definitely sweating when all this started. The boss-man, who I'd met before, introduced me. He told them what we made, pointed to me and sort of said, *"Get on with it,"* and that was it. I was literally thrown in at the proverbial deep end to talk to these 20-odd men. And women. I think there were one or two women.

I did my best. I gave it, as they say these days, my best shot. I'd written down notes and I told everybody all I could, in French, about this product and that product, and t'other product would do. What it could do for their sales and how their customers, the electricians in their areas, would absolutely love it. Have you ever sat down to silence? Because I did. I sat down to absolute silence. I don't know if I was expecting either a round of applause or a load of catcalls, I'm not quite sure, but I sat down to silence, and that meant I didn't know what they thought of the product, what they thought of me. Nothing, I had no idea. They gave nothing away. Their faces never altered. I didn't know what to make of it.

We then get to the point where the meeting comes to an end, these people go off for their tea and biscuits or whatever they have in France, coffee and whatever, and I'm left with the boss man to have a chat to, and he was very kind. He said that I'd done very, very well, the original response from his brief words were good.

People liked the product, they thought they could sell it. I said, *"But they were so quiet."* He said, *"Well, if you went to the number of meetings that they go to, you'd probably be quiet as well. You wouldn't find anything to be getting really excited about."* *"Oh. So we can now be expecting an order from each of them, can we?"* *"No, that's not the way our system works."* *"Oh? So we don't get an order following this meeting?"* *"No. You have now got to go to all the branch managers within the 25 regions and sell to each branch manager what you've just sold to them and hopefully they will buy tens and twenties off the head office, their regional head office, who will then place an order with me, and I'll place a big order with you, if it goes well."* I said, *"How many branches have you got?"* and he said, *"300 and something."* I said, *"But, I haven't even got so much as an agent in this country, and I don't live in this country, and you're saying I've got to, to get anywhere, visit 300 branches and hopefully get orders out of them."* He said, *"I'm sorry, but that's the way our system works. I can't do anything more for you than that. You've had your opportunity, it's now up to you to take it."*

We thanked him for his words of advice, got back in a taxi, I thought, *"We might has well spoil ourselves,"* back to the hotel, and we went out for a nice meal. I said to the man I'd gone with, his name was Paul, I said, *"We'll chat about this over a meal tonight. We're not chatting..."* And we chatted over a meal that night and we just decided that with me, and me alone, and me trying to do the rest of Europe and the UK et cetera, et cetera, to go round 300+ branches, some big, some medium, some small, was just, well, it was bordering on the impossible, and that we wouldn't be rude and ring up tomorrow and say, *"Thanks but no thanks,"* but we'd give it a week or two and then write back and say, *"Well, sorry. Although we think things went well and we think you could do a lot with us, we just haven't got the staff, we haven't got the personnel in France to sell our products to your branch managers."* And that's what we did. And so, my fear of what was going to happen happened, but not for the reasons that I had anticipated.

One final part of this story, and there's got to be a relatively, hopefully, amusing bit at the end. We were going, the next morning, we were catching the train back to Calais. It was before the days of the Channel Tunnel. Catching the train back to Calais and then the ferry and my car was near the ferry Terminal in Dover. We were both on the same floor of the hotel, and we agreed to meet downstairs and I would pay the bill after breakfast.

As luck would have it, I came out of my room virtually the same moment as Paul came out of his, and we went to get in the lift, which only would take two people and two suitcases, that was about it. It was quite a fair number of rooms in this hotel, so the lift would go up passed you and down beyond you but not stop for you. We were there quite a few minutes, or it seemed that way.

We're stood at the lift door, facing the lift door. To our backs there was a door to a bedroom, and our attention was drawn almost immediately by what appeared to be the sound of a woman being strangled or murdered, and it sounded very, very, very, very dubious and bad indeed what was going on in that room. She sounded to be in a great deal of distress. I looked at Paul and he looked at me, and we didn't know whether to intervene or what to do, but in the end I said, *"There's something wrong in there,"* and I turned and I was just going to knock on the door when, and all the gentlemen amongst you who are reading the book will realise, a male voice suddenly let out a... and I don't wish to be rude, long moan, and we realised that we had nearly spoilt two people's day for them. We went downstairs and paid the bill and went home.

# Chapter Twenty-Five

As I've said many times, I love France considerably. If Bob Genier loves the UK, then I love France. If there's any country that I would go and live in, there's only one I've ever been to, that I would go and stay, and that is France. In actual fact, I decided at one stage to have a French office, and to support the French office by living in France for a period of time while other people ran the UK operation. I hunted around, I wanted to be in the north of France, I wanted to be somewhere where it wasn't too difficult for my wife to get home to see her family, because she wasn't really keen on the idea of going, but because she was going with me, and we were getting married, she went along with it.

We eventually settled, after going to two or three towns, on the city of Metz in eastern France. Metz is a city of maybe 350,000 people. It's got a lovely cathedral. It's got a football team which makes it better. We found a house to rent which was absolutely gorgeous. The village that we were in was called Charly-Oradour. Small village, typical of France. No matter how small the village, they've always got a town hall and a mayor. Normally, they've got a restaurant of some sort, a little bistro-type place, but Charly-Oradour doesn't. At that time, there wasn't a bus service. I believe there is now a bus service. We were about eight or nine miles away from the office that we rented in another small ex-steel town.

I remember going over there six or seven weeks before we actually got married and I recall everything was due to be delivered to the house by the time I got there, everything should be just exactly as I wanted it, as we wanted it. It was the strangest feeling of my life getting off... I went on the hovercraft which used to run at those times from Dover to Calais. It was the strangest feeling to go into the Hertz place there and hire a car, or pick up the car that I'd hired, and drive that car about 350 kilometres down to Metz.

I got to the house, because of course I'd been to the house before, I got to the house after dark and went in, fingers crossed. I went in and everything that had been promised by local retail organisations to be delivered, because we'd left a key with the next-door neighbour, was all there, it was all in its place. I was absolutely delighted. Just to ensure everything worked, this was the beginning of a little bit of a downfall, I switched everything on. The television. The heating. The fridge/freezer. The fridge. All the lights in the house. I switched absolutely everything on. I'm sitting watching the television, just playing around with the channels, with everything switched on in the house, and then suddenly everything went, blew, out, gone. Oh dear.

Now, I didn't understand the French system, and I did my best by ringing the French electricity people, who sent out a little van and a man came and I told him as best I could what had occurred, and he looked at me as if I was some sort of idiot, which I suppose, on reflection, I was. He led me into the garage and there, they had something in all garages, all buildings, that we don't have here. They had a major circuit-breaker, and it was 25 amps. If you wanted more than 25 amps, you had to ask for it. It didn't cost more, you just had to ask for a different device. I think the next one up was 40. When I switched everything on, I exceeded 25 amps, and the whole thing just went out, bang, gone, finished, I'm in the dark, I don't know what to do. But he came and he did the difficult task of flicking the switch back up, telling me to reduce the consumption that I'd got on at the moment by switching off a load of lights and switching off this, that and the other, and making sure that I was burning less than 25 amps, and that was the end of that. The next day, an engineer came and he fitted a 40 amp mains breaker and we never, ever, in the time we lived there, had any bother.

I had six weeks over there, prior to going back to get married. I've got to say this. I've never had six weeks when I've enjoyed myself or been as content outside marriage in my life. I used to go to work, I tried my best to build up a customer base in France, and at weekends, Friday nights I went shopping, and on Saturdays I went into the city, into Metz, just whiled away the day. Did nothing on Sundays, apart from cook a meal, watch the television. I took my Sky dish and all the rest of it with me, got the local engineer fella to come and have it facing south into the direction of where it needed to face to be of any use to me. I loved that period, that six weeks.

I made mistakes galore in not knowing the difference between living there and living here. One that I recall, one I look back on with amusement, is that one day I went into the local Leclerc supermarket on Friday night, and I decided I was going to buy myself a nice steak for tea that evening. I looked around and I picked one and I took it to the counter and I paid for it, and got back and I'm cooking the chips, and I'm cooking this, and I'm cooking that, and I'm just going to put the steak under the grill when I noticed that it said, *"Horsemeat,"* on it. I'd picked up horsemeat instead of beef steak. Couldn't face that. My father used to tell me they ate it in the war when the horses were killed by the Germans in the raids. I couldn't face that, so I had a meal of tinned something or other, plus the veg and chips and the what have you. I went out the next day and had a proper lunch in the city.

We lived there for short of 18 months. It was incredibly difficult to get French electrical wholesalers customers to deal with us, incredibly difficult, because our product, which was of very good quality, but it was more expensive than the market leader which came from Germany. That didn't do us any good at all. Eventually, after zigzagging all over the place, getting some customers, don't be misled, of course some people said, *"Yes,"* of course some people wanted the quality, and of course some people bought, but not enough to pay the wages of myself and the part-time wage of my wife. She used to come in now and again when we'd got an order to get out, an order to book. It wasn't enough and the logical decision was to come back. But I enjoyed my time living there. I would go back. I found it fun to have to go in to shops for my wife and buy tights, knitting needles and such things, because she couldn't speak French. It sounds all very boring and mundane, but it wasn't. It was quite amusing. It was quite nice.

The people in the building, that we shared with, maybe a dozen other companies, they were all small companies, were all so kind, and they were all very sorry when we gave up the ghost and came back, but nobody more so than I. I wanted that to succeed. I was really determined that that should succeed, but unfortunately it didn't. But I'd try it again. Or I would have tried it again. Not now. The Grim Reaper has caught up there and I'm too old to do it. But it was worth the effort. It was worth the experience and I'm glad I did it.

# Chapter Twenty-Six

The village in France where we lived, Charly-Oradour, was originally called simply Charly. An interesting fact about it, if any of you are historians and you think about the Oradour bit and you think that it rings a bell, well, it will, because about 1940 the Germans had run riot in Holland, marched straight through Belgium and Luxembourg, seen us off at Dunkirk and were on the verge of just putting their jackboots straight through France.

Metz, from the sound of its name, has changed its nationality on more than one occasion over the centuries, sometimes German and sometimes French, but for some considerable time now, I think all of the last century certainly, it has been French. The people of Charly, small village though it might be, had something like 20 young children living there, and very much as per here when the Blitz occurred in cities like, well, obviously the obvious one here was London, the children were evacuated out to counties like Dorset and Somerset to be safe from the bombs. Metz was never bombed but it was obviously going to become very much in the hands of the Germans, and the adults sent their children down to the south of France, or south of Lyon, for safety. What they thought was safety.

Many years later, the war was coming towards an end, and the village where the children had been sent in the south was called Oradour. The Germans were in retreat, and the French Resistance killed a German soldier. Now when that sort of thing happened, the Germans were not known for their niceties in the ways of war, and they decided they'd tracked him down, the killer of the soldier, to the village of Oradour, where there were something like 15-20 children who were not from that village. There were also the children of that village, and all the people. They... What word can I use? Massacred everybody, absolutely everybody, for the death of this soldier, with the exception of one young man, one young lad, who played dead and laid under the bodies of the ones who had been massacred. To this day, the French have never rebuilt the village of Oradour. It stands as a monument to what man can do to man and what, in particular, at that time the Germans... I refuse to just simply call them Nazis... The Germans were prepared to do to their fellow man.

Word, of course, got back to Charly at the end of the war that the children would not be coming back. They were dead, bar the one, who I met. He was an old man then, and he will have been long gone now. He was an old man then, and I shook his hand and we said a few words, but it wasn't a subject that either of us particularly wanted to get involved in a conversation on. They built in Charly-Oradour... They decided that they were going to change the name of Charly to Charly-Oradour to commemorate the deaths of the children of Charly. This they did. It is a very, very small village. In the middle of the village, they built a cenotaph, a monument, and on that monument are the names of the children who were massacred by the Germans, and it stands there to this day. When we moved there, we had no idea of this story of course. We just thought it was the name of the village. It's the name on the map.

It was only through talking to a man who became a good friend of mine when I was over there, a man called Thierry, which is French for Terry, who helped us no end with all the dos and don'ts of French life, like getting an identity card. I'd lived over there six months without realising you're all supposed to have an identity card, and he asked me where I got mine from and I said, *"What identity card?"* He said, *"Well, if you get stopped by the police for speeding or something like that and you haven't got an identity card, you'll be in bother. They might take a lenient view with you being a foreigner, but I suggest you get one quickly."* That identity card didn't run out until 2008. I used to jokingly say that I'd got dual nationality. It wasn't true, but I did have a French identity card. I've been back twice. The house hasn't changed one iota. The gardens are as bedraggled as ever because the French are not gardeners. My wife could never have put up with that. It's always a mess. They're not great DIY and garden people. But, we found them to be so friendly that it was absolutely untrue how friendly they were.

I tell you one little instance. One morning... Actually, my father-in-law and mother-in-law and my father-in-law's sister-in-law, if this isn't getting too complicated, my wife's auntie in other words, they all came across for a week, and they picked a very good week when the sun just shone. We took them to Paris, but they didn't like Paris. I knew they wouldn't like Paris. Too big. We were soon back out of Paris. One morning, I'm getting up and I'm going to work of course, and that left my wife, her mother, her dad and her auntie in the house. He'd got up for a walk round the village, and when he came back he noticed that we had a big tree which wasn't on our land, but it overhung our land. He looked up and there was, overnight, had appeared a great big nest of wasps. That nest had got to be got rid of, otherwise somebody was going to get badly stung and it wouldn't be pleasant at all.

Well, as I said to you before, the village has a town hall. It had a town hall with a staff of one. There was the mayor who was a local farmer, who used to zoom around on his tractor, and when he saw me, he used to wave at me and shout at me, and he used to call us, *"His English,"* in English. He used to say, *"You are my English,"* and we used to say, *"Yes, okay, fair enough. We're your English."* And, there was a woman, a very nice lady, who was the only member of staff in the town hall. She worked eight o'clock in the morning till twelve. Twelve to two was lunch. Two to six, go home. Five days a week.

This particular day, my father-in-law has seen the wasps nest up in this tree overhanging our land. The only thing I could think of was, was it a fire brigade job? Because I certainly wasn't going to tackle them. I mean, good God, it would have been impossible for one man, or me and my father-in-law, or me and all my neighbours. Nobody wanted to know. All people wanted to know was it was going. So on my way to work, I went to the town hall, told the lady. I had to look in the dictionary what *"wasp nest"* was. I still remember it, but I won't bother telling you what wasp nest is in French. I went off to work.

When I came back home for lunch, because don't forget I had got the twelve to two thing... There was no point being at work. You couldn't ring anybody. Nobody would answer you. Wherever you rang in France, they were all having lunch. When I came home at lunchtime, I came back to the news that the fire brigade had been, been up the ladder with their masks on, visors or whatever, gloves, popped the nest in a bag and taken it off and, I presume, destroyed it. That was a day of excitement in Charly-Oradour. A day of excitement indeed.

Travelling up and down France, in the car... France is a lot bigger country than the UK. If you come up this part of the world that I live in and you think that you go from Hull on the east to Liverpool on the west in a couple of hours, that's not bad. France is great for motorways, as long as you're driving in straight lines up and down. Motorways going sideways, east, west, west, east, don't exist in such numerous quantities. In those days, they were very few and far between. It was okay up and down, north, south, south, north, but east, west and whatever, it was a shocking idea.

I once went to Lyon, to visit a potential customer, who I had known from day's way back. It was in a place called

Villeurbanne, an outskirt, nonetheless a separate town to Lyon. I went there and I saw the gaffer, who I've known for years, and his sidekick who was the engineer I suppose you'd call him, because they made light fittings as well as buying things in as well. I went down to tell him that we'd opened up in France, near Metz, which he thought was crazy because most people did. They used to say Metz was for dying and praying, and I didn't realise that. You don't go into countries the size of France and open up your only office fifteen minutes from the Luxembourg border, because that means you are a very long way from Bordeaux for example, or Marseille, or even Paris for that matter. You are very long way away.

This day I went down to Lyon and told them what we were doing and they promised they would have a look at supporting us if they possibly could, but the fun part of the day came at lunchtime when these two fellas too me for lunch. Now, Lyon sits on two rivers, the Saône and the Rhône. The Rhône is much better known than the Saône, but not if you're from Lyon of course. If you're from Lyon, and you live on the banks of the Saône, then you don't think much to the Rhône, and vice-versa.

That day, I was going to see them. I'd driven down the day before, stayed overnight and then gone on the last bit. But after I saw them, I determined that I was, because it was a Friday, I determined that I was going to drive all the way back to Metz, which even with motorways was an extremely foolish thing to do, or to contemplate doing. At lunchtime, when I'm thinking, *"Right, let me get a head-start on everybody and get away,"* oh no, oh no, these two fellas had known me too long for that. Business or no business, they were grateful that I'd made the effort, *"We're taking you for lunch Chris."* There was no way that me, hoping to get business out of a major French manufacturer was going to turn down their offer. So off we go in separate cars. They're in one car and I'm in mine because obviously after lunch I'm going to make my way back to the motorway and drive north, and they're just going to nip back to the factory or go home.

We went into this restaurant, and we had a beautiful meal. I can remember it well. Now, as I said, there are two rivers, the Saône and the Rhône, and they grow entirely different wines on both banks of the rivers. They all think theirs is better than the other. We sit down and they both ordered a bottle of red wine, a good quality red wine. So, we've got a bottle from the Saône and a bottle from the Rhône, and there's only the three of us, and bearing in mind I've got 350 kilometres to drive after this. We got towards the end of the meal and the two bottles were empty, and one of them, I don't remember which, said, *"Well then, which..?"* and the question was posed of me, *"Which of the two bottles do you think..? Which of the two wines do you think was the better?"* *"Oh hell,"* thinks I, *"I haven't got a clue. They were both, I thought, absolutely gorgeous. How can I come down on one side or the other without offending the loser? The one I didn't choose."* So I decided to try and get out of the whole thing as diplomatically as I possibly could by saying, *"I thought they were both equally good, and I enjoyed them both very much. Thank you."*

I thought that that was the best way of getting out of it all, getting in the car and getting away before the traffic built up and before I got anymore worse for wear. Their answer was exactly the opposite. *"Fair enough. We'll call it a draw,"* to use an English expression. Clicked his fingers, the wine waiter came across, the sommelier came across, *"Another bottle of each please."* And I thought, *"Pardon? Another bottle of each please? Oh dear, oh dear, oh dear. Now what am I going to do?"* We had to consume it. I managed to work it that they got as much of the two bottles... They got about a bottle and a half of the two bottles to my half a bottle, but even then I'd had more to drink than I would certainly have nowadays. But, in those days, in France, nobody bothered a great deal about drinking and driving.

I came out thinking, *"I don't know how I am going to keep my eyes open. I don't know how I am going to drive all that way."* I got home at something like midnight with my wife waiting up for me, and I told her the story, to which she called me a bloody fool, but when you're in the situation, it's a bit difficult to get out of the situation.

Another man that I loved almost as much as Bob Genier in France was a man called Henri Baudoin. He did so much business with me over a period of time that it's absolutely untrue. He sold these infrared sensors by the absolute bucketloads. He had a company in a town called Valence. The firm was called SFPP, and he supplied security companies the length and breadth of France with sensors for burglar alarms and for all sorts of things, and we made all these things. I used to go down there time and time again, always come away with a massive great order. I never drove. I went on the train. I flew to Paris and then took the train to Valence, the TGV, and the next morning... I stayed in a Novotel, always stayed at the same place, and the next morning somebody would come in one of their work's vans and pick me up.

I always remember one lad coming to pick me up in a work's van. They're big rugby union followers down there. Well, rugby union to me is, well, it's not my sport at all. I once heard two fellas from Halifax talking about rugby union and they called it *"Kick and Clap,"* where you kick it out and everybody claps, and I thought that was a pretty fair assessment. But down in that part of the country, that part of the world, this lad was playing rugby union, and he'd recently been over here, as an amateur, just playing a few games on tour down in the south of England. One team that they'd played against, one town that they'd played against, was in Surrey. East Grinstead, I think it's in Surrey isn't it? East Grinstead. Well, this lad, on the journey between the hotel and SFPPs office, was determined to tell me that he'd been to East Grinstead. East Grinstead is not easy for a Frenchman to say, believe you me. It really isn't. It's very, very difficult. It took me a good ten minutes to work out what he was actually saying, that he'd been to East Grinstead, and that they'd won or lost or whatever they'd done.

That same day, I went in to see his gaffer, Henri, who was, without a doubt, a friend of mine. We got on well. They always liked the ability that I held the conversations in French. I made it easier for them and more difficult for me. That gave them a certain respect for me. This particular day was a Monday. If any of you know France well, you will know that Mondays are a day that most shops are shut. That's the weekend, Sunday, Monday. They all open Saturday, but they shut Sunday, Monday, and I was there on a Monday. We always went out for lunch. Different places. He always wanted to just change things around a little bit.

On this particular day, we went out and we're driving down this road out of the industrial estate in his car, and I could see something was bothering him, and what was bothering him was where were we going that would be open, because they just close Mondays. So, we get into the centre of this small town. This is not Valence. This is another small town away from Valence, driving away from Valence, where he normally took me for a bite to eat and it was always extremely good. Everywhere was closed. We went to a particular restaurant, and it was closed, and Henri hammered on the door until eventually the owner came to the door, saw who it was, obviously realised that Henri spent quite a few quid with him in the year, and he opened the door, let us in and prepared a meal for me, Henri, and his brother. Now, his brother here would be known as a dozy so-and-so. He hadn't got a lot of brains. If it wasn't for Henri, he'd have been sweeping the streets I think because he just hadn't got anything in him at all. Henri was the brains of the family without a shadow of a doubt.

We had the meal, we came out, and we got in the car, and Henri's fidgeting about. He always smoked, and smoked heavily.  He's fidgeting about, trying to find his cigars.  He used to smoke small cheroots-type cigars. He hadn't got any.  Well, we'd both had a fair amount to drink, but he was driving not me.  I recall him pulling up...   There were one or two shops open.   Usually tobacconists stayed open because tobacconists and the like, they stayed open because people want cigarettes and what have you every day of the week.  They can't do without just because it's Monday, and that's a fact. I recall him saying...  He gave me some money, pointed at the shop and said, *"Go in there and get a pack of my usual,"* or words to that effect.  That's how we would say it.  I went in and I said to the man, who didn't know me at all, never seen me before, never seen me since, *"Henri Baudoin, pack of cigars,"* and he served me, I paid him, went back to the car.  It's one of the daftest tricks I've ever done in terms of making sense, but do you know, it never crossed my mind that it was stupid. It's funny what a few drinks will do.

We decided then we were going to drive back to his building and then he would get the lad with the van to take me back to the hotel, I'd have a night at the hotel, get on the train and come back north.  As we're driving back towards his building, we come to some traffic lights, and he's absolutely steaming.  He's not fit to drive, not really at all, but he could get away with it in a sense, because it was Monday and there wasn't much about.  We pulled up at these red traffic lights.  I'm amazed he even stopped.  I'm amazed he even saw the traffic lights.  A French motorcycle police officer pulled up alongside us, and Henri wound the window down because the policeman suggested he should, and

I thought, *"Oh dear, we're going to be in trouble."* No, we weren't in trouble at all. It was Henri's brother-in-law who was a policeman, and he knew that he was full of drink. We had a quick chat, ten to fifteen seconds or so, the lights changed to green, he went one way, we went straight on, and nothing more was said.

We got to the industrial estate, and the road that he was on was a one-way street. I tell you no lie when I say to you that we got to the end of the street and we should have gone round the block and come round from the other end to drive up the right way, but he couldn't be bothered so we drove straight down the one-way street in the wrong direction, and he pulled into his yard. I don't think I was compos mentis enough to realise what we'd done quite at the time, and of course he was the local dignitary and if anybody had have stopped him, he would have told them where to get off. Last time I saw him alive.

He didn't look well that time I saw him, and he drank a lot at that lunchtime meeting. Well, it wasn't a meeting. We'd had the meeting. He never stopped smoking. He smoked one after the other, after the other, after the other. I used to say to him, *"Look Henri, as a friend, for God's sake, it'll kill you man. It will kill you,"* and he just used to smile at me and ignore me, and that drive down the one-way street was the last time I saw Henri Baudoin alive. I got a message to say that he'd died of lung cancer. I went to the funeral, which was a long way to go for a funeral, but he was a friend. He was a friend, a good friend, and a man I will never forget. The sad side of this, the sadder side of this, is that the daft brother took over, and within months the firm was struggling. We weren't getting paid. They were losing customers hand over fist, and they just went bust. To most people in the world today, they won't remember him, but I always will. He was a tremendous influence on me. He helped me no end, and I thank him. I thank him deeply, from the bottom of my heart.

# Chapter Twenty-Seven

Living in France was, to me, a dream come true. I've always loved the country, and I've always had an inkling for speaking the language, which I'm told I speak reasonably well. I can get through on most things. I enjoyed my time there. I enjoyed it very much indeed. I, because I was working, had the privilege to meet some rather important people in the French lighting and electrical trade, people who I will never forget, people who I admired at the time and who did all they could to help me with orders, and they were kind.

One particular man was a man of over 90 years of age. His name was Baltzinger, and he had a son who was Michel Baltzinger. Now, old Mr Baltzinger, he had three languages, and the preference of speaking them was German, Alsatian, and French. Now, the Baltzinger very large warehouse and factory unit was situated in Strasbourg. Now, Strasbourg is like Metz, where I lived, a name which is Germanic in nature, not French, and it has changed hands on several occasions through wars, and changes of government, and all sorts of things, and is divided from Germany by a river. The other side of the river is in Germany. Not far away is the city of Karlsruhe, in southern Germany.

Mr Baltzinger, as I said, spoke three languages, in the order that I gave you, but when he spoke to me, and he was always extremely polite, and kind, and gentle with me, gentle in the sense that he didn't speak in a way I couldn't understand with a strong accent, he helped me out no end, he always used his weakest language, which of course was French. His son only spoke French. We got a conversation going there where I found it very easy to understand the old Mr Baltzinger, and the oung one, Michel, was much more difficult to follow because, although he was an extremely eloquent, well-dressed man, he did speak with a considerable Alsatian/ Strasbourg accent. They were, in that part of the world, in Alsace, the big electrical and lighting wholesaler. If you wanted to make headway in Alsace, you either sold to Baltzinger, or you tried somewhere else. It was as simple as that. We were holding stock in Metz, on the outskirts of Metz in our warehouse, and so it wasn't difficult to supply them in reasonably small numbers when and if they wanted things. They helped us. They did sell, from time to time. They did organise trade meetings with their customers to promote our products, and they always paid on time. I can't say much more about them, because there wasn't much more to say.

When I came away from France, when I came back to the UK, the relationship ended, except for a couple of occasions when I was at exhibitions in Paris and they had a stand and I bumped into them and had a quick word with them. With the younger man I should say. The old man wouldn't travel to exhibitions because he was a bit frail. If the world was full of Michel and his father Baltzinger, the world would have little or no problems. They were kindness itself. They were helpful, and I thank them for all that they did for me. It was only a great, great shame that I didn't get to know them better and for longer.

Living in Metz meant that you couldn't spend the entire time in the office. You couldn't spend the entire time working. You had to find other things to do, other than going out eating and what have you. And being a football fanatic, which I am, I decided that I would become a one man British Metz supporters' club member. Metz, I discovered, was a town, in terms of the football team, not very dissimilar to Barnsley. Very similar to Barnsley. Never good enough for one league and too good for the one below.

I used to like going to Metz to watch the matches. I saw some good players there, mainly playing for the opposition I'm afraid I need to add. The only thing that I found about going that I found difficult to get used to is that when they were in the first division, which they were for the whole time I was there, their matches at home used to kick off, local time, at 8:00PM. Now 8:00PM in a Lorraine winter, with the wind coming in over Germany, from Poland and Russia, can be a bit cold to say the least. I used to go alone, because my wife has never, ever been a football fan and it was too cold for her to want to go anyway.

The major difference I found between British and French football was, when I was watching British football, particularly at Barnsley, there was a great deal of cut and thrust, and we scored a goal, they scored a goal, and it was all go for 90 minutes. Watching Metz was completely different. Remarks such as watching the fire go out could be sometimes levelled at games I went to. I remember going to watch them play a team called Valenciennes, which is in north-eastern France. I can honestly say that it must have been the most boring 90 minutes that I've ever spent in my life, and before you ask me, yes, you've guessed it, it was nil-nil. It was pretty dreadful.

I used to go sometimes with a local chap who was a Metz supporter called Thierry, French for Terry, and he would go to most of the home games. We'd meet up and he would show me the way into the ground. They don't have turnstiles like we do, or they didn't at the time. You went to an office to buy a ticket and then you went from the ticket to the turnstile and then you went in. It all seemed a rather convoluted way of paying your money to get in to watch a football match to me. Nonetheless, he was a very kind man, a very helpful man, he answered a lot of questions that I needed answering concerning life in France, and he showed me various little snippets of information that were helpful in my day to day life, as well as going with me to the football. But, we never went for a drink after or anything like that. That sort of tradition in Metz just did not exist. I'm not saying it didn't exist in the rest of France, I'm not sure, but in Metz it didn't. It was really you went to the match and then you went for a meal because the restaurants would stay open until midnight, one o'clock in the morning, to allocate for the football fans who were, I must say this, a darned sight better behaved than the ones that we had here at the time.

I said my wife didn't like football, and that's true. She doesn't, to this day, really. Well, how can a Huddersfield Town supporter possibly like football? It's a total impossibility. One night, mid-winter, I don't know why but she said, *"I'll go with you."* Metz were playing Toulon. Toulon is a town in the south, very much better known for its rugby union connections than it is for its football connections, and as far as I know, today they're in the French third division, but I wouldn't swear to that. But I went with my wife to watch them play at Metz one night, eight o'clock, and believe me, it was cold.

We went into the main tribune, which is just French for stand, and we sat on plastic seats with no backs to lean against. The plastic seats were screwed down onto concrete and they ran the length of the stand. Well, the Valenciennes match was poor, and at half-time, this was just about worse than the Valenciennes match. Too many teams in that league go away to draw nil-nil. Their appetite for scoring goals, at that time, I think it's improved considerably since, at that time was not really something that they were interested in. They came for a point. They were quite content to draw nil-nil and go home. We watched the whole 90 minutes, which I would say was a tad better than Valenciennes but only a tiny tad, and then we went home. My wife said that it was rather appropriate that they were playing Toulon, because the whole thing, from her point of view, lasted too long. I'm afraid I've got to agree with her. She was spot on right.

I continued to go. I continued to support them. At the end of the season that we were there, they narrowly avoided relegation. We then left to come back home and I noticed that at the end of the season, they had been relegated. You may not believe this, but I promise you that it's true. Every weekend, sometimes they play Saturday, sometimes they play Sunday. It depends whether they're in the first division or the second. I always look to see how my favourite French team have fared. It's very much hard work for them to show much in the way of success. Success to them is avoiding relegation from the first division, and if they get relegated, success is about coming back up the following season. Football was something I looked forward to over there, but was distinctly disappointed by what I saw.

I was, for 20-odd years, a football referee, and I decided that I would approach the local football association here and see whether they could get the football association in London to recommend me as a referee to the French football association. They did, they gave me a letter, and to cut a long story short, I didn't take it up. Before I showed the letter to anybody, who would be the secretary presumably of a local or regional league, I went to a couple of games just to see what it was like, didn't think much to it, changed my mind about wanting to referee in France, and never did, and that was the end of that. I regret it. I regret it intensely. I should have done it. I should have just seen their faces when an Englishman went on the field with a different interpretation of the rules to what they got from their normal French fella on a normal Sunday, because all the football is Sunday at local level, but I didn't do it. Can't give you an explanation as to why. I just did not do it, and I'm sorry that I didn't.

One of the main things about being where we were is that everybody goes out for a meal on most Saturday nights, when Metz are away. But, no, seriously, they go for a meal either before... If they're a football fan, after the match, or if they're not, they go during the match. I remember once going to a restaurant in the middle of Metz with my wife and we had a very nice meal. Metz is a city which a lot of people in this country know of, but know nothing about. It's because a lot of these touring parties on coaches cross over the Channel into France and a decent drive down on the first evening when they're going to somewhere like Austria or Switzerland, is Metz. The following morning after breakfast, they carry on down to their final destination.

I recall being in this place in Metz once. We were in the restaurant and it was probably two thirds full. What I had noticed was that the events room, if you want to call it that, was full, and I could overhear the accents and they were all very familiar to me. I went just for a look outside, and there was a bus outside from Bradford. So, adding two and two together, I concluded that the people in the annexe restaurant, if you want to call it such, were from Bradford. Now, what they usually did, they usually put on a cheap meal for them, basically chicken and chips and peas, plus a dessert, coffee, and then most of them, because they were too shy to come out into the open and speak, went to bed. But, this particular night, a group of them, maybe eight or nine, came into the bar area where we had gone for a drink after the meal.

One man was in his mid-60s and he'd taken control of ordering from the waiter. It wasn't going well. He was asking people what they wanted, the people from Bradford who were with him, and they were telling him, but he could not get it across to the French waiter who spoke no English whatsoever. They were getting frustration on both sides. So, much against my wife's better wishes, I went across and I said to the man who was obviously the organiser of this little group, *"Can I help you?"* and he looked at me with considerable surprise and said, *"Well, you speak extremely good English."* I said, *"Well that's because I'm from Barnsley."* And of course, he then proceeded to inform the rest of his little group that here he had with him to help him, he had found, which he hadn't, a fellow Yorkshireman from the Broad Acres. I said, *"Now, what do you want to order?"* He told me and I told the waiter and went to sit back down. A few minutes later, the waiter came back out with a pal and on the two trays they had the drinks. They gave the drinks to the people concerned and that was that.

The man in charge came across, in front of everybody else, French and the people from Bradford, and said, in the broadest of Yorkshire accents, *"You'll never guess what we've got here. We've got somebody that can talk to them,"* as if I'd suddenly discovered penicillin or something, or I'd come up with a cheap way of getting men to the moon or some such thing. He said, *"This fella's from Barnsley and he can talk to them. Ee, tha're a clever lad,"* he said. *"Tha're a clever lad."* I said, *"Thank you very much. You could do it yourself if you tried."* He laughed at me, sat down, we went and I never, ever saw them again.

A similar incident occurred, but not the same. A similar type of incident occurred in town call Thionville. This is the town near Metz where we banked. The reason we banked in Thionville and not Metz was quite simple. It's called parking. In Metz, it's like all major cities. You can't get your car anywhere near where you want to be. Thionville is a small, medium-sized market sort of town. There's no yellow lines. There's no parking meters. You can park your car up and it was always, always, I can't recall a day when it wasn't... I didn't go to the bank very often, but I would go maybe once a week. It was always possible to get parked up virtually outside the front door. The people inside the bank were terrified of me, not physically but linguistically, because I used to burst in, open the door, burst in, and say, *"And who's speaking English today then?"* Well, that used to get a sort of rat-run-type effect on the staff. They all went everywhere bar near me, because they thought I was being serious, that I couldn't converse with them, but I could. After a while, they realised the true situation, and it just became a little bit of a joke, *"Who's going to speak English today?"*

One day, I'm in the bank and I am at the desk talking to one of the tellers, just handing in a few cheques and things like that, and suddenly a man comes in from the street and in the broadest of Yorkshire accents, even broader than the man from Bradford, he said, *"I've just been down to the bank down the street and they tell me that you will cash some travellers' cheques for me, because I'm running out of money."* Now, remember, in those days, hole in the wall wasn't a thing that was everywhere, not everybody had a card and a PIN number, and it was much easier to carry travellers' cheques. Well, after his outburst... Sorry, not outburst. After his initial remarks, the rat-run effect started to happen again. Everybody found they'd got something to do, disappeared out of the way, because they weren't going to tackle him, for the simple reason they hadn't a clue what he was talking about. He was another one from the Broad Acres. And of course, I had the great advantage, or disadvantage, depends on your point of view, of being able to understand exactly what he'd said about cashing some travellers' cheques.

Madame Schmidt we'll call her... I did know a Madame Schmidt just down the road, by the way, she was our accountant, but I can't think what this other one was called, so we'll have two Madame Schmidts... Looked at me and I looked at her, and she said to me, *"Do you understand him?"* and I said, *"Yes."* She said, *"Will you help us and will you help him?"* and I said, *"Yes."* He came, and I said, *"Excuse me, can I help you in any way please?"* although I knew exactly what he wanted. Again, I got this, *"My word, you speak good English."* And again, we came back to the, *"I'm from Barnsley. I live here. I speak French and I speak English."* Now, this fella was from Swillington, which is on the outskirt of Leeds and Wakefield, it's between the two. I know that because he was waving his passport around like a flag and I just happened to notice that his place of birth was Swillington, Leeds.

Well, it wasn't difficult to understand what he wanted. I asked Madame Schmidt, *"What do we do?"* She says, *"Get him to sign the cheques,"* he signed the cheques for however much he wanted, *"And ask him for the passport."* Well, he's waving that around, so the passport was easy. He gave her the passport, he gave her the cheques. I don't know how much he cashed and I wasn't interested. It wasn't my concern. A great beam came across his face because what he'd come in for, he'd got. He came in for some money and he was going out with some money. He got to the door and I turned back just to finish off what I was doing with one of the tellers, and he turned, and when he turned he said, *"It doesn't matter where you go in this world, you'll always meet a bloody Yorkshireman."* I was his bloody Yorkshireman, and proud of it.

# Chapter Twenty-Eight

As you will recall, I had an unfortunate experience with a suitcase with Air France in Lyon, and part of the following journey took me up to Paris and eventually into... At some time during the journey, I ended up in Kaiserslautern, in southern Germany, where I was visiting the UK/German headquarters of a very big customer of mine in Doncaster. I had made this appointment to see this man in Kaiserslautern. He was in charge of something in the region of 100-120 branches of this UK wholesaler over in Germany, and as such I thought that it would be perhaps my likeliest way into the German market.

Just to briefly explain to anybody who has never tried to sell anything electrical or lighting to the Germans, they are great believers in using their own equipment wherever possible, and defend that stance behind something which has been introduced by them into the European Union, and it won't change with us leaving, we shall still carry on doing this, called the CE mark. You may have seen these two letters, CE, on all sorts of products. It's French. It stands for Conformité Européene, which is simply translated into European Conformity in English. The Germans hide behind the CE mark very, very successfully, by always claiming that all their products comply and anything that anybody else is trying to sell into their market doesn't necessarily comply, and therefore their choice is already made for them. It's baloney of course, because when you go out of the head offices, and you go to a local branch in a town, you will find that the branch manager has done what the branch manager would do in any country, he's gone and bought the one that makes the most money for him, CE mark or not, although everything carries the CE mark.

I got to Kaiserslautern without my suitcase, obviously, I should think, by now somewhat high in smell and not to be followed downwind. Or is it upwind? I don't know. I can't remember which. My father used to say, *"You smell like a country closet."* I've never smelled a country closet, but I can imagine what he must have meant. First thing to do, I'd got my 400 Francs, which I'd changed into marks, because of course, this is before the days of the euro, and I booked into the hotel that I'd arranged through my travel agent here in Kaiserslautern, and I thought, *"Well, the only thing I can do here with the 400 Francs converted into marks is to go out and buy some new underwear."* Sorry to mention that particular topic. It's not that sort of book. But, it was the obvious and logical thing to do.

Not too far from the hotel was a gent's outfitter where I went, clutching my marks in my hand. I went into the shop. Now, of course, in many countries in Europe, Holland, Belgium, Denmark et cetera, English is spoken freely and very, very well. In France and Germany, this doesn't apply, particularly Germany. I go into this shop in Kaiserslautern, this men's outfitter, and I have to describe what I want. Now, putting your hands down by your side, wiggling a bit and pretending to pull something up is one way of doing it, but not necessarily a very successful one. There was another man in the shop at the time, and he was watching these antics with quite considerable, not amusement because the German's don't laugh, amazement I think would be a better word.

But what I wanted dawned on him, which it had not done on the assistant who was serving me, which was a lady, a lady in her mid-50s I would say. He said something to her and used the word *"unterhosen."* Now, my German was good enough to know that *"unter"* is under, *"hosen"* is trousers, and I, *"Ja. Yes. Unterhosen."* *"Ah."* So, she looked at me and my considerable size and thought to herself, *"I don't know that we've got any unterhosen that'll fit this fella, but we'll try. We'll see what we can do,"* and the largest that they had did fit me. They had one colour, white. They had elasticated bands round them which, my word, were tight, and I spent the next two or three weeks getting these things washed intermittently in the laundry of hotels where I was staying for a couple or three nights. That gave the laundry time to get the garments back to me.

So, I'm kitted out for next morning, and off I go, by taxi, to the office of this company in Kaiserslautern. The man's expecting me. We sit, we talk, we chat, in English because he came actually from... From Coventry he came. It was a very easy, very simple appointment because of the language situation. Told him what we were doing, told him what we were selling, and he was quite willing to help a fellow Brit trying to do his best into Germany, and was prepared to consider giving me an order.

He said that evening, would I go to his house and have dinner with his wife, because he understood that I was there a couple of nights and that I was alone? At the end of the day, we got in his car and we drove off to his house. Well, his house was some way away. It was at least 45 minutes, and that's excluding the traffic. That's out of the traffic. We were up in the hills, not quite mountains, way up into the woods. I suppose we would be in The Black Forest, wouldn't we? I imagine we would. We would probably be on the edges of The Black Forest, without the gateau.

We eventually pulled into a drive, with very impressive gates, electronically controlled, a very long driveway and a two-storey building, a massive house at the end of the drive. I go in, follow him in, I'm introduced to his wife who is equally from Coventry, or somewhere. She knew I was coming. They had a maid. The maid had prepared dinner for the three of us. He said, *"We'll sit down and have a drink,"* so I did. He said, *"Would you like to have a look round the house?"* I said, *"Very nice of you. Very kind."* We looked round the house, went outside, massive swimming pool he had. The weather was quite warm. He asked me if I wanted to go in and I said, *"No."* To the swimming pool that was. I said, *"No,"* for one very good reason. Not because I'm shy, but because I can't swim and I didn't fancy drowning in The Black Forest.

He then decided that it would be nice for me to look at his wine cellar. Well, he had a bigger wine cellar than most restaurants than I've ever seen in the UK. It was massive. His selection, his choice, was absolutely enormous, not only of German wines, but of French, and of New Zealand, and Australia, and then Spanish, et cetera, et cetera. The man was living the life of a baron, a huge land owner. This didn't really tally with the situation that he was the German area manager for an electrical wholesale group. I have no doubt that he would get paid a nice salary for it, but I couldn't see where up in the forest, with a drive of about a quarter of a mile, with a huge swimming pool, and a marvellous house, plus the wine cellar, I just couldn't see how he could finance it. It just seemed quite remarkable to me.

The next day, I went back down to the office, we chatted a bit more and he popped me back to Kaiserslautern railway station and off I went to somewhere else in Germany. A few months later, I was discussing with a friend of mine who worked for the same company, but for the UK head office in Doncaster, and he sort of whispered in my ear that the guy I'd been to see had in fact been sacked only a few weeks after I'd gone because, as my mum used to say, he had problems identifying his money and the company's. We won't take it any further than that because I don't want to be sued. So that was where the money had come from, and that was the end of a very promising relationship.

I've just remembered where I was off to actually. I was going quite some way and I had to change trains about twice. I was going up to Bremen which is the north of

Germany to see somebody who I'd again met at an exhibition, again they'd expressed an interest in dealing with us, and the CE mark didn't have anything to do with it. I went up there to Bremen, and I got an address... The man was an oldish man, and his son, and they were not manufacturers, they were agents for the type of product that my company was making and supplying throughout Europe. I think he must have seen something or other in an advert we may have placed, and he also saw the stand at Olympia, at the annual exhibition.

I had the address and I got a taxi and went out to this address, having left everything behind in a local hotel in Bremen, except my briefcase. I went out and I got to the address and it was just a small door in-between a line of shops. I got out of the taxi, paid him, he drove away and I walked to the door. Now, I knew what the name of the company was, and I knew what the address was. We'll say it was number ten whatever the street was. I walk to the door and there was a ten on the door, but there was no mention on the plaque on the side of the door of his company. There was a plaque on the side of the door, but it wasn't his company. The plaque was the Irish Consulate for Northern Germany, and I was completely puzzled by this. I've come to an address where I think I'm going to see a man about lighting or electrical equipment, and I've gone through a door that says Irish Consulate. This really had me perplexed. Well, it would you, wouldn't it?

I went up the stairs. There was no lift. I walked up a couple of flights of stairs and at the top there was another door with another plaque, Irish Consulate. So, I knocked, and I thought I was going to be confronted by an Irishman or two, but I knocked and went in, and when I went in, there were the two fellas that I recognised from the exhibition, smiling and waiting for me, and expecting me. Put the kettle on, as we would say here, and we had a drink. I said at first, *"Please, I'm a little confused here. I've come to see a company called so-and-so but I've walked through the door of the Irish Consulate. You're not Irish. I'm not Irish. What are we doing?"*

He said, *"Oh, it's quite simple. I love to go to Ireland two or three times a year, southern Ireland, fishing. I met an Irish government official, diplomat-type fella while out fishing, said that I was from Bremen in northern Germany. They said that they were looking for somewhere to put just small premises for a Consulate to help any Irish people in distress, and did I fancy doing it, and being paid an honorarium each year?"* He said yes, and that's what he did. I said, *"I understand. That's fine. So, you're not Irish, but if anybody is Irish and they get into any sort of scrapes round and about, you come and you sort them out and you help them and the Irish government foots the bill."* *"Spot on."*

Then we turned to business, and we talked business and he actually placed a small order, just to see how things went, and we did business over the years. Not a great deal. The type of products we were selling were not his strong point. He was basically really into external die-cast aluminium lighting, not into what we did, but nonetheless he did a bit with us, and eventually

I remember him moving out into a warehouse out in the countryside. Unfortunately, he died a few years later and that was the end of that. I started on my own, and never thought that I would see anything more of them again, until one day when I was in my office in Barnsley. One of the girls who worked for me came in and said, *"There's a Herr something-or-other from Germany just turned up to see you. Will you see him?"* I said, *"Yes. It must be the son."* This guy, this son, walked in, no appointment, just by chance, and we sat and we chatted, but what I was doing then of course was a million miles, in many ways, away from what I was doing before, so although it was nice to see him, there was nothing we could do and we just agreed to keep in contact, but like most cases, this contact was never kept.

The biggest lighting exhibition in Europe, the second largest in the world actually, is in Frankfurt and it's every other year, and I used to go, simply because the Chinese who I dealt with always had stands there and it was one very good place for them to display new products. It was also a very good place for me to pick up samples. I used to go by car. I used to take my car, rather than fly. It was a very good place for me to go, pick up samples at the end of the exhibition, put them in the car and drive them back, and save myself a few quid and a bit of time waiting.

Now, most German cities - and Frankfurt is no exception, have a... How can we say it...? Have a red light district, and I had an Irish friend who was rather... An Irish customer who became a friend who was rather keen on the red light districts. One night, during one of my visits to Frankfurt, we, the pair of us decided to go out for a meal. We went for this meal, and it was nothing special. It wasn't expensive. It wasn't cheap. It was just an ordinary meal. We came away, got in a taxi and I asked for a ride back to my hotel and I assumed that he would do exactly the same.

# Chapter Twenty-Nine

We were driving back to where I was staying, and this part of Frankfurt was a huge one-way system, so we're going back in a different direction than we came and I didn't recognise any of the buildings, because we'd gone one way and we were going back following the one-way system, which was fair enough. I noticed as we were driving along that the buildings that were around and about us were by and large a giant Soho if you like. They were a red light district, and it struck me that my friend who was with me, who for the sake of argument we will call Jim, rather knew this part of Frankfurt a lot better than I did.

The next thing I know, we come to some traffic lights. The traffic lights are red. Jim throws open his door and he's gone, he's out, he's disappeared, he's gone, he's left me. I quickly paid the driver whatever we were owed and I saw where Jim was idling about looking in these various buildings. I walked up to him and I said, *"What on earth did you do that for?"* *"Well,"* he said, *"I didn't know whether you'd want to come."* I said, *"Nay Jim, you're the Catholic lad amongst us, not me. You're the one who shouldn't be doing this, not me. What are we doing here?"* He said, *"Well, I'm going in that place over there,"* and he pointed to what can best be described as a three or four storey block house, with lights blazing around all over the place, and he said, *"Come. Come on. Come on in. Come on in. Nobody'll ever know."* And I thought to myself, *"No, nobody'll ever know. It's just my luck, it has been all my life, that I'll walk straight in and somebody'll shout, 'Chris' out no sooner than we'd got through the door and they'll recognise me."*

In we go, and it was the weirdest place that I've honestly ever been in, I think, in my life. There were four corridors along four flights of... What's a nice word for it? Flats, apartments. I can't think of another word. Each of them had doors like stable doors, that you find with horses, in other words a bottom and a top. At each of these doors, leaning out over them were naked women. Well, almost naked women. Certainly, the top half of them was rather poorly-clad. They'd run out of material there, that was a fact. This was a bit beyond me. I'd never seen anything like it in my life, and I didn't really feel very comfortable, and I wanted to go, and I kept saying to Jim, *"Come on Jim. We don't want to be in here. Come on. It's not where we want to be."* But it became quite obvious that Jim had been in here before, and this exhibition only takes place every two years, and I know he'd been three or four times before in the past, so he knew exactly where he was. When he jumped out at the traffic lights, he knew where he was. The surprising thing for him was that I didn't stay in the car, the taxi, and carry on and just leave him to it.

So, he's wandering up and down. He's examining the goods. It was like being in an antiques shop, examining what was on offer, because some of them were quite old and that's why I used the word antique. Nobody had a smile. In Germany, smiling seems to be illegal. I've never come across anybody with an explanation as to why they are so damn miserable, for people who are so rich, by comparison to us. And he's walking up and down the aisles, and he's deciding, and we come eventually to a door and I just turned away for a moment, just a moment, I don't know what for, I can't think why, and when I turned back, I'm on my own! He's gone! He's disappeared! He must have nipped in to one of these places, shut the top half of the door before the horse could bolt, and left me without a please or a thank you, stuck outside in the corridor, all on my own, with a, *"What do I do next?"* look written, I suppose, all across my face.

I thought to myself, *"I don't know. I'm not stopping here. I'm going,"* and I walked down the stairs. Most of the people, who were men, were all walking up the stairs. I'm going down the stairs. I, thankfully, saw nobody from the UK or, more to the point, somebody from the UK that I knew, and eventually got down onto the street level and went and stood across the road. I went in a bar and I sat outside, so that when he came out I could see him and we then, presumably, could go back to our respective hotels. I gave myself half an hour, and I thought, *"Well, if he hasn't come out in half an hour, then I'm off."* Half an hour went by, there's no Jim. I gave it fifteen more minutes, 45 minutes, three quarters of an hour gone by, there's no Jim. Taxi pulls round the corner, drops somebody off, I'm in, gave him the piece of paper in German with the address of the hotel, and I went. I didn't see Jim again until the next time I went to Dublin. I didn't see him again at the exhibition, and I didn't speak to him. I didn't think it was any of my business, and I kept out of it.

The following night, I'm still in Frankfurt, and of a more sort of serious and sober nature. A Scottish customer of mine had turned up, and being from north of the border, and being a typical Scotsman, he'd come with his son and he fancied finding some obliging supplier to buy him dinner. Well, you're reading the book of the bloke who bought him the dinner. We got in a taxi and we went off, said to the taxi driver who spoke a bit of English, *"Decent restaurant, not too expensive,"* and he took us somewhere, and it was fine. It was okay.

I had a quite interesting conversation with this chap and his son, because it was completely different from the night before. There we are in Frankfurt, sat in a building which was 100 years old, I would think, at least, and the man I was with just suddenly turned to me and said, *"Isn't it difficult to understand how, if this was in the mid-1930s or a little before, early 1930s, just looking out at this window, those buildings across the street would be just the same. They would be there. They're all way older than that. Can you imagine the scenes outside in the street, the Stormtroopers, the SA men, Hitler's gang, all marching up and down with swastika flags?"* And it was strange. It was a sobering thought.

I've said in the book, yeah, they're not very amusing, they're not very light-hearted, but they are extremely intelligent, the Germans, and they do a good job, and they get on with work, and they make a lot of money, and they make good products, like motorcars.

It was really odd to sit there and just sort of look out the window, or close your eyes even, and just imagine what it would have been like at some of these little shops across the way if you were Jewish, and it was 1931, 32, and the aggravation that you would get, the threats that you would get, the damage that you would get to your property, and eventually the doom that would engulf not only you and your family, but you and your race in the vast majority of Europe, east and west. It brought a lot of things home to me.

I never knew that the chap I was with was so serious minded or ever gave such consideration to things as he did that night, but I must say I admired him for the difference in the way that he approached the situation to the man who I'd been with the night before. It made me look at him, the Scotsman that is, in a whole new and different light, and to realise how right he was in what he was saying and how careful we must all be not to repeat what happened in Frankfurt and in Hamburg, and in Bremen, and in Munich, and in Nuremberg, and whatever. We mustn't repeat that ever, ever again.

As I've said, the major European light show is in Frankfurt. Hall 10 of the light show, I can tell you this if ever you're considering going, Hall 10, I'll tell you now, is 100% Chinese. Because my business was 100% Chinese and Hong Kong, I never went to any other hall than 10. I used to, on the last day, go round all the stands that were interesting to me, where I'd seen something new, and when they started to take down their stands...

This is an interesting feature about the Chinese at exhibitions. At an exhibition, even right to the end, five o'clock shall we say, on the last day, Friday usually, nobody took their stand down. At five to five the stand was as it was at nine o'clock on the morning of the first day, except for Hall 10. At lunchtime on the last day, they all got tired and fed up, and at whatever exhibition, whether it be in Hong Kong or whether it be in Frankfurt, or whether it be in Guangzhou, the stands came down at roundabout one to two o'clock, despite the five o'clock finish. There you have people who are strangers to these exhibitions from the west, going in to the Chinese hall on the last afternoon to find the Chinese banging and clattering away at taking the stands down and getting ready to go home.

The reason they're all in the same hall is that the Chinese lighting authorities, association, put on jumbo jet aeroplanes and they all fly in to Frankfurt together, and they all fly out of Frankfurt together, so much so that they want to have a good night out on the last day prior to going home. One way of doing this is to make sure that by three or four o'clock in the afternoon, you've cleared everything away and you're out of the building.

They never take the samples home with them. One of two things occur. One I had never seen in my life and I found extremely amusing at the time, and extremely bizarre. Because the Germans realised what the Chinese do on the last afternoon, they permit German retailer/wholesalers/importers to come freely into the exhibition, and these people go onto stands and offer cash, cash money, to the Chinese for what they are going to leave behind, because they just cannot be bothered. They're making thousands of these things, why should they be bothered to take one home?

I recall once being there on the last afternoon and this was happening. A lad called Anthony, I don't know what his Chinese name was; was taking his stand down along with his helpers. Well, he wasn't doing much. The helpers were doing all the work. He'd got some decent looking fittings on the stand, but of course it was always one each, one of each, one of each. A woman came onto the stand and saw all this stuff laid on the floor which was presumably going to be binned, thrown away, by the organisers once the Chinese had gone. The organisers did not take kindly to the Chinese taking their stands down early. They just realised that typically with the Chinese, it's a waste of time asking them to stick to the rules. It's like asking the Chinese to play football without the offside rule, and they would agree to do it.

This woman came onto the stand, and I was stood chatting to this lad, Anthony. This woman came on and they were using euros by now. He's got all this stuff that he's just going to simply leave for the Germans to skip and to throw away. This woman came on the stand, and she offered him 400 euros, which is quite a lot of money, to clear the lot for him. I'd never known anything so odd. He said, *"No, I want 500 euros."* She said, *"I'm not giving you 500 euros, I'm offering you four. You're only leaving it behind. You're only, effectively, throwing it away. I'm just giving you something for it."* The logic of a Chinese is simple. He wanted five because that's what he rated them as being worth. Our logic would be to take the money which was on offer, rather than to take nothing and lose out. But with the Chinese, you either get the 500 that you want, or you take nothing. It's quite simple. You demand 500, you're offered four, you refuse it, and you walk out without a penny and the 400 euros is lost to you. I'd never seen anything like this in my life. I thought it was stupid. He was asking for the real value of the product. I walked off and left him because I just couldn't really understand what he was about.

I had a very good friend, and I still to this day contact this man. He had a stand, and his name was Liu Fei. Now, Liu Fei was a Chinese, from the same city as the Anthony fella we've just been talking about, but so completely different as to make him rather odd and strange to understand. Liu Fei had a sense of humour. Liu Fei could crack jokes in English. Liu Fei thought his own countrymen were so much short of a shilling. He would have taken the 400. He'd have taken 300 would Liu Fei for all that he'd got on his stand, except for one thing. He'd promised me all the best stuff. What I'd agreed to do was, with him, cart it all out to the taxi rank, put it into the boot and the back seat of a taxi and get the taxi to take me back to the hotel, put the stuff into the hotel lobby, and I would get the hotel staff, plus me, to put it in my car, and I would drive it back.

We're taking all the stuff that I want, and we decided that we could, between the two of us, we could just about manage these two boxes, one each. We're walking across a huge courtyard in the middle of the exhibition hall area to go back out to where all the taxis were. Getting a taxi at this time wasn't difficult because this was still two or three hours before the scheduled finish of the show. As we're walking out, across the courtyard, Liu Fei who'd had his fill that week, I could tell, of the exhibition. It had either gone not so good for him or, as I found out later, his wife had gone mad in Frankfurt with the credit card, and he wasn't too happy.

As we're walking across the courtyard, and I'm saying, *"Thank you very much for doing this and helping me carry this,"* he just looked at me and he said, *"Do you know Chris, I'm flipping,"* except he didn't say flipping, *"I'm flipping knackered."* I couldn't do anything else but to smile at him and to laugh. I couldn't imagine the Chinese, anybody else, many foreigners, never mind Chinese, who spoke better English. He just turned to me and he said, *"You know Chris, I'm flipping knackered,"* and I've never forgotten that, and I always remind him. If I speak to him on the phone these days, which I do occasionally, just to see that he's okay, and everybody else is, and his wife is, and he's got the credit card in his pocket, I always say to him, *"Do you remember the flipping knackered day?"* and he laughs. It's nice that he's well, and it's nice that his business is going, from what I can gather, from strength to strength. One day, I hope he comes over here. One day, I'd like to see him again. I liked the man.

# Chapter Thirty

One final thing about Frankfurt. It really is two things about Frankfurt, although they both hinge around the same hotel. A couple of years after the *"flipping knackered"* day with Liu Fei, I went out to Frankfurt again and I, as per normal, took the car. Not because I'm frightened of flying, but because it lets me bring back samples. But at this particular time, flying was a bit of a problem. If you recall, we had the problem with the ash, the dust, call it what you like; that was coming out, to use a Yorkshire word, puthering out of volcanoes in Iceland. This stuff was lingering around in the atmosphere over here and flights were being cancelled et cetera. Now the Chinese all got here, but they couldn't get back. They went by jumbo. The jumbo flew back to China, and then the jumbo was again supposed to come back to Frankfurt to pick them up, to fly them home to China. But, because of all this dust from Iceland, the return flights didn't arrive for a considerable number of days until it was considered safe to fly.

But of course, the same thing applied to anybody flying back to France, or back to Britain, or back to wherever, but I was completely different to almost everybody else. I'd got the car. Now, I suddenly became, to all my UK customers, Mr Popularity, because... And I got calls galore from people over here who were stranded and couldn't get back to the UK. They could try all sorts of things. They could go to Holland and try and get a ferry, or to Belgium and do the same, or to Brussels and try to get on the Eurostar, or even go to Paris and try and do the same thing. But, of course everybody was trying to do this, and there weren't enough seats on the trains or cabins on the ferries for them all to get home, so they were getting stuck. But I wasn't, because I'd got my ticket booked back. I'd got my car. I was driving to Calais and I was coming back on the train, on the Eurotunnel and coming home. I'd got nothing to worry about with Iceland. I'd got the car.

Word got round that I'd got a car over there. I was on my own and I'd got two or three empty seats. Well, the number of people who rang me, who didn't want to see me when I was at home, because they didn't want to buy from an agent, et cetera, et cetera, et cetera suddenly disappeared, and they all wanted to talk to me. They all wanted to see me. They all wanted to get in my car just to get home. Of course, it wasn't possible. I could squeeze two of them in, because the rest of the car was full of luggage and samples. I brought back a customer from Birmingham and a customer from Leeds, so it ended up with us driving to Calais, under the tunnel, out at the other end, at Folkestone, up to Birmingham, drop him off at home, and then up here.

These two guys, these two men, arranged to meet me, but strangely enough, I'm doing the favour, but it's me that's got to go to their hotel, looking for them, when

I deliberately stayed at a hotel that was near the motorway for me to drive easily away on the Saturday morning back home. So, I dug my heels in and said, *"No, I'm sorry. You will have to get in a taxi or two,"* because I didn't know whether they were staying together or not, *"and you'll have to come here. I'll give you the hotel address, you come here, put your stuff in my car, and we'll go from here."* They did that and off we set. Off we go.

It was a Saturday. The sun was shining, it was a beautiful day, everything was reasonably alright in my world, and we're going up the autobahn, the German motorway back towards Belgium, and then into northern France and home. We go round a corner on the motorway and suddenly in front of us we see stretching for miles across all three lanes traffic, traffic, traffic, and more traffic. Somewhere up there in front of us, way beyond our sight, there had been an accident or something, or roadworks, I've no idea. Never did find out. Eventually, in a few moments, we get to the back of the queue and I have to stop the car.

Well, after about ten or fifteen minutes, we weren't going anywhere. We weren't moving at all, and looking into the distance, hundreds of cars and wagons weren't moving either. At the side of me was a van, and they were just in the same situation as we were, and I looked at the van and it was, my German's good enough to know, that it was a van carrying a load of dancers, boys and girls, males and females, obviously going to do some sort of display or show somewhere up the motorway. Much to our surprise, they managed to get the cars round and about to move up a little bit, move a little bit left, move a little bit right, move a little bit back, and that left them, these boys and girls, enough room to do an impromptu show for us on the motorway, and they did. They danced. On the motorway. And we all sat and watched. When it was over, we applauded and cheered them.

The gentlemen amongst us, and I admit to being one of them, happened to see at the side of the motorway, a farmer's field with a gate, and we went over the gate to satisfy the call of nature. What the ladies did, I do not know. But it wasn't very long after that that suddenly this whole lot started to move, and we were away, and we were gone, and we never saw an accident, we never saw any roadworks. We had no idea why we'd been delayed. But the impromptu dancing from the boys and the girls was something worth seeing, because they were good. They were really good.

I'd arranged to stop the night actually in southern Belgium, in Liuk, Liège in English, and we'd arranged to stay the night in a hotel. I'd booked the hotel room for the three of us, for me and a room each for the other two. Got there. It was a Novotel we were staying at so I thought it won't be bad. We got there and we parked the car up, went into the reception, got the keys, I asked what time the evening meal was served, and on a Saturday night believe me, the answer was, *"The restaurant is shut. The restaurant is closed."*

The two gentlemen who were with me, who I hadn't explained before, were both of Indian extraction. They asked for an Indian restaurant and off they went, and I saw them again at breakfast the following morning. I went into the bar and found that there were a few bar meals available, and I had a bar meal and a few drinks, went to bed, watch the telly for a while, got up the next day, had breakfast and drove on to Calais. Never forget the dancers. Never forget their kindness. Never forget the fact that they took the boredom out of what is a terrible thing when you can't move on a motorway. For their age, they were very considerate people indeed. That's Germany.

We continued to do well with the branch of the UK customer in Kaiserslautern, except it was moved to Aachen. Aachen, if you recall, was mentioned earlier in the book about the chap who had suffered from a severe bombing attack at the end of the war, and it was strange, to say the least, that this customer also decided to move their head office in Germany to Aachen.

I want to add just one little thing. This company, and I'm loathe to mention names of the people or the company, because people may get the wrong idea, but when I was in the house of the man in Kaiserslautern, with the pool and the wine cellar et cetera, he had given me the home telephone number in Switzerland, of the big boss worldwide, because they have a lot of branches in America, but that's no good to us. They have a load of branches in America. They are probably the largest electrical distributors in the world, and they are definitely, definitely, or they were at the time, definitely the largest in Europe. This man in Germany had said to me, "*You want to ring that number. That's the home number of the boss man."* We'll call him Mr Tom for the purposes of the story. I thought, *"Oof."* This man was so important, so big in the trade, that just receiving a call out of the blue from me, I just didn't know whether it was right or whether it was wrong. I really didn't know whether to chance my arm or not.

One day when I'd got back home, I still had this piece of paper with the phone number on, and it was Saturday, and I thought, *"Do I ring it or do I not? Am I brave enough or do I bottle it?"* And I thought, *"I'll give it a go. I won't get through to him. I'll get through to a flunky, or a servant, or a girl, or something, who will leave a message and I'll never hear any more about it."* So, I rang. I dialled the number, fully expecting it to be ex-directory or... When I say ex-directory, I mean nobody to answer it, the wrong number or whatever. But it rang. It rang out in Switzerland, and it only rang a couple of times, and a man's voice answered, and I said, *"Can I speak to Tom?"* and mentioned his surname. I said Mr Tom, and his surname. He said, *"Speaking."* It was the man himself. He was at home, and he'd answered the phone.

I explained... He asked me where I'd got the phone number. I told him. He recognised the name, of course, of his manager in Germany. *"And he's given you my number?"* I said, *"He has."* *"Bit of cheek, doing that. I don't normally speak to suppliers."* I said, *"I appreciate that, and I didn't really expect that it would be you yourself who would answer. I do apologise and I'm sorry to have disturbed you."* He said, *"Do you supply our people in the UK?"* Well, at the time, the answer was not much, and the reason it was not much was because I didn't have the name of the right man. You've always got to have the name of the right man, otherwise you're just barking up the wrong tree. This gentleman said to me, *"Well, I admire your cheek in ringing me, but I can't help because I don't get involved at the level that you are looking for. But, if you write this number down, and you ring this number, and you ask for a man called Neil Mantovani, and say that I have told you to ring him, you never know, he might like what he sees. You may do some business."* I don't know how many years we did business with Neil Mantovani, but we were doing it when I retired when I was 66, so it was a long time.

I speak to Neil on a regular basis now. Nothing to do with work. Nothing at all. It's none of my business what he does work-wise. He's still there. He's been there, I think, 30 years or more now, or maybe a bit less than that. Neil, you might not be that age. I may be doing you an injustice there. But he's been a good friend to me for a long time.

There is one little secret that I will disclose as perhaps to why we get on so well, and as to why we've always done business. People deal with people they like, and invariably they like people with whom they share an interest. My great love in the winter is football. My great love football-wise isn't Manchester United, or Liverpool, or Chelsea, or whatever. It's very easy to support winners all the time. It's the easiest thing in the world. The hardest thing is to support the ones that don't have many good days, but you know when they do, they mean more to you. More than anything to you. I support the Super Reds. I know it's a joke. We play in red, yes, but super we most certainly aren't. We have been on two or three occasions, and I've never forgotten those occasions, because I've always maintained that those three occasions that really spring to mind, beating Manchester United in the cup, beating Chelsea, and of course in 1997, 26th April, getting promotion to the Premier League.

I support Barnsley. Neil Mantovani supports Barnsley. So, we're both mugs together. If we win, we're both elated together, and when we lose, and over the years we've lost an awful lot, we're miserable together. Those three days will stand out in my mind as being three wonderful days, and the three wonderful days that I've shared with Neil. And with anybody else who supports the Super Reds. It's too late in my life to change anything of that nature. I will support them forever and when I eventually do leave this mortal coil, that's where I want my ashes, down at Oakwell, because it's been my life, outside my home. It's been my life.

If you think about it, a lot of that came from having the nerve to ring Mr Tom, who gave me Neil's number, who created a friendship. Neil, thank you.

# Chapter Thirty-One

The first time I went China alone, where I had it all to do myself, when there was nobody to speak to other than the people I met, was in 1997. I took a flight to Hong Kong, arrived in Hong Kong, came out, got a taxi to the hotel where I'd booked just for the one night, and spoke to porter and told him that I was going to a city called Foshan in Guangdong province in southern China. In other words, it's the border province to Hong Kong.

The next day, I have breakfast and I go, and I find that the train is two o'clock in the afternoon every day to Foshan. At about half past one, I roll up at Hong Kong railway station. Very impressive. Very new. Very modern. Bustling with people, both taking internal trains within Hong Kong and external trains to take them as far as Beijing or maybe even further north. I went to the desk to buy a ticket, and it was confirmed, yes, two o'clock was the time of the train to Foshan. Showed my passport, gave them the money, they gave me a ticket.

I went through the emigration I suppose it is, down an escalator, onto the platform, looked at my ticket, saw that there was a carriage number. Went to the carriage, got on, via showing the ticket to a bunch of young girls who obviously worked for Chinese railways. This was not a Hong Kong railway journey. This was a Chinese railway. They weren't allowed anywhere above the platform. The reason is simple. I found all this afterwards. The reason they didn't allow them to go up to the major concourse was that they thought they might run off, and having seen China over the years, I'm damn sure that given half an opportunity, they would have run off. I know if I'd been one of them, and I can't run, I'd have walked as fast as I could to get out the way of them and leave them forever.

Get on the train, look at my seat number, sit down. The train starts to fill, and bang on two o'clock, we set off. The train would have something in the region of about a dozen carriages. The seats were reasonably comfortable, it wasn't uncomfortable, but they were old. Very old. We set off, and this engine took great exception at being put into first gear and told to move. We rocked backwards and forwards two or three times while the driver actually got the wheels to turn in the right direction, and eventually off we go at a very steady pace out of Hong Kong station. The train goes out of Hong Kong, up through the northern territories of Hong Kong and across the border into China.

Now, what became absolutely obvious from the word go was that the railway line was surrounded on both sides by huge fences with barbed wire topping. Now, I'll leave it up to your own imagination to work out as to why they'd done that. The obvious reason is that they knew people might make a jump for it to escape into Hong Kong. If you were Chinese, you escaped into Hong Kong, you're gone for good. You're never going to be seen again by the Chinese authorities where you live. But they'd even made it worse than that. There was no means of getting from one carriage to the next. They'd locked all the doors, so therefore if we had a fire, for example, in the carriage that we were in, well that was it, it was frying tonight as they say. We couldn't get out. We were stuck. We were lumbered. That was it. It was the end.

I'll always recall, and I bet it's still there today, as you got towards the border, there was quite a large, a very large in actual fact, electrical fuse box. Big metal, grey, enclosed thing. I always remember that the speed we were going at, you could read what it said on the side. It said, *"South Wales Fuse Gear."* If any of you are from South Wales, then I am not in any way knocking South Wales, I am just saying that was really, seeing that big box, year-in, year-out, as I did, I knew that we were coming to the end of civilisation as is known to man and we were about to enter into an area where quite frankly, the lunatics run the asylum.

We get to the border town on the Hong Kong side without any bother and we trundle through. I suppose that's because they don't want to check your passports, they're just glad to get rid of you. We then come to Shenzhen. Shenzhen is quite a modern city by Chinese standards, but of course it has to be because it's absolutely facing... It's touching... It's the next door neighbour of Hong Kong. But in terms of the way they treat people, it's nothing like Hong Kong. It's nothing like anywhere I'd been in my life. We pull up in Shenzhen railway station, which was painted, as is most of China apart from the lorries, a miserable grey colour. It looked a little bit like a prison. I think, in actual fact, China is a prison, but that's for another day. When I say nearly all the paint is grey, the other colour is blue. All lorries, no matter who's they are, private or otherwise, and there aren't many private ones, are all painted blue for some reason. There must be, as in American buses, an excess of yellow paint, there must be an excess of blue paint in China.

There we are, we're all sitting in the carriage. There's just me and a lot of Hong Kong people. There were two sorts of people it became clear to me, and I was told about this. One was people who were Chinese who had been to visit relatives in Hong Kong, who were going home, and the other were Hong Kong people who were going to Foshan to visit Foshan people in the hope that one day they'd be going home. All of a sudden, immigration people come onto the train, and they're checking everybody's paperwork and stamping it. The Chinese have a wonderful habit. If they can stamp something, they do. They absolutely love stamping things.

They came to me and took one look at me and obviously realised that I was a Westerner, a foreigner, and in all probability British. I showed them my ticket, waved that away. Not a word said, just waved it away, it wasn't the ticket they wanted. It was my passport they wanted. So, they started to look at the passport. The fascinating thing about looking at the passport was that

I noticed that the man who was trying to pretend to be extremely knowledgeable and clever and wise and show the others that he was the boss, he had my passport and he was reading away at it, or pretending to.

Well, it would have been rather difficult because I realised that he'd got it upside down. He's reading English upside down. I didn't know whether to laugh or cry quite frankly. Eventually, he came to the page with my Visa on which was in Chinese and English. Of course, when he got to that page, he promptly turned the passport the right way up because he knew what a mug he was making of himself by reading it upside down. Well, if he read it once, he read it six times. He kept reading and looking, and looking and reading. I'm thinking, *"Is he ever going to give me this passport back?"* But he did. He eventually decided that I wasn't James Bond, I wasn't on a spying mission and I could be let in.

We carried on on the train through various towns, which all looked the same to me. They seemed to have no particular identifying monuments or process or anything. The only place I noticed was that when we went through one particular town, it seemed to be the headquarters of the local Guangdong, that's the province, it used to be called Canton many years ago, Guangdong television station. Everybody stared out the window in great admiration of this mini Emley Moor thing that was out of the window to the right.

We carried on and it turned out that Foshan was actually, after Shenzhen which was just a border check, the only stop that this train made, was at the end of the line. We slowed down many times to go through stations, but we never actually stopped anywhere until we ground to a halt. Nobody announced that it was Foshan. There was no sign on the platform in any language, Chinese, English or anything, to say that it was Foshan. It was only when they all started to get up and I just said to somebody who looked as if they might have a brain cell, *"Foshan?"* and they looked at me and nodded and I got off.

I went through… I just simply followed everybody else, but I went last. I thought, *"I'll be last. I'll be last."* I went through. My case, I'd left it with the ticket people in Hong Kong, and I'd got a ticket for the case to take off the carousel, but you couldn't do it yourself. You had to give the ticket to somebody who would check the ticket against the stub on the case and then give you your case back. This is finding work for finding work's sake quite frankly.

I come out of the station, eventually, and all I'm looking for is a taxi. Somebody in Hong Kong had kindly written down for me, in the hotel, a Chinese, had written down for me, the name of the hotel which was called The Golden City. As the years went by, I'll leave it up to your imagination what most Westerners nicknamed The Golden City. I went to a taxi driver who looked completely bemused by me. I don't think he'd ever seen anything as big as me in his life. He was most concerned, from the way he was waving his arms around, that I was going to bust the springs on the back seat of his car. When I got in, it became patently obvious there weren't any blooming springs. It was like sitting on a wooden plank, although it looked like a seat.

The Golden City was ten minutes at the very most through a lot of crawling traffic. We got there and dropped off and that was it. I booked into the hotel. It had a western restaurant of sorts. I had something to eat, and I spent the night in the hotel.

The next morning, I went to the factory that I was going to. Now, I'd found the factory in a magazine that I contributed to for Chinese suppliers, and it turned out from speaking to one of the girls on the desk who had some English that this was only a five or ten minute walk. Go out the door, turn right, just keep going and you would go passed it. In actual fact, she was quite right. I went down to this place and went in, and they were expecting me, and I introduced myself. There was a boss, his wife, and a translator. The boss and the wife spoke no English, but the translator, it turned out, worked at Foshan University as a Professor of English.

There was nothing particularly unusual about what happened in the meeting. We talked about what we needed, what I needed to be supplied by him. This was over two days, a Thursday and a Friday. We discussed what we would pay. We came to an arrangement and I gave him an order for about 10,000 pieces. He was absolutely over the moon at this, thought it was wonderful, and said to me on the Friday, *"Tomorrow, on the Saturday,"* this is all through the translator of course, *"I've just bought myself a brand new car."* When I went out onto the street to walk back to the hotel, I noticed this... I'm no car man, I've said that before, but there was a brand new white Toyota something-or-other which was quite clearly brand new outside. He'd just taken receipt of it. He said, *"Come back in the morning and we'll go for a ride. We'll take the translator and wife, and I'll bring my..."* He had a son I think with him. So, that I did.

I walked back to the hotel, nothing eventful at all happened that night, and the next morning, I set off a little early just to walk back, stroll back, to his factory. I had noticed on a couple of previous mornings when I'd been walking on this road, that there was an organisation called the Guangzhou Trading Company, with a plaque on the door, in English, on the right-hand side. I thought, *"It's Saturday, I can be ten minutes late. I'll just pop in."* So, I did, and there was an old boy at the desk who spoke no English. He'd got a face that looked like leather. But, he was pleasant, and he indicated to me, *"Sit down. Wait. Wait. I'll get somebody to speak to you."* It was quite clear what he was going to do. And he did.

A minute or so later, almost running, a young man appeared from down one of the corridors. That young man was to figure in my life for the next eight, nine years. He was an agent. The Guangzhou Trading Company is what they call a trading company. It's a layer of employment we don't have in this country. They stand between the importer, that's me in the UK, and the manufacturer over there in China. Because they speak English and the factory doesn't, they handle everything.

This young man was called Timothy, and Timothy and I became friends, and for years after, when I was going anywhere, anywhere, within a 30 or 40 mile radius of Foshan, I stayed in one hotel or other in that city, and he would take me to various factories, we would source products and I imagine that Timothy... I'm pretty certain that Timothy was receiving a commission from the factory. I didn't mind that. Saved me an awful lot of bother. Anyway, I left him and said, *"I'll see you again tomorrow,"* on the Sunday, *"If you come to the Golden City and ask for me, we'll have a tea or a coffee."* Timothy never drank alcohol, *"Tea or a coffee, and we can talk about things a little more, because I've got an appointment down the road."*

I went to the appointment, and there everybody was, all in their best clothes, all waiting to take me out in the car for a ride. They put me in what in China is known as the *"death seat."* They are the worst drivers in the world. There's absolutely no doubt about it, and the *"death seat"* is what would be the driving seat here. It's the front seat on the right-hand side, because they drive on the other side of the road. Well, in actual fact, they drive on any side of the road, or straight down the middle. They ain't too fussy about that. Laws that are made for them to follow are, by and large, just ignored on any subject, never mind driving, and driving, of course, is one of the most dangerous ones.

We get in the car and I notice immediately, I have a look round at the interior, very nice, and he's bought himself an automatic. We set off in this automatic in the general direction of where he was going to take me. The translator had explained that he was going to take us up into the hills above Foshan and we would look at various things that were of interest in the area. One of them was called TV City. We went up and away, but I noticed that what he did when he set off, he put the car into second gear, obviously thinking that he drove it... Instead of putting it into drive and letting it choose its own gear, he's used the manual system of driving.

We drove for miles and miles in second gear, and I looked and we never got above the equivalent of 20 miles an hour. I could see he was getting more and more frustrated with this car, in as much that he was revving it up, putting his foot to the floor, but it wouldn't go any faster. Well, of course it wouldn't. We were stuck in second. It would go to the maximum speed in second gear and that was it. I thought, *"I can't just sit here and leave this as it is,"* and I just went and put my hand across, tapped him on his elbow and beckoned him to watch. I just flicked the gear control into automatic, put it into drive, and we shot off down the road like a bat out of hell, and he thought I was some sort of wonder man after that, that I could do something with the car that he couldn't do.

We drove, and drove, and drove, and we got up this hill, and we came to TV City. Now, TV City is where a lot of these... The Chinese are very keen on watching films about their past, medieval past, where there's the king and his servants and they all kill and destroy the enemy that wants to get them down and all the rest of it. Everybody, if you notice, if you've ever seen anything like this, can jump the height of a double decker bus.

They all seem to be able to do anything that defies science, or the logic of science. So, I watched them filming some of these actors, not understanding a word about it, and to be quite honest with you, a little bored by it all, but nonetheless, it was something he wanted to do and I appreciated what he was doing.

The translator woman said, *"We're going to have lunch and then he's going to take you back down into the city."* I said, *"Thank you. That's very nice. Thank you very much."* So, we did that, and she said to me on the way back down, and only she and I could understand, *"Would you, this afternoon…"* This was Saturday afternoon when I was looking forward to a little bit of relaxation, *"Would you come and speak to the English language students at Foshan University?"* Quite frankly, I'm not often lost for a word, but I was then, because I didn't know in actual fact what she wanted me to do, but because she was such a nice lady, and because she had persisted for two or three days to translate every word for me, then I said, *"Yes."*

Some bus turned up at the Golden City at about three o'clock in the afternoon, and she took me to the Foshan University, and she told me that there would be about 30 students who had volunteered to turn up to listen to me. The reason they wanted to listen to me was that they had never heard an Englishman, a live Englishman, speak English in their lives. They'd only heard Americans or people like David Beckham on the telly. He was very popular, as is Ronnie O'Sullivan by the way, the snooker player, which is just a matter of interest. Snooker is a big sport in China, a very big sport. They'd never heard an Englishman speaking English live.

I follow her to, well I suppose in English we'd call it a classroom, and inside there were about 25 – 30 young people, both sexes, and she'd told me on the way to it that she wanted me to read something to them, read something she had, a part of a book, and at the end of this reading, which turned out to be a chapter from the book, she would invite them to ask questions. She told me the first one that would get up would be the girl in the far corner because she was the best and she liked English as a subject, maybe four or five more would ask me a question. The other ones were so... Well, let's put it this way. They probably didn't understand a word I'd said.

I'm put there before them. I'm introduced to them by name. I'm given a round of applause. It's the only time I've had a round of applause in my life that I can remember. I'm given this book and asked to read this chapter. Well, the book was something, from the looks of it, which was printed, I would have said, somewhere in the 1930s. A long time ago, that is a fact. She turned to a particular page, and she said, *"Would you read these two pages to the people who are in the room?"* I said, *"Yes, fine,"* and then I looked down at the book and saw that the two pages that I'm about to read are entitled *"Good Manners in Great Britain."* I'll repeat that. *"Good Manners in Great Britain."*

So, I set off. But when I'm reading this, I find myself transported back to the days of Sir Walter Raleigh chucking a cape in front of Elizabeth I so she doesn't have to walk through a puddle and all this nonsense, and they thought that we still did it. They literally thought that we still did it. Well, I don't know about you, but it's quite a while since I threw my cape in front of a puddle for my wife so she wouldn't have to walk through it. I really found that it beggared belief did all this nonsense that I was reading as if it was true and happening every day of the week.

Eventually, I come to the end of all this. She asks, in English, *"Has anybody got any questions?"* and as she had forecast, the girl in the far corner jumps up immediately, waving her hand, *"I have a question. I have a question."* Now, I thought I was going to be asked a question about good manners in Great Britain. Far from it. She jumped up and she said, *"Do you like Princess Di?"* Now, that took me aback. I've just been talking about Walter Raleigh and his cape, and I'm now being asked about do I like Princess Di. Do I like Princess Di? Well, you don't know whether to give them an honest answer or what. I have no feelings one way or the other about the Royal Family. I don't like them. I don't dislike them. I tolerate them. They're there. I'm here. Fine. That'll do for me. But I had to say, *"Yes, very nice lady,"* et cetera, et cetera.

The next question, and I thought, *"Oh no, I don't want more questions about the Royal Family, please."* The next question was, *"Do you like John Major?"* Well John Major, of course, was our Prime Minister at the time. I think I shared one thing with John Major, the love of cricket. My politics couldn't have been much further away... I'm sorry for giving the game away again. My politics couldn't have been much further away from his and I have never voted in that persuasion. I've never voted that way in my life and I never will. My father would turn in his grave, as would my grandfather on both sides. So I gave them an honest answer, which totally threw them, because you see, in China, everybody loves the gaffer, whatever the president of the place was at the time. But I said, *"No, I don't like him, and I don't vote for him,"* and that concept meant nothing to them.

They could not get their heads round the idea that I could actually choose not to like him. I mean like in the sense of politically like. I'd never met the man in my life. He's probably a very, very nice gentleman. But it was fascinating to them that I would be abroad and would actually say, *"No, not much."* *"Oh."* That killed the questions. That killed the questions stone dead. Nobody else could think of anything then. I had really surprised them. I don't know what was supposed to be coming next, but it didn't.

The lady said, *"We've arranged to take you out in the bus shopping this afternoon."* Hmm. Now, I am to shopping what Eddie Waring, if you remember him, was to ballet dancing. I can't abide it. I never go, only when I am absolutely forced. I detest it. If I'm sent anywhere to buy anything by my wife, I buy the first thing that remotely foots the bill, and I'm out and I come home. I don't care whether they've got a green one, or a blue one, or a red one, or a purple one. I'm not interested. I just buy the first one and I'm out. But, she was kind and I might need her help again before leaving Foshan, so I agree to go.

Now, we were taken into...  This is the absolute contradiction of China.  You are driven through the poverty ridden areas to get into the town centre, or to a shopping mall as the Americans love to call them, and you suddenly find yourself going from poverty to the exact opposite in a matter of moments, and all the modern things that you would find in the shops here, you find there. It's difficult to understand. Very difficult to understand.

We go in and we have a look round the ground floor of this departmental store.  We go through the ground floor and there's not much there really, but they encourage me to go up the escalator.  This was a start of something that I should never have started.  We go up the escalator to see what's on the next floor.  Clothes, television, I don't know.  As we got onto the escalator, I stumbled over the first step, and they all rush to prevent this huge man, that they'd never seen anything like in their life, falling and hurting himself.  I was nowhere near falling or hurting myself, but I did stumble. I just said, *"In English we say mind your step."*  I know that's probably more used with underground trains in London than it is anywhere else, but it'd do. I didn't realise that for the rest of the afternoon, wherever we went, somebody would rush up to me and say, *"Mind your step."* Wherever we went, it was, *"Mind your step."*  At the end of the day, I must have been told 20 times to mind my step.  If nothing else, the students learnt all about Walter Raleigh and his cape and minding their step.

I went many, many times to Foshan and the relationship with Timothy grew and extended and expanded, and actually in terms of a source of income for me, and I suppose for him, he became very important to me. I was introduced to various factories. We sold their products over here and I made a commission and made money, and so did he I suppose.

We had one chappy who we decided to call... He hadn't got an English name and I never... I don't to this day know what his real name was. They decided to call us Big Chris - that's me, and Little Chris, because he was a small fella. Little Chris - that was him. He and Tim were very, very close. Very, very close. But of course, whenever they were together, they spoke Chinese and I don't know what they were talking about. They were probably doubling the price or something. I'm not sure.

We always used to finish every day by having a meal. Now, I can't say I was a great lover of Chinese food, but there was one dish that Timothy introduced me to which was a fish, quite a large fish, a scaly-type fish, and covered in a delicious sauce. An absolutely delicious sauce. I used to wait for the full day to go by so we could have this fish. Tim always used to look at me as if it was some sort of working class dish, and he wouldn't normally buy it unless I was there. He wouldn't eat it. But Little Chris, he liked it. No, I'll be more correct. He liked a part of it. I liked the meat on the fish, what we eat, the meat of the fish. The fish was always presented, always served with the head on the plate. I didn't like looking at that. That put me off a little bit, but then I used to think, *"Well I like the rest of it, I'll forget about the head."*

Little Chris didn't like the body or the meat of the fish, he liked the head, and he used to pick up with his chopsticks... I never used a chopstick in my life. I dropped more stuff messing around with chopsticks to the extent that I said, *"Look, I'll eat it. I'll eat anything you put before me within reason, but I want a knife and fork."* It's no problem. The restaurants always have knives and forks. He used to pick up, and I used to be amazed by the skill at which he did this, the head of the fish, which was quite large. He had the ability of stuffing the whole head into his mouth at one go. His jaws and cheeks all seemed to move in various directions and eventually he would start to spit out bones, all over the place. Never mind the plate, all over the place. On the floor. On the tablecloth. On the plate. Anywhere you like, he'd spit them out. He wasn't bothered. This used to happen every time I met him, and over the years I met him many, many times, always in the company of Timothy.

There was another man that Timothy introduced me to who, again, was a lighting manufacturer. He had every appearance of being a very nice man, and he had a daughter who was called... Her English name was Jessica. I used to go with Timothy to this factory and we would talk about products and we used to sell a lot of stuff via him, from him, into the UK. One day he said to me, we were having a drink, again tea or coffee or whatever, no alcohol in the Golden City. We were having a drink and he said to me, *"I want to send my daughter to university in the UK. Can you help?"* Oh dear. Thoughts of Walter Raleigh and the cape came flooding back. *"Could I help? What do I do? What on earth do I do?"* I don't know. I wasn't clever enough to go to university. I didn't know what on earth to do. He suggested that first and foremost, I should get her into a Chinese school where they spoke only English, not too far from where I live, where she could improve her English and then I would choose a university which wasn't too far away, and he would then, via the government in China, get her into this university.

Well, I came back here and really was hoping that it would just die a death, but it didn't. He kept persisting and pestering. In the end I'm searching things out and I find out that in the middle of Manchester, somewhere in the middle of Manchester, there was a Chinese school. I visited this Chinese school on behalf of him and his daughter, Jessica, and it became obvious that everybody there was Chinese, and they were all there for the same purpose, improve their English, move on to university. I didn't really take much notice of the area that it was in. I took absolutely, well, very little notice of the area that it was in, in Manchester. I said to him, *"Found a place. She can go whenever she wants. It's just a question of money. You pay, she learns, and then the nearest university that I've had a look at, I'd been, was Keele, which is in Staffordshire."* So, we agreed that this would be a good way of going forward.

She goes to this place in Manchester. I remember picking her up from the airport at Manchester. Took her to this place, and they had found somewhere for her to live. I took her, she introduced herself et cetera, et cetera, et cetera and we then went to the address in the suburbs of Manchester, quite a leafy area, but not an expensive area, where, it was a weekend, where she met the man and the woman who owned the house. He was a postman, she was a sister at a local hospital, a theatre sister at a local hospital, and they had two children. I think there was a boy of ten, and a girl about 8. I introduced Jessica and everything was agreed. They'd spoken to Jessica's father via... I don't know... And agreed how much she would pay, that he would transfer every month this money, and everything seemed perfectly okay. I left her. She was a bit tearful at losing me because I was the contact that she knew, but I said, *"I'm only 40 miles or so away. I'm not too far. I can always come and have a chat with you from time to time."*

A couple of weeks later, I got a phone call and it was from the postman in Manchester to say, in no uncertain terms whatsoever, *"If you don't get over here and get this..."* Well, he called her a bitch. *"If you don't get over here and get this bitch out of here, I'll turn her out in the street. We are not having her behaving in the way that she does. We've got two young boys who we intend to bring up to behave correctly and properly, and she is doing exactly the opposite to what we want them to see. You get over here and you either sit her down, put her right, or she goes."* Well, I've got my life to run, I've got the business to run, I've got... I didn't need this. I didn't need all of this nonsense. But because he was a friend, her dad, he was a friend, I went across to Manchester, and we all sat down, and I said to him, *"What is she doing that is so offensive?"*

Now, you could have knocked me down with a feather, as they say, when he turned round to me and said, *"She just simply walks round the house spitting on the floor."* *"Oh no."* *"And now my kids are doing the same. They're spitting on the floors, spitting on the walls, spitting on the table. I can't have it and I won't have it. It's not our way of behaving."* And I looked at her and I said, *"Have you understood what he's been saying?"* and she said, *"Yes."* I said, *"Well, you either behave yourself, stop all the spitting, it's not done in this country, or we'll get your father, we'll get a ticket bought and you fly back to China. I'm sorry."* She said she would behave herself.

Another couple of weeks go by. I hear nothing. I think everything has settled down. The postman rings me up and says, *"Do you know she's walked out and left us?"* I said, *"No, I'd no idea. No, she hasn't been in touch with me although she has my phone number. She has my home number and my works number."* I don't think I had a mobile phone at the time. I may have done. It doesn't matter. It was quite easy for her to contact me. I said, *"No."* He said, *"Well, by talking to some lad that she knows, I've found out where she is,"* and he gave me an address and directions as to how to get there. It was ten minutes away. It wasn't next door. Now, his house was neat, and tidy, and clean, nice front garden, very good. Nothing wrong with it.

I drive to this other place. Well. There hadn't been a lick of paint on this house, I don't think, since Harold Wilson was Prime Minister. It was a shambles. I knocked on the door. The garden was full of old rubbish that anybody had just chucked over there, the grass had never been cut et cetera, et cetera. I knock on the front door and all my worst expectations were met. The place was awful. It was a mess. She wasn't in. The character who came to the front door, I can't remember if it was a man or a woman, I'd lost interest completely by then, couldn't have cared tuppence.

# Chapter Thirty-Two

I never saw the girl when I went to this second property and quite frankly I didn't care less whether I saw her again or not. She was obviously just wasting dad's money, wasting dad's time and above all else because I'd got a business to run, she was wasting mine. And it was only a couple of months or so later when I get a call from Timothy in China who said to me, *"Oh, Jessica is studying at Keele. She'd like you to go and see her."* And he gave me her mobile number which I rang and she answered and we arranged a date and my wife and I went across. And I'd said to her on the phone, *"We'll take you out for... We'll come on a Sunday and we'll take you out for lunch. It's a tradition in our country, Sunday lunch, and I'll take you out for lunch."*

We found out what apartment or flat number she was in at Keele – some gate man told me – and we get to her and I forget what she was studying. Oh, business studies, that's what she was doing, business studies. And I was in this flat with my wife and her and there was about as much sign of any work going on as there were pictures of the man in the moon. It was quite obvious that she didn't attend lectures. It all came out in conversation that she'd been to a lecture or two, hadn't understood a word that was being said that mattered to her, and so consequently just stopped in the room. But one thing that was evident from looking round the room were some extremely good drawings – pencil drawings. I know nothing more about that type of thing, but that's what they were. And I asked her, I said, *"Who did these?"* and she said, *"Me."* Well it was quite obvious that our Jessica was studying the wrong subject. She was a quite excellent artist. Whether she was much of a business expert, I never found out.

A few months later when contact with her had really dropped off altogether, I get another call from our friend Timothy in China to tell me that Daddy had paid to send Jessica onto another business study university and it was the Sorbonne in Paris, of all places. I don't know how long she stayed there. I didn't nip across there and buy her Sunday lunch. As far as I know she did a year or so, I have no idea, and I never ever saw her again as far as I can recall. But talk about money wasted. Talk about time wasted. That was Jessica. Her dad died a couple of years after. He was a chain-smoker, one of the biggest chain-smokers I've ever seen. As one came to an end, he lit another. Now never having been a smoker in my life, I see no point to all this. I just call them coffin nails. I really think they're a waste of time, money and your life.

But he was a nice enough man until one day, I was asking him over there if he would mind paying me the commissions, about four or five thousand dollars that he owed me off several jobs and I rather foolishly took a cheque signed by him and drawn on a Hong Kong bank. It all turns out that this was quite deliberate. He was getting me out of China, back into Hong Kong, straight down to the bank with the cheque and the bank teller told me... because it had been made out to cash. The teller told me there wasn't a red cent in that account. It was empty. It hadn't been used in years. So he'd got me out of China, he hadn't paid the $4,000 and he never did.

I only suffered twice in that way in all the years that I dealt in China through people not paying me and the other one was our friend Timothy. I'm not going to go into great deal about it, but he did me for $7,000. So between the pair of them, that was $11,000 and that was $11,000 that I shall never, ever see. Timothy was a compulsive gambler. He'd bet on two flies walking up a man's trouser leg, would Timothy. He really would. He just bet, bet, bet. And of course there's only one thing wrong with betting and that is, I'll ask you the question, *"Have you ever seen a poor bookmaker?"* and the answer's no. And Timothy had obviously blown the lot and in the end, he got hold of $7,000 from a supplier; another supplier, not Jessica's dad, in the same town, who I dealt with. Well, to tell you the truth, it was the fella I've called earlier on 'Little Chris'. And Little Chris gave him the money to give to me. He never gave it to me. He used it to pay off his gambling debts. I never, ever saw him again. I spoke to him a couple of times when he somewhat sort of foolishly answered his phone, but I never, ever saw him again and I never got my money. You live and you learn. It's life. And if you learn more than you get wrong, you'll survive and you won't do too badly.

I remember once Timothy had a sidekick, a girl called Susan. Now Susan was just reasonably good at English and she was paid by Timothy – one assumes that he paid her – to take me and other foreigners who turned up, to various places that they'd ask to go to. And one day I'd asked to go to see a factory that made emergency lighting. And Timothy didn't know anywhere. Susan, of course didn't know anywhere, but one of the people who worked for Timothy and who understood some English knew the name of a factory; a factory which became one of the mainstays of my income for years and years and years and is still there today making emergency lighting for all round the world including the UK. They have a fabulous new factory. It's much too big for what they need, but nonetheless that's the Chinese way.

But when I went first time, it was – oh, a little old dump and we had to go up two or three flights of stone steps to get to Mr. Liang's office. I had a colleague with me from Leeds who wasn't interested in emergency lighting. We'd been somewhere else in the morning. This was the afternoon. And he came in with me and he said, *"I'm not going to sit in listening to all this. I'm not interested in emergency lighting. I'll just stand on the balcony and I've got a couple of calls to make back home. I'll do that and then when you're ready for off we'll go."* And I sat there and this man looked at me thinking that I must be totally crazy. He'd never contemplated the idea of selling or creating a product which was suitable and legal to sell here, but I talked him into it and he's made a fortune out of me and he's still doing it. To this day, he and his son and two or three more others along with many hundreds of workers who all live in dormitory accommodation at the side of his factory. But this time we're still in the old building, and I mean old and decrepit, really a shocking place, not fit... In this country it would have been closed down, it really would. It was awful. But they will work anywhere some of these people in China. My friend is on the balcony behind me, but he's not taking any part in the conversation. I'm sitting on an old settee and about the only thing I could think of, apart from the business, was how the devil was I going to get myself up off this very, very low settee which had no springs. It was completely, as they say in Barnsley, black lacquered.

And it was a rather odd meeting, but nonetheless it turned out to be a very successful and good meeting. After the meeting was over, we exchanged niceties and I said, *"When I get home, I'll send you samples of things we need and then you can make something similar and the next time I'm in China I'll come and see you and see how you're going on."* And that was the end. We went down the stairs, very gingerly because I'm not great at stairs and I hate these stones ones - chipped they were, all these stairs. They were dangerous, they really were. And we go down the stairs and we get into the people-carrier which has been driven there by Timothy, and we're off. We go through the gates.

We've only gone a hundred yards or two and the chappie from Leeds who was with me said to me, *"You know when you were sitting on that settee in his office discussing whatever you were discussing?"* and I replied, *"Yes, why?"* He said, *"Well do you know that a damn great big rat came and sat underneath you while you were sitting on the settee?"* And I said, *"No, I didn't."* He said, *"Yes, it came out of one door, came and sat under the settee and then walked across – walked across the general office where there were boys and girls…"* – and I use the word in the sense of young men and young women – *"…working at their desks at their computers and none of them who… all of them saw it, none of them took the slightest notice and it disappeared down a hole in the corner of the office."* So I'd been to a meeting – a successful meeting and Roland Rat had been sat round the table with us, if you follow me.

We then drive with Tim driving. We're going back towards the hotel in the middle of this city, which is called Ningbo and we're driving back towards Ningbo and it's a fair old journey. It's a good hour, hour and a half. And as is typical in China, we're driving all over the road. We're doing anything we please. We're not stopping at red lights. We're just pleasing… they just drive as they feel fit. Well you see, the police do. They drive that way. So if they drive that way, what possible compunction is there for Joe Public to drive in any other way? But we did in actual fact on the way back, much to my surprise, actually stop at a red light. It might have had something to do with the number of great big wagons that were crossing our path and Timothy deciding that it wasn't the best of ideas to try and weave in-between them.

So in China they have a system where you've got your red light and if you look up in the air in the middle of the junction, there is another machine which is counting down the seconds that you've to wait before you can go.

And we had something like 60-odd seconds to wait while it got down to zero. I, then look out of the window to the right and I see what you see thousands of, I'm afraid in China, awful little hamlet-type places with filthy streams running through them. The streams are, I'm afraid, open sewers and a mouthful of that and you are dead, I should think within minutes. And there was a young girl squatting on her haunches, who I would say would be 15/16 at the most at the side of this stream that went through this hamlet.

The stream would be five/six yards wide and heaven only knows how deep, but certainly deep enough to kill you. And this girl who's sitting there had a baby in her arms. You don't need languages at times to know what's occurred. Mum and dad have kicked her out for what she's done with some lad. She's got the baby. She's got no money coming in. She doesn't know what to do. She's sitting at the side of the stream and she's thinking about throwing the baby in. And I don't speak a word of Chinese. And I couldn't have heard her from where I was anyway. And I tapped my translator on the shoulder and pointed to her.

And I cared, my friend from Leeds cared, but the two Chinese, that's the driver, Timothy and the girl, Sue, looked, shrugged their shoulders and simply looked straight in front of themselves at the machine to see how many more seconds we had to go. I was tempted to say to Timothy and to the girl, *"Turn right and go into the hamlet. Turn right and go into the hamlet and here is 100RMB. Give the girl this."* It's worth about £10. 100RMB would have been more money than she would ever have seen in her life and I... well, I suppose, soft as people would say I am, was greatly tempted to give her 100, to give her 1,000. It was in my wallet. Human life was at stake. *"For God's sake Chris, do something about it."* But it was too late. The number went down to zero, he put the thing into first gear and we've gone. I don't know what happened. I have no idea. But it looked so sad.

I've tried to talk about amusing things – the rat under the chair and all the rest of it, which didn't seem amusing at the time, but it does now when you think of who you were actually sharing the room with. But it defies me to think of anything other than sadness when I think back to this young lass and what she was thinking and what she may well have done. Who knows?

A couple of days later after a few more trips round factories selling this, that and the other, we go to another factory and this time Timothy couldn't get. He might have been having to go to the bookies, I don't know. And Susan went with me to this factory and they made some sort of electrical device. Something cheap which the local wholesalers all sell thousands of and I'd been looking for a supplier for some time. And it's way out in the middle of nowhere and we go off in this people-carrier thing. It was only then I found out that Susan could actually drive. Well, when I say 'drive', she pointed it in the right direction and eventually we got there. And we went round the factory. Wouldn't have passed muster here. It was a bit of an old dump, but nonetheless you couldn't think that way too much when you were in China. You had to accept what you were given. And we had a look round and we talked price and I said I would do my best for him and I had orders for him back home.

He said round about 12 o'clock, *"Lunch."* He had a few words of English and he wanted to take us for lunch. So he, two or three of his cronies, all men, Susan and me are all in the people-carrier. It's a boiling hot day. It must have been 40 degrees and the humidity was topside of 90% and we go to an absolutely fabulous looking restaurant. What it would have cost to build that place here, I couldn't even guess. And we went in and we were shown to a private room. He'd ordered a private room. I thought he'd ordered the private room in deference to me. It turns out he'd ordered the private room because we were in the south of China and they liked watching Hong Kong TV soap operas and there's a television in the private rooms. There isn't if you're just out in the restaurant.

So we went into this private room and we're all sat round the table. You will have seen, obviously, pictures of a table with a revolving middle part and they put dishes on and it revolves round and you take a bit when you want it.

Most salespeople out there, by the way, call it the revolting table, but the correct expression, I suppose, is the revolving table. And we had a nice meal. We had a nice meal. And we came to the end of the meal and I'm expecting, well that's it, we've done now. We always finish with oranges and melon. That was how it always finished, oranges and melon. And we had the oranges

and we had the melon and I thought, *"Right we're off."*
But the soap opera from Hong Kong hadn't finished
and it was quite clear that they wanted to watch it to
the end, so we weren't going until it finished.

Now I'm sitting there and I'm gently getting bored out
of my mind because I can't understand a word of what's
going off on the television, A, and B, I couldn't care
anyway because it's not something I'm going to watch
tomorrow. So I'm just idly staring round the room.
And in the far corner was like a dressing table-type
thing. A dresser, not a dressing table. A dresser. The
girls who had been serving us were doing was knocking
on the door, coming in, putting the dish on there and
then carrying it to our table and putting it onto the
revolving bit. And then they would leave us and shut
the door behind them.

So we, the five or six of us, are sat round the table and
they're all watching the TV and listening most intently
to their equivalent to 'Coronation Street' and I'm
thinking I wish I was anywhere in the world bar here.
And a moment later I thought it doubly because the
reason I mention this cabinet thing that the food was
perched on from time to time, is that out from
underneath the cabinet with five or six people in the
room, plus the two waitresses coming and going, out
comes Roland Rat's brother – another one – to have a
look at us. And it wasn't in the slightest frightened of
us. He took absolutely no notice of us whatsoever. I
find them the most revolving things that you could
possibly imagine to look at and this thing looked as if it
was carrying more fleas. Oh dear, what an awful sight.

And of course as soon as I see this, I start shouting, *"Hey, hey, hey, look at that, look at that,"* and they all turn round and believe it or not – and this included the girl, Susan – they laughed at me as if it was something amusing that was occurring. And one of the men, he got up, he stood on the table. He took off both his shoes and threw them at the rat. The rat looked at him as if, *"Nobody does that. Why are you being so unpleasant?"* Turned on its, not inconsiderable tail, and waddled back underneath this cabinet. And I am going mad. I just want out. I'm going mad. The girls outside, the waitresses, must have heard the kafuffle, the noise and they came... I wouldn't say they burst in. Nobody in China bursts in, not in 40 degree heat, although inside the room we had air-conditioning of course.

But they just came in and looked and could see nothing wrong. And they were wearing cheap, plastic shoes, these two girls and a very, very drab uniform. And as they were standing there wondering what on earth was going on, because this lunatic was still stood on the table laughing and joking and whatever and pointing, the rat came back out and walked straight across both sets of feet. I tell you no lie. It walked across both sets of feet to the far wall. Now I know what my wife would have done. I know what my assistants, female assistants.... I know what anybody would have done back here. They would have screamed, they would have... Oh, I don't know, hell would have let loose.

The girls showed no sign of emotion or disgust or anything. And they turned and went back out of the room as much as to say, *"What's the big fat one..."*

that's me, *"...why is he making such a fuss?"* The rat then tootled back under the dresser. I picked up my briefcase. I'm out. I've gone. I found myself... the next thing I know I'm outside, stood next to the van that we've come in and it's 40 degrees, it's absolutely sweltering and the humidity is terrible and I can't stand it.

A couple of moments later I find that Susan, who is there to protect me and look after me and see everything's all right, she arrives enquiring of me as to what was wrong. And I said, *"Well do you normally have lunch with a rat?"* Well that brought no response whatsoever. I then said, *"Well where's Mr. so and so then?"* That's the driver of the van, the owner of the factory. And she said to me, *"He's paying the bill."* We have just had lunch in a room infested with vermin and he's paying the bill. I know she didn't understand me. *"Is he right in his head or not this fella? If this was happening where I live, I'd be straight down to the environmental health and our friend here with his fancy restaurant wouldn't be opening in the morning."* Well he probably wouldn't be opening in half an hour's time. *"You must be mad. They carry disease. It's awful."* And I'm lecturing her all about this and it's going absolutely over her head. She's taking no notice whatsoever of me. Can't see what the fuss is all about.

At that point, Mr. whatever his name was, turns up – makes no remark, no apology, no nothing. We get in the van and we drive back to his factory and in all the years I dealt with him after, the topic was never brought up again. Utterly, utterly remarkable.

# Chapter Thirty-Three

M ost of my business in China was done from a city in the east called Ningbo and I found, off my own bat actually, a decent hotel in the city. A city, by the way, of five million people. In other words, five times the size of Birmingham and there's nobody here ever heard of the place. I found a decent hotel and I stayed there... I think I've got the long-service medal for staying there over the years. I stayed there so many times, the staff all knew me. This was in the middle of Ningbo, just off from where the major shopping streets were, and as I've said before, when you're on the outskirts of these places, these cities, there is poverty – oh absolutely everywhere. But when you get into the middle, it's just like advancing hundreds of years in time. And Ningbo was no different to any other. There are lots of boring stories I could talk about of going to factories and finding this and finding that and finding t'other. Yeah, it's quite true, I did and I did quite well from my visits to Ningbo. It's more thinking about the people who I went with and the people that I met and the things that they did and the way that they behaved.

There's a suburb of Ningbo called Cixi. Now Cixi is where most of... at least 70% of the industry in Ningbo is situated. The other 30% is in a place called Yuyao and to get from Ningbo city centre out to the factories and Cixi, there was only one road; one big, main road. And the type of road that I detest is a two-lane, two-carriageway thing but with nothing in the middle to stop them crossing over to your side. And this thing had got two lanes going in each direction and in the middle they'd just painted two yellow lines.

Now I've never met a Chinaman in all the years I went there who took any notice whatsoever of these yellow lines. I think they just thought they'd done it for fun. It certainly didn't seem to apply to any of them. And on the number of occasions that we have been going up on the right-hand side – bearing in mind they drive on the other side of the road to us – and I've found that we're in the outside of the two lanes and coming towards us is some great big wagon who's decided that he's going to overtake everybody on his side and therefore he's in our inside lane. Miraculously the two yellow lines don't stop him. And I wish I had a quid for the number of times I've grabbed hold of the steering wheel and dragged some driver over to the inside out of the way because we were playing chicken. We were playing chicken with the drivers of these wagons and they knew they would win and they didn't care. It's got the highest death rate in the world on the roads, so why would they be bothered. Kill a few more, particularly if one of them is a foreigner. That doesn't matter. Foreigners are ten a penny.

# Chapter Thirty-Four

Some days going out to Cixi on this road, oh my God, if they were new people and I didn't know them and I wasn't aware of what the address was, I might go as many times as three times up and down this road. And the locals used to nickname it death road and they weren't wrong. It was an absolutely dreadful place; a terrible, fearful place to drive. And what I could never grasp about my Chinese drivers/colleagues/friends, call them what you like, was the lack of fear or concern that they showed for their own lives driving in these places at such speeds and on the wrong side of the road. They would see me deliberately covering my eyes because I thought this was it. I think I'm the luckiest man alive to have had so many flights in China and driven so much in China, to have come back from China without a scratch. I know people who've ended up dead or at least in hospital through the way that they drive.

One day I'd had enough of Ningbo and I was being driven with a Chinese colleague who was acting as an interpreter. We were being picked up at the hotel in the middle of Ningbo to go to Shanghai. Now Shanghai at that time – they've built a big bridge since – but Shanghai at that time was, if it had been me driving, something like a five and a half to six hour drive; being driven by one of the lunatics was about four to four and a half. And this particular day, this particular morning, we have breakfast and we're waiting outside the front, cases all ready, and this taxi turns up that my Chinese colleague has ordered and they'd got two drivers. One was to drive the car to Shanghai and the other one was to drive it back. That was about one of the few bits of common-sense I ever saw on a Chinese road. We get in the car and we go out the car park, onto the main road and we head in the direction of the motorway junction.

Now if I tell you that before we even got to the motorway, this woman that was driving us – and I am not talking about women drivers and male drivers; they're all crazy. It doesn't matter what sex they are. By the time we've got virtually to the motorway, she has terrified me about three times at the way that she drives and I'm now contemplating four hours or more on a motorway – no service station; no service station whatsoever, so we could stop and have a drink or a rest. No. Non-stop with her at the wheel. And I just did not fancy this one little bit. And we'd been on the road ten minutes up on the motorway and I knew why I was not wrong. She was crazy. Absolutely, completely and utterly crazy. We're going from lane to lane, back to this lane, over there – oh whizzing in and out. We're not caring less whether anybody's overtaking us. The speed is fantastic that we're doing. We haven't a hope in hell if anything goes wrong, of stopping the vehicle.

There is one city between Ningbo and Shanghai and that's Hangzhou. It's quite a bit city. And I did have two big suppliers in Hangzhou but I wasn't planning to see them on this particular visit, and nor did I. About two hours out of Ningbo, Hangzhou came up on the signs. And not long before we get towards the Hangzhou turnoff, I am so frightened I'm writing my will in the back seat, I quite honestly am. I've had enough. I can't stand any more of this. I can't do four hours of this. And I was just saying to the Chinese fella who was with me, *"I just can't sit in there four hours with her driving. I've never been used to it and it's just unbelievable,"* and of course typically Chinese, he just laughed and went back to sleep.

As luck would have it, I have a very good friend; his name's Grenville Firth. He's from Barnsley, but at that time every winter he used to go out to Australia and get two summers and two cricket seasons. And this would be, I don't know, something around January-ish, so it wasn't cold because it never really gets too cold in many parts of China. But there was a bit of rain about which worried me even more. And my mobile rang. Now it was a strange time of day for it to ring because they were still in bed at home and I never actually thought that it might be Grenville ringing me from Australia. Well it wasn't a ring actually. It was a text. And I looked at the phone, read the text, said to the man who was with me who spoke very good English, *"I've just had a message that I've got to call off... we can't carry on to Shanghai. I've got to call off and see one of the factories in Hangzhou. Would you tell her to take the next exit and go into the centre of Hangzhou?"* And she did. And then I said to the man who I was with, *"Just find a good hotel. We'll go there first and then we'll sort out the visit to the factory after."*

The reality of the situation – well I can tell you the truth now because it doesn't matter – was the text actually said, *"England 133 for 3; we look like losing."* That's what the text said. It was about cricket. And since I had no intention of trying to explain to the Chinese anything about cricket, I told a lie. And I had another friend who knew both Grenville and me and one of his mottos in life was, *"I only lie when I have to."* And I copied his motto on that particular occasion, simply to get off the motorway and get out of her clutches. She then disappeared. We paid her and she disappeared on her way back to Ningbo, never to be seen again by me.

And he said, *"Oh, when are we going...?"* I said, *"We're not. I'm sorry, but that was just my excuse to get off the motorway. I could not stand any more of being driven like that. Go into the hotel. We're not going to any factories. We're going to have an afternoon of peace and quiet. We're going to have a meal tonight and tomorrow we're going to carry on to Shanghai, get in touch with the people in Shanghai and tell them we shall be there tomorrow, not today."* And I said, *"And another thing, in 1.3 billion people, there must be a taxi company where the drivers are not all insane, where they drive properly, where they drive in the correct lane, where they stick to the speed limits. You've got to have one."* He said, *"Oh yes, of course there is. They're called the blue taxis."* I said, *"Well I've never seen a blue taxi."* He said, *"No, it's the jackets that the drivers wear. They're blue."* I said, *"Well can you get one for tomorrow and he or she in their blue jacket can drive us to Shanghai?"*

And he did. And it was safe. It's one of the few times I've ever felt safe on a Chinese motorway. But it was safe. And I did it again and again. I don't mean telling lies, I mean just asking for a blue taxi. And it worked every time and I could relax a bit. So if ever you're in China and you're terrified of the taxi driver, just ask them to get a blue taxi. It'll put years on your life.

# Chapter Thirty-Five

When I was in Shanghai, eventually getting there in the blue taxi, went to various places. We did business with quite a few of them as the years went by. I met a young man whose name was Huang Tao. His English name is Job. I'm not sure whether he thinks he's called himself 'Jobe' or 'Job', I'm not quite sure. Just an aside from that, I do know one in Ningbo who gave himself an English name and believe it or not, and I know you won't believe me, but I can promise you it's true and it's the most difficult thing I've ever had to do, is to sit opposite somebody across a desk and call him, *"Machine."* Can you imagine calling somebody, *"Good morning Machine and how are you? Oiled up well today are we?"* That was quite true. His name is Machine.

Job was an intelligent lad. Job is an intelligent lad. I started a little business with him called Shanghai Pacific Electronics Limited. We didn't use the whole mouthful. The Chinese do to a certain extent. A lot of them love business names which are so boringly long that it borders on the ridiculous. So SPEL – Shanghai Pacific Electronics was born. I owned it. I put the money in. It wasn't very much. It was only about a thousand quid. And he ran it for me over in China. He helped with the sourcing and he did help a little bit with manufacturing because he was a clever lad. The only problem I found with it was that I had a big customer in Walsall. Walsall's a fair way from Shanghai and the problem was that the bloke in Walsall who sells emergency lighting, has a division of emergency lighting and he called it SPEL and I'm sure to this day he thinks that I copied the name SPEL off him, just for the sake of it. Well the reality is that it wasn't me that gave it the name SPEL; it was our friend Job that gave it the name SPEL.

Anyway, one day I was having lunch at a Crowne Plaza, the hotel in Shanghai and he asked if he could come and see me. And I said yes and he came along and saw me with his wife, Gloria, which isn't her real name of course; it's just a name that she uses for speaking to foreigners. And he asked me straight out, no messing, straight to the point, the question, *"Can I come and work for you?"* And I said, *"Yes."* According to every Chinese that I've ever met, I overpaid him. But he was good for me. He never let me down. He never let me down and that was important for me in China. And if I said to him I wanted him to get on a plane and travel to the other side of China to meet me, then without any ado he would do it and we would meet.

One of those meetings turned out to be my – I won't say claim to fame – but it was in Hangzhou in southern China and in Hangzhou there is a very nice hotel called The White Swan and I'd booked the hotel through my travel agent here for two nights; a room for him and a room for me. I go from Hong Kong to Hangzhou by train, he flies down to Hangzhou from Shanghai and we meet in the lobby at The White Swan. That was all right on the first afternoon and we went out to see a man that made something or other. I think they were electronic timers, I can't recall, but I think they were.

When we came back there is such one hell... the third world war has broken out in the car park of The White Swan. I've got a room, my suitcase is up in the room and so has Job. Oh no we hadn't. Our suitcases were still there, but when we came back and asked for the key to get in our rooms, we were told, "*Well there's the key. Go and get your suitcases and out you go.*" "*Why? Why are we being turned out? We haven't had chance to run off and not pay you yet. We don't owe you a penny. Why are we being told to go?*" And they pointed rather sheepishly and, I must say, they looked a bit frightened, at a gang of people who were men and women of all ages, but quite a few of them; I would say about 100, who were virtually occupying the restaurant. And I said to Job, "*Ask the girl on the reception who this lot are. Are they the reason we're having to move, find another hotel at such short notice?*" And he asked and she said, "*Yes, they were.*" I said, "*Well who are they and why are they so important and why are we being kicked out, even though I, months ago, booked these two rooms for you and I?*"

Now you know this crackpot that runs North Korea, Kim, whatever his name is, he thinks he's a pal of Donald Trump or Donald Trump thinks he's a pal of his, I'm not quite sure. I'm not quite sure who's the saner or maybe the word is insane and I'm not certain. But he's a young man and all of us on this planet need a mum and a dad because no matter who you think you are, you need a mum and a dad to get here. And it transpires that this gang who have taken over the restaurant, taken over all the rooms – well most of the rooms – but decreed that nobody else shall stay in the hotel, they are all the entourage of this fella in North Korea today, of his dad who was Kim Jong something or other. And he was pointed out to me as being at the top of the table. And what he'd done, it came to pass, was that he had... As you know, Korea is a peninsular. It's a boil on a part of China. It's connected by land, in other words.

He had hired some great big train. I reckon it must have been the only train that North Korea had. And he just simply piled it full of all his generals with all the medals. You've seen them on the television. They've got more medals than... well, I was going to say the Duke of Edinburgh, but I'd better not say that. He had piled all these generals on the train and the women weren't the generals' wives. Oh no, they weren't the generals' wives. Job, after a bit of persuasion, told me these were Chinese prostitutes who'd been lined up for all these generals and for our friend in Korea's dad.

Went up to the room, went into the room. My things had been put back in my case out of the drawers and there was a note on the bed saying 'Please go down to reception and leave'. And five minutes later I find myself down in the reception with Job who promptly asked me, *"How much do you think we should pay?"* to which I gave him an old English answer. And we went out and got into a taxi and he said to the taxi

301

driver, *"Can you find us a good hotel to stay at?"* and he did. So there's my claim to fame. The dictator of North Korea was instrumental in getting me kicked out of my hotel room in Hangzhou, lock, stock and barrel. Nobody seemed surprised except me and the other westerners.

We went to a hotel that we found through Job talking to the taxi driver and it was quite nice; very nice actually, probably better than this White Swan, but I wasn't going to tell Kim Jong-il, or whatever his name is. The funny thing about it was, the day we left. It was only two days. The day we left, I had agreed... I couldn't be carrying all this cash around all over China. I went to the desk to pay with a credit card, which they said on the desk they accepted, which in actual fact they did accept – eventually. When I offered the card to all these girls who were at the other side of the desk giving me the bill, I seemed to have enough people watching me to fill Wembley Stadium. Credit cards were odd to them and they were puzzled at the sight of one; the sheer sight of one. NatWest Bank meant absolutely nothing to them; nothing at all. But pay with a credit card I did.

We then decided we were going to fly from Hangzhou to another place called Wenzhou.

# Chapter Thirty-Six

So we got on this aeroplane from Hangzhou to Wenzhou; it would be about an hour, an hour and a quarter flight, up the east coast of China. And at the time there was a thing just starting to happen in China. It was called the SARS epidemic. It was a bit like the Coronavirus thing in a sense, but nothing like as bad as Coronavirus. And we're on this plane to Wenzhou and again an uneventful flight and we land and we're put... They always bus you to the Terminal building in these old airports. And we're all being herded onto a bus when suddenly a load of young doctors roll up in all their white smocks, boots, hats, masks, and the bus which Job and I are on, plus the other one which meant everybody on the flight – bar one person – was whisked off to the far side of the Terminal. An ambulance turned up and we were told later that one man was taken off the plane and rushed away to hospital.

Apparently this fella, when the plane was landing, had said to one of the stewardesses, *"I've got a cold."* The stewardess panicked, told the captain. The captain said he'd got SARS. He radioed it on and we ended up in what was the old Terminal building just sat on old chairs while all these people dressed in white with just their eyes peering above the top of the mask at us, gave us forms to fill in, which were in English and Chinese, thank goodness, and we were given these forms to fill in and also they asked to take our temperature. By the way it was the conventional way – under my tongue. And before they took my temperature, I had completed the form and on one of the questions was 'What is your normal temperature when at home?' Now me being an older man and not really used to all this metric stuff, I wrote down 98.4, which those of you who are old enough to know will remember that this was the figure in Fahrenheit for a standard normal temperature, 98.4. This is us, the British, never doing anything the simple way; always doing it the hard way. Well this Chinese doctor comes up, takes Job's form, looks at that, yeah fine. Takes mine, jumps three miles up in the air and shouts, *"He should be dead. Your friend, he should be dead."* And I said, *"Why should I be dead?"* *"You got temperature 98.4."* I said, *"For God's sake Job, quickly explain that I have given him the temperature in Fahrenheit. I do not know what the equivalent in centigrade or Celsius is."* And he explained. *"Oh,"* and the doctor came back down off the rafters, shoved this thing under my tongue and got 36 and he was quite happy.

It then turned out that this bloke; he'd just got a bit of a tickle, the man in the ambulance. He'd got a bit of a tickle in the back of his throat, over-reacted, thought he'd got SARS and was not ill at all. The alternatives were two. One, they either let us go to our hotels or to their homes or whatever these people were doing or two, we were kept in quarantine for two weeks. And I thought, oh no, we can't have that. I can't be here two weeks. That's way after the flight back. But as luck would have it, they said, *"No, you can go to your hotel. But when you get to your hotel, every morning before you go down for breakfast you must take your temperature with the thermometer provided by the hotel. We shall make sure they have some and some forms to fill in just asking for your temperature and you must take your temperature and you must leave the form completed on the pillow so that the woman doing the room can pick it up and take it down to the reception."* This of course is the Chinese again.

I said earlier in the book that they love stamping things. Well they love having bits of paper. What they do with these bits of paper that they accrue throughout the country, I have no idea. But what I decided to do was rather than bother with all this and because I felt perfectly okay and I was more bothered about eating something that upset me rather than not being very well in terms of my temperature, we were three mornings and I put 35.9 on one, 36.1 on the second and 36 on the third and they were collected because when we came back to the hotel at the end of the working day they'd gone. These pieces of paper were collected and presumably somewhere in China to this day they are hidden away, kept for posterity, my temperature, which was a complete load of nonsense because I never took it once properly – or improperly for that matter – I never took it once, was recorded between 35.9 and 36.1. The moral of the story is when you're in China, for God's sake be metric. Don't be imperial. You're looking for trouble and you'll find it.

# Chapter Thirty-Seven

I've said many a time in this book that I've done a lot of travelling in and out of China whether it be by air, by sea or by road and I've been very fortunate inasmuch that experiences, bad experiences have been extremely few and far between. But I have to say that on one occasion I rather thought that my time was up.

I had a very, very scary hour or so in... I said I'd been in Ningbo and I'd found a nice hotel where I always stay and this particular time I'd been talked out of staying there to stay at an American owned hotel group called Howard Johnson, I think it's called. It was more modern than where I'd been staying before and anybody who knows me will tell you that I don't like modern particularly and I didn't like the Howard Johnson Hotel very much. But it was okay. The quality of it was good. But I just didn't like the environment. Breakfast was held either on the ground floor as we would call it, floor number 1 as they would say, or on the 19th floor. Now because our two rooms were both on the 17th floor, we decided to eat at the breakfast bar on the 19th floor, which was as high as you could go without going into the staff quarters. And I was sitting there talking to a potential supplier along with Job, the sales manager and we're eating and we're talking business.

The sales manager suddenly turned to me and said, *"Don't look out the door now, but all I can see is smoke."* And I did look out of the door and there on the 19th floor of this very large hotel was smoke so thick you couldn't see anything. And we didn't know where it had come from. We had no idea. Now the staff were I'm afraid typical of the Chinese. They panicked immediately and just simply did what you shouldn't do, because at the side of every lift it'll tell you in a hotel 'in case of fire do not use lift'. The Chinese, on a rather lighter note, don't put 'if' they put 'when'. In other words they're expecting a fire. They always put 'when there is a fire do not use the lift'. The staff just shouted, *"There's a fire,"* ran to the lift, got in the lift and went down and chanced their arm. We were left.

There were the four of us and I recall there were two other men there who turned out to be two Dutchmen who were on business. And the six of us headed towards the fire exit at the far end of the corridor, which we could just about glimpse as the smoke was increasing. It was a very funny smoke. It smelled. It was a very odd thing. And we went on to the end where the fire door was and I was thinking... *"Well, all fire doors should not be locked, but since we're in China it's a very fair bet that this fire door will be locked."* And we got there and somebody pushed it and thank goodness it wasn't locked, but it let us out onto the fire exit which was a series of staircases going all the way down to the ground; stone staircases with a green painted bannister to guide you. And on each floor as you went down, in green, was the number of the floor. Well I, with my poor heart and what have you, was not too sure whether I could manage this.

We thankfully were going down and not up and we began to go down and down and we put handkerchiefs over our mouths to keep out this awful smelling smoke. And we went down and down and down and eventually we got down to – and I could see it – just – the number 8 and I felt that that was it for me. I just felt that I couldn't go any further. And I remember saying to… I don't know where the Dutch people were, but they'd gone. They'd disappeared. Whether they'd gone quicker than us, I don't know. I presume they must have done. And I just said to the two people who were with me, *"You go on lads because I'm not going to get out of this. I will not get out of this."* And they were most encouraging and said, *"Come on, come on, get up, get up, get up. You must. You must try. Get up."*

And I did and we staggered down and down and one of them was holding each of my arms. And we got down and eventually we got down to 2 and the sales manager chap looked down and he said, *"I can see the sun. I can see sunshine at the bottom."* And when we got down another floor, we'd walked out of it, which meant that the fire, the fumes as it turned out, were on floor 2 and once we got beyond 2 we had fresh air. We were saved, we were fine; we were okay. We never saw a fireman until we got outside. They could have come in with all the equipment these people carry to cover their faces with masks, but we never saw anybody until we got to the bottom.

When we got to the bottom there was a very small fire engine; a very small fire engine and lots of equally small Chinese firemen running around with absolutely no control, no common-sense, no means of going about the job. Just running around like headless chickens, going in all directions, just shouting at one another and nobody seemed to be taking any notice. And when we came out, nobody came up to us and said, *"Are you all right? Are you okay?"* to the Chinese man; because we had a Chinese man there so he could speak to them. And we came out and we came out at the back of the building and we walked round to the side of the building where there was a little pond affair and that's where the windows started for where the customers sat on the inside on what we call the ground floor drinking coffee, tea or what have you and just having meetings. And when we got down to the bottom, we sat on the edge of the pond on the little wall and believe it or believe it not, there we are with a hotel that's got some sort of fire which hasn't been evacuated with the people that we wanted to meet still inside. We could see them and they were waving us into the building. And we're saying, *"No."*

The man came to the door – Anthony his name was. I said to him, *"Don't you know that there's a fire?"* And again, like Chinese do, he laughed and giggled. I said, *"The place is on fire. We've come down from the 19th floor."* *And we weren't even sure whether we were going to get out with our lives and you're sitting here drinking tea. Has nobody from the staff told you to get out of the place?"* *"No, nobody's told us."* And we actually went in and I don't know what happened.

I didn't know what they did. Nothing was ever said to anybody who was a customer. The one solitary fire engine drove away and that was the end of that. Nobody realised, nobody knew how near us three and the two Dutchmen, wherever they went; I never saw them again, how near we were to losing our lives. At the end of the stay there, a friend of mine who was one of the people that we were visiting over there, a factory owner, came to take us to the airport...

# Chapter Thirty-Eight

Enough of being miserable in China. Let's have a bit of a laugh – or what I thought were two laughs actually.

We're in Ningbo, me and a couple of men from a customer – the big one in Doncaster. And the three of us plus a man called Liu Fei, who was a very, very nice man, he'd taken us somewhere in the morning to look at some sort of factory that was working in conjunction with him and was hoping to supply these people in Doncaster via me. And we went there and then off we go to go to a factory which made lamps – that's bulbs to you, but lamps to me. Bulbs come from Holland and come up in the spring.

We're driving along from one factory to the other. We didn't need to go onto any major roads or motorways, just an ordinary road between one town and the next. They were only about half an hour apart. And we never got up much of a speed because there was so much traffic on the road. We're going through this town and we eventually catch up with the back of a blue painted – because I said earlier that everything is painted blue – a blue painted lorry, but with no sides, just a flat platform with a tractor, as they call it, at the front pulling it. And we're behind it crawling along at 25/30 miles an hour because it was about his limit.

And on this platform for the world to see were six cows – two, two and two at the back. Two at the front, two in the middle and two at the back. And round this platform were ropes and staves. It looked a little bit like a boxing ring, if you know what I mean, but you don't often see cows in a boxing ring. But that's about all that was keeping these cows on this lorry. Now we get towards some traffic lights and I saw the lights change to red and surprise, surprise, rather than go straight through them, which is the normal thing for the Chinese to do, the lad who was driving must have put his foot on the brake and stopped the wagon rather sharply.

Now bear in mind I've said that these were cows on this here wagon, a cow's foot, all four of them are not exactly made for standing on a wooden platform that's moving. To say that they were not at ease and were wobbling about all over the place would be to put it mildly. And the two from Doncaster and me, but not the Chinese driver, Liu Fei – no, he thought it was a perfectly normal sight, which it presumably was in China – he was taking it all very seriously and we didn't know where to look and we were laughing and laughing and laughing at the sight of six cows on the back of a moving truck. In footballing terms, two centre-halves, two midfield players and two strikers up front.

# Chapter Thirty-Nine

Visiting Foshan which was on my regular route when I was in China – I nearly always went to Foshan because... well Timothy's been very good to me. He made me feel very welcome and he in fact introduced me to several of, what turned out to be long-term suppliers. However one day I was in the hotel. I think it was a Saturday or a Sunday. I think it must have been a Sunday because there were so many families about and Sunday is a very big family day in China. And he rang me in the room to say that there was a man who had been a professor of Chinese studies or something of that nature at Hull University and that this man had got to hear on the grapevine that there was, if you like, a 'fellow Yorkshireman' in town and would I care to meet him for lunch. And I saw no reason to say no, so I said, *"Yes, I'll meet him. What shall I do?"* He said, *"I'll come and pick you up, but I can't come with you. I've got to go somewhere."* I can only think that he was going to the bookies to have a bet on the 1:30 at Newmarket or something, but he couldn't come with me. *"Don't worry. This chap speaks very good English,"* because as he'd explained, he had lived and worked in Hull.

Along comes Timothy, we get in his car, five minutes' drive just off the city centre and he drops me and he points to a man – a distinguished elderly man, over 70 – stood in the doorway of this eating place and he said, *"There's your man in the suit with the tie. He's expecting you. When you've finished, if you want picking up, just give me a ring and I'll come and collect you."* So I got out of the car, walked across the pavement, of course much to the great entertainment of the local gathering because they were all utterly amazed to see a westerner, particularly a big overweight westerner waddling his way across the pavement of their hometown on a Sunday lunchtime. I approached the man, explained who I was. He spoke to me in English, gave his name, which I'm afraid I don't remember, and we go inside the restaurant. The restaurant will be familiar to many of you and totally unfamiliar to another great many of you.

My Sunday lunch was at McDonald's. But it didn't matter because at least I was going to get something to eat that I recognised and didn't have to worry about what it was. Over there – just a slight aside – I had rat, cat, dog, snake. You name it, I had it. And they always told me – eventually told me – what it was that I was consuming, with one very notable exception, which I did eventually prise out of them what it was, for the simple reason that I knew what it was because we eat it here. But they thought that this would be beyond the pale for me and that I wouldn't want to know what I was eating. And that, strange as it may seem, was black pudding. They didn't think I would like the idea of pig's blood. And I said, *"Oh we eat this quite a lot,"* – or some of us do. I do. I like a piece of well-prepared black pudding. There is a habit, particularly in the south of England to cook it until it's like shoe leather and then plonk it in slices onto a tray and say, "*Well help yourself.*"

I go in with him and it might have been half full. It wasn't over-full. The Chinese tolerate KFC, McDonald's and the like, but they are far more loyal to their own food and restaurants – far more loyal than we are. Never saw... for example, in all the years that I went, never saw an Indian restaurant. Never smelled the delightful scent of curry, which I can't abide, whether it's from the next-door-neighbour or from an Indian restaurant or a takeaway. No Italian, no French... a French restaurant or two in Shanghai, I tell a lie, but basically speaking it was a choice of Chinese or one of these American – KFC, McDonald's-type places. They have their own KFC by the way – a copy of it. There's a surprise for you!

It's exactly the same sort of an idea and it's run by Major Sanders or something because they haven't got a great deal of imagination when it comes to copying. They just do it and hope they don't get sued. Well anybody who's tried to sue in China and get a verdict that goes with them has got nothing to do but spend money because you're not going to win. So there we are, we're sat down at a table and we've got the menu which is in both Chinese and rather poor English, but nonetheless I could understand what it was about. He asked me what I wanted. I told him and a drink to go with it and he went off to the bar area, the counter area to order.

While he was ordering I noticed a young many in overalls who quite clearly worked there. Or if he didn't work there, he was working at a lot of places like it because he looked to me from the things he was carrying to be in my trade. He looked to be an electrician, not that I have any pretence to be an electrician, but that I sold a lot of goods which went to electricians, so I'm familiar with their appearance. I sat down and I said to the man, *"Local electrician?"* *"Yes, local electrician."* He said, *"Let's see. What is he doing? Oh..."* And you know those insect killers with the ultraviolet tubes? They've usually got two tubes in a fitting and I think in the old days they used to be... 18 inches was the size of the tube. And the lad had got a pair of steps – steel steps – and I noticed on his feet he'd got a pair of boots with steel soles. And one of the tubes of the ultraviolet fitting wasn't working and the other one was doing its best to work, but just to prove that there was electricity to it, it was flickering and it was annoying and it was bad for your eyes. And somebody had obviously told him after about three months of this happening – because this was the norm in China – not that things flicker is the norm; the norm is that it takes three months to do anything about it. Somebody had obviously given him a phone call or whatever they do and he'd come down and he'd got under one of his arms a brown cardboard box with a line drawing of one of these insect killer units, which obviously was a new one and was inside the box.

So here we are, and this is fascinating me and it's fascinating my professor friend from Hull, who now by the way, had gone back to China to Foshan and retired and that's where he was living. But he just loved the idea of being able to speak to somebody from the UK and particularly from our part of the world. He did tell me that he'd never been to Barnsley but he'd heard of it because it's in Yorkshire and – another gambler – Hull City had played us at football. That was another couple of wins for Hull City. And he said, *"Watch. Don't speak, just watch."* And the lad never turned off the mains supply. He went up with his steel boots on his steel steps. He disconnected the one that was flickering and then took it back down the steps, got the new one out of the box. Everything was live. He hadn't disconnected anything at all. He went back up the steps, attached the new one – live, earth, neutral et cetera – and it came on without him having to go down and flick it on, the switch, to ensure that it was working. His face never altered. He never batted an eyelid. He simply picked up the discarded insect killer, put that into the box that he'd brought the new one in, took it away and came back for his steps and went.

Now my friend the professor said to me, *"What do you think to that then?"* I said, *"Well is that a regular occurrence? Do they all do things like that?"* *"Oh yes, perfectly normal. We try to tell them to adhere to safety. We lecture them. We talk to them. We tell them they may not be going home to see the wife and kids tonight if they do it wrong, but they never take any notice and they never alter. And at the rate we're going, it'll be a thousand years before they alter."* And I always recall something he said which was extremely wise... *"You don't have to have a university education..."* although he had of course. *"You don't have to be a genius. You don't have to be some sort of member of the Royal Society or whatever it's called, to talk common-sense.*" There's only one trouble with common-sense. As an old mate of mine used to say, *"It's not so bloody common."* And he said to me, *"You..."* and by you he meant the western world, *"...are buying so much off us. We're building factory after factory after factory after factory. Every day of the week another one opens selling something. Money is no problem because we print our own and so therefore money is easy come by."* He said, *"You are expecting us to go forward 50 years in manufacturing capability in five years and that's quite true. But you are also expecting..."* and he pointed to his temple and touched it and he said, *"You're also expecting us to move that..."* and he meant the brain, *"...forward the same 50 years in the same five and that Chris we cannot do. We cannot promise and you've just seen the result of it."* I've never forgotten that expression he had. *"You can't move the mind forward 50 years in five,"* and it's true. It's very true.

We talked. We chatted about his days in Hull. The Humber Bridge. And I'm desperately trying to think of other things that they have in Hull. North Sea Ferries, the prison. I've been on North Sea Ferries but never in the prison. I'm desperately trying to think of things in Hull that I could talk about. At the end we spoke I suppose for a couple of hours, two and a half hours. He kept getting up and renewing the drink. We'd eaten the burger and the chips some considerable time ago. And he eventually said, *"Well it's been lovely to meet you."* And I was going to get out a business card. I went to my pocket to get a business card out and he said to me, *"No, no, no. I don't want to be rude, but don't waste your card. They all cost money,"* and he's talking about one business card. *"We've never met before. This is the only time we will ever meet. We will never meet again, so what is the point of me having one of your cards that you've had to pay for? It's been lovely to talk to you. I've enjoyed meeting you and I wish you every success."* And he stood up, shook my hand. I stood up. We both stood up. We shook hands and he went.

I'd got part of my drink left and while I was drinking that I rang Timothy to get him to come back and pick me up. He told me to go and stand on the street corner so that he could just pull up, pick me up and we'd be off. That I did. I stood on the street corner. It was a nice warm day. And I was surrounded by another thing in China which they haven't eradicated and is a real bind, a real pain to visitors, and that was beggars. And the parents normally send the children to tug at your clothes and to hold their hand out and they want one or two RMB. Well I never carried anything less than notes because the coins were virtually valueless and Timothy had told me many times, *"Give them nothing because the more often you give them, the more of their mates will come to bother you and to demand. And if you don't give them money, they then get nasty. They then get aggressive. You have to do your best to keep your temper and to ignore them."*

Timothy had got a brand new car and I kept looking down the road at all these cars that were coming past looking for his just to get me away from all these people who were trying to induce me to give them money. And eventually he turned up. I think it must have been after the 3:30 at Newmarket. And we got in the car. Absolutely typically Chinese, Tim never asked me whether I had enjoyed the afternoon, whether I'd liked the old gentleman, whether we'd chatted about things in common – nothing. It was almost to Timothy as if it was so unimportant. It was almost to Timothy as if, *"Why should I be bothered whether they've enjoyed themselves? It's nothing to do with me."* And I got in the car and he drove me round the block and back to the hotel. And I saw him again the Monday, the following day morning when off we would go again to look at more factories, more factories and more factories.

He didn't only stick with electrical and lighting. Oh, he would take me anywhere. I remember him taking me to a place that made children's clothes. Jeans and t-shirts and the like – for kiddies. What on earth he'd taken me there for, I'll never know. I had no contacts in that industry whatsoever, and as such, it was an utter and complete waste of time. But it all came out that what was really happening here of course, that he worked for this Guangzhou Trading Company and they were acting as agents for people in all sorts of different industries and electrical and lighting was one; kiddies' clothes must have been another. That's how I ended up going into all sorts of factories.

Extremely recently one came to mind which was useful - or could have been. He took me to a place that made... what did they call it in this virus situation that we currently find ourselves? PPE. And I'd no interest in smocks and gloves and masks and what have you. But I did keep the business card. And when there was this shortage of PPE, they must have kept my business card because they sent me an email quoting me all sorts of prices and I wrote to the Secretary of State for Health – Hancock – I dropped him a line telling him that instead of buying from Turkey, who were buying from China and just putting 'made in Turkey' on it, any fool who knew China knew what was happening there.

Instead of doing that, I knew the name of one at least factory that actually produced these goods and that if he wanted anything quickly, they'd got the stock and if he paid the right price, ten pence apiece for a pair of gloves... You look how much they are in a supermarket or a chemist, or should I use the American pharmacist word – you look how much they are over here and he could have had them for ten pence apiece. I never got a reply. Only an electronic one. And they decided to send a vacuum cleaner manufacturer to do the job instead.

I've every admiration for Mr Dyson except he's shifted all his manufacturing outside this country. I couldn't see what the point of sending him was. Why didn't we just contact these people directly? I didn't want anything. I didn't want a commission. I didn't want a knighthood. I didn't want anything. The country was in a mess and there was the name. Get in touch with them and see what they could do. But I never got a reply. And to be fair, I will also tell you that I sent exactly the same email to Ashworth who is the Labour Party opposite number and I'm a member of the Labour Party and he never answered either.

So I didn't think much... well I thought nothing of... to be brutally Yorkshire, I thought nowt to either of them. And I don't know what they're paid, I've no idea, but they weren't interested in people who could help them who knew China. As I've said before, I've been 64 times to China. I think if you were to add up the number of times that the entire cabinet plus the Labour front bench have been anywhere near China, you probably wouldn't come to more than 20. And I'd been 64 and they knew more about it than me. Yeah. I don't think so. I don't think so.

# Chapter Forty

If you looked at cow's feet, they're hardly suited for wobbling around on the back of a wagon and going left and right and backwards and forwards. It's a recipe for disaster. Now, during the journey as we're following these six cows on the way to their maker, we christened the two at the back Gert and Daisy. Now Gert and Daisy were the most uncomfortable of the lot and they didn't like it at all. And when he braked and he braked hard to stop at the lights, Gert, who was the bigger one of the two on the left, in footballing terms, shoulder-charged Daisy with considerable force and poor old Daisy, God bless her, flew straight over the top rope and out onto the ground, onto the road. And you know how they say, well that's something I'll remember the look on his or her face for as long as I live, there we have laid on the floor in front of us, a cow on its back, four legs in the air, a face that's saying, *"What the devil's happened here?"* which then realises, *"Hang on a minute, there's freedom here."* So Daisy wobbles about from left to right, left to right and manages to retain her feet before these two lads who were driving the wagon had been alerted by people who were in the street that he'd lost one of his cows, and Daisy gets back to her feet and she set off at an enormous gallop, past our car and down the street, to be followed by the two lads who were in charge, running for all they were worth to catch up with her.

Whether they ever caught up with her, I do not know. The three of us couldn't stop laughing for love nor money. The Chinese fella saw nothing at all amusing about it whatsoever; couldn't understand why we were laughing, pulled round the wagon, the lights had changed to green and off we go. Off we go. Whether he ever caught Daisy, heaven only knows.

We hadn't been gone more than about two or three minutes further on the same road... By the way, everything looks alike in China. Every block of shops look like the next block of shops. I've often wondered how they know where they are, quite frankly. There are no identifying things at all. It's all just sort of one miserable place after another. And we're wandering along the street there and he's not sure where this factory is that we're supposed to be looking at that made lamps and his mobile phone went off. And he answered the mobile phone. It wasn't a hands-free and even that's illegal in China, but nobody takes any notice of things like that. You don't want to worry yourself in China about the law, I mean good grief. That was just written down to give somebody something to do. And he answers the phone, realises who it is and to my amazement and surprise, starts to speak to the person in English. So I looked at him thinking, *"Hello, he's pinching one of our customers here"* or something, but no, he just mouthed at me, *"Brazil."* It was a customer from Brazil apparently and they were talking about some order that hadn't been dispatched, et cetera, et cetera. Once I realised it was nothing to do with me, I didn't take a lot more notice.

We go down the road and we come to another set of red traffic lights which Liu Fei would normally have motored straight through, but he didn't because there was a policeman stood on the corner. Not that a policeman would have bothered him. They wouldn't have cared tuppence. But it gave him chance to stop the car and talk to the man from Brazil while the lights changed. So he put the phone in the central well between where the gear lever would be and talked for a short while – only a few seconds – to this fella from Brazil. But then we have to set off because the lights have changed. So off we go driving down the same road. And we drive down there for about, I don't know, 10/15 minutes before he sees some sign in Chinese, which obviously was the sign to indicate to turn right because the factory we were looking for was down this little lane.

And just as we were turning down the lane, I turned to Liu Fei and I said, *"You do know you've got the bloke from Brazil still on the phone down here and it's costing him a fortune?"* *"Oh, I'd forgotten."* I said, *"Well I think you'll find he's not still on there now,"* and he'd gone. So we had Gert and Daisy and Brazil all in one afternoon and I'll never forget laughing about all the lot of it with the two people who were with me. But Liu Fei saw absolutely nothing funny in it whatsoever. To him it was just in a day's work. To us it was – well, how shall we put it? Something rather unusual.

Another time in Ningbo, Liu Fei and I had arranged to do some business with a man who ran a garden lighting centre; a garden centre which did lighting is perhaps a better way of putting it and that was in Lutterworth. And this fella came across once that I remembered, just the once and we went to see Liu Fei and what this man was asking for was actually somewhat unreasonable. He was wanting nigh on the impossible out of poor Liu Fei just for about 50 or 60 fittings of each design, of each type. It was an awful lot of work costing an awful lot of money for no particular reward for him. But this guy who was called John didn't seem to realise this or want to realise it. Liu Fei said to me in a private moment, *"I don't think I can do this order because I don't think I can buy and assemble such small quantities of raw material for him. Do you think you could have a word with him about getting up the quantities so that it's worth my while and it's worth the while of the other supplier, the raw material man, to help me out?"*

That night in the hotel that I was back now using having deserted the fire station that I'd been staying in – I never went back to that Howard Johnson by the way; that was the end of that – we were having a drink which tended to wander along a bit into the night. John, although his business was in Lutterworth, was a fellow Yorkshireman, but you wouldn't have known it from his accent. He was rather posh with a capital 'P' – and I wasn't. But we got on and we did business. And I had to ask him that night if he could possibly multiply up his quantities by about three or four times to make it worth Liu Fei's while. Because if Liu Fei didn't do what he wanted, then nobody else would.

Believe it or not, he agreed and he increased his order by four-fold and we carried on drinking this… well I'm not keen on lager of any type, but that was the only thing that they'd got. And we carried on drinking this stuff for quite a long time, well beyond the average Chinese person's bedtime and the girl in the bar wasn't at all happy with us. And I was ready for bed, but John was really into it by now and he was off and he was away and he was talking and he was putting the world to rights and all the rest of it.

One thing that I noticed about him as we were having this meeting or this discussion – it wasn't a meeting – was that the posh accent suddenly became a Yorkshire accent. Bit by bit by bit he started to drop all his Hs, which by the way for anybody who isn't from Yorkshire, it's a very good way of identifying us. So much so we became, like my dad always used to say, there were three towns in Yorkshire, 'Ull, 'Ell and 'Alifax. And he became 'Ull, 'Ell and 'Alifax by about midnight. And the business with him went on for several years. The orders were never very big, but 'Ull, 'Ell and 'Alifax was always his nickname in the office when we talked about him. I believe he's sold up and gone to live… somebody told me, I think it was Malta and I presume the accent's come back and he will be talking upper crust again, no doubt. But I nicknamed that little escapade *"Ull, 'Ell and 'Alifax.'*

# Chapter Forty-One

A man who has remained a dear friend of mine for many, many years, who helped me start to get decent orders and recognition in the lighting industry and electrical industry – and I'm going to name him by name because what else could I do? – was my dear friend Peter Scott. Peter was a southerner and he came from Surrey. I believe he lived in Surrey. Where he originated from, I do not know. But his original factory was in a military town in Hampshire where when you got there... you were going out into the countryside where his factory was in a small industrial estate, you had to dodge the tanks. I don't know whether they were carrying or firing live ammunition, I'm not sure, but I was always glad to get away. But these are things about meeting him in China, not in Hampshire.

I recall one day meeting him in the hotel that I liked in Ningbo. I'd flown in from Hong Kong probably or somewhere like that and he maybe had come down from Shanghai. He didn't do all his business with me by any manner of means, but he did a fair amount of it and we were looking for a simple plate metal shop that could bend bits of metal. This is how technical I am of course. Bend bits of metal to the shape required by Peter and Peter would buy them by the thousand. Well that was the end of that really. So I said to my dear friend Liu Fei, because it would have to have been invoiced through somebody with an export licence and I'm quite sure that where Liu Fei was going to take us wouldn't even have probably heard of the UK, let alone have an export licence to sell to us.

And one fine and sunny morning, off we trot in Liu Fei's car. He'd found just the place. And you've got to bear in mind that Peter's place down in Hampshire was 'la crème de la crème'. He had machines that cost a fortune. He had staff from the UK and a lot of them, I think, from Poland and nothing could be called sort of old-fashioned about Peter's factory. But there we are, we're in this car of Liu Fei's and we're trundling off and we wander down death row just for a bit of fun and... I didn't tell Peter about death row of course, otherwise he probably wouldn't have wanted to go. But knowing Peter, he's so laid back, he probably wanted to go twice just to see whether he lived. But we get out there and we turn right somewhere and down into a yard way and we went in a gate and – that's it, there we are and there isn't a great deal to see. There's a building in the far corner. There's two fellas who turned out to be father and son, clanking away on some old machine and a woman who turned out to be mother to the son doing some sort of cleaning work around the house. They knew we were coming and Liu Fei introduced us and they were so friendly, so, so, so friendly. So willing to do anything that was necessary to get his business.

Now nothing could have resembled his business less than this place in downtown Ningbo. I've no idea why they call it 'downtown' by the way. It's always puzzled me. Downbeat maybe, down mode, downhill are probably better words, but nonetheless there we were. And Peter who will always give – and this is one of his major things to his credit – he will always give everybody a chance to prove his strengths, his rights to have the job, his opportunity. I never saw him ever once just turn his heels on somewhere and say, *"Chris, what the hell have you brought me here for? We're off."* And this particular day was a, *"Chris, what the hell have you bought me here for? We're off,"* morning, if ever there was one.

But he was prepared, because he recognised in this chap, who would be in, I would think his 60s, early 60s, he recognised in this chap a blooming hard worker; a man who if told to make something this way, he would make it that way. He wouldn't please himself what he did like a lot of people who are in manufacturing want to do and want to give you their advice about your product. No, he wanted to listen. And before I know where I am, there's Peter and this fella with drawings out on a surface in this office area and they're talking like bosom buddies. Now whether either of them understood a word the other one said, I'm not quite sure, but it was quite clear that it was getting through to him. They had a mutual respect. It was quite obvious that he thought, *"Well it is a dump. It's a hell of a dump, but this guy he'll make what I want, so let's give him a go."* And I thought that was lovely. I thought that was a lovely way to treat people.

The old lady – I won't use this word, 'old' – the lady. My word, at my age nowadays she'd be a young woman.

And she brought out morning coffee if you like but it wasn't coffee. Well that didn't matter to me because I don't like coffee, but she brought out the old green tea. Now Peter would have a swig of this green tea; I wouldn't because I knew where the green tea would eventually send me before very long and believe me, public conveniences are scarcer in China than they are in the UK. So, I hope, gracefully declined the offer of tea, but she also brought out a plateful – and I mean a huge plateful of the biggest grapes – black grapes – I have ever seen in my life. To be honest they were big enough to be damsons, but they weren't damsons, they were grapes. And in our honour, they'd washed them. Well that, I'm afraid, wasn't great news because you were well advised to steer clear of the water. What do you think the green tea was made of? And this was a difficult one for us. And we proceeded... we really felt we had to eat a few of these things just to show willing. So I took my hanky out of my pocket, dried the grape as best I could, bit into it and I found that there were so many pips inside, there's no wonder they spit on the floor. They do that because of the pips that they put in the grapes. But we did our best. We tried to be English gentlemen. We treated them fair. They were kindness itself to us and business was done with them.

And I recall saying to Peter as we came out the gate in Liu Fei's car, in a joking way, *"Where do you want the 'CE' sticker putting on the final product Peter?"* I don't think CE actually ever came into it. But yes, he did business with him and yes, he treated him as an equal. Now Peter was no equal. Peter was a brilliant, and is, a brilliant man. He's retired now. I'm told he's running...

well I do occasionally have text conversations with him and the last time he was telling me when I actually met him that he'd sold the business and he'd bought into a brewery in Limoges in France. And it was a brewery, not brewing French beer, but brewing good old Barnsley Bitter. And apparently the youth of France are getting a bit tired of drinking wine. Now I never will get tired of drinking wine. I never drank bitter, so there's probably the reason. They're wanting an alternative and he was telling me that Limoges bitter is doing quite well. And good luck to you Peter. I hope he succeeds. Don't drink too much of it. Don't become the only customer.

He was the boss man, 'El Presidento', whatever you want to call him, I don't know, of the British Lighting Industry Association, which meant that he was an important man. Now I was never a member of the Lighting Industry Association because they wouldn't have me in it, I don't think. I don't think they were too keen on jumped up blooming Osram reps – I used to work for Osram many, many years ago – becoming members of the LIA and then therefore being able to claim that they were LIA members when approaching other customers – other potential customers.

Peter was the one that actually, quite amusingly, pointed it out to me that there had been a joining together of the Lighting Industry Association or something and the Lighting Federation in the UK to form the Lighting Industry Association and I looked at him and was sort of thinking, *"Oh well I'm very pleased to hear that."* It was only when I saw the twinkle in his eye that I realised that LIA spells liar and he knew it did and I knew it did and we laughed about it. And he's no longer the Chairman or President or whatever of LIA, but he remains a man whose opinions I value greatly and will, I hope, be a friend 'til my dying day.

But of course Peter wasn't the only top man in lighting that I knew. There is a very big lighting company in Gillingham, down in Dorset. There's Gillingham in Kent and Gillingham in Dorset. I don't know how you put that in writing, but there is a difference in the pronunciation of the letter 'G'. And this company down in Dorset, the boss man, who took a shine to me when I approached them about sourcing for them in the Far East was called Rupert. And Rupert was a man of considerable wealth and in Gillingham if you don't work for his company or somebody supplying his company, then I don't think you work.

It is so modern it is unbelievably true, but I was there to supply all the fiddly, nasty bits. You know when you see a light fitting, there may well be a piece on either end which is a metal bit. That's my technicality coming to the fore again. Well the metal bits were a bit messy for Rupert and his lads and his main fella that I dealt with who is a director of the company was called Nigel and Nigel is a... he shares something with me. He's a keen football fan. Unfortunately my team is about to descend into League One and his team, Southampton, is a Premier League side. But I've told him there'll come a day when he'll get on the wrong end of a tanning from Barnsley and you can expect a phone call about ten minutes after the referee's blown the final whistle. Every dog has his day. It's a devil of a long time since

I remember Barnsley beating Southampton, but nonetheless we'll keep trying.

Rupert – oh Rupert – he was a gentleman of the highest order. I suppose politically – I can say these things now because they're not customers and I don't rely on them anymore – I suppose politically we couldn't have been much further apart if we'd tried. But you know, it never mattered. And I was always gratified to know and it was always a lovely moment, that even though some of these meetings with Nigel and the buying staff used to drag on interminably or used to seem to do to me, interminably but justifiably, Nigel was always under instructions that before Chris went, *"Bring him into my office."* This is Rupert telling Nigel, *"And I'll have a quick word with him just to ask how he is et cetera."*

Rupert was a great lover of horseracing and he always used to talk to me about his horses that were in yards; trained in yards round about where he lived. And this was a great disadvantage to me because I've got to be honest, I find that any sort of racing, whether it was men, dogs, horses or whatever, cars going round and round in blasted circles, does not appeal to me one iota, not one iota. But when you're with a customer, GEC always taught me, act as if you're interested. Look on the wall. There'll be photographs. It will give away his interests. It gives you something to concentrate on, to surround your selling pitch by; an opening gambit of horses, in this instance horses.

I had another man who used to have a picture of Leeds United. Well Leeds United to me, even though I was born in Leeds, is nothing, but we always used to talk about Leeds United. I had another one in Walsall who was a massive customer and he had a Wolverhampton Wanderers shirt. Wolverhampton Wanderers meant nothing to me. But what he didn't know was before I used to go down and meet him, I realised that the first hour of any meeting would be talking about Wolverhampton Wanderers.

So I used to get out Google and have a look at who all their latest signings were, et cetera, et cetera so that I could talk knowledgably, I hope, about Wolverhampton Wanderers. Rupert was one of these and I remembered one day he said to me... It was getting near Christmas and I always used to go there in an afternoon and believe it or not, all the way from Dorset, after I'd seen them, drive all the way back to Barnsley. It's a long way and I used to come home very tired. And he said to me, *"I've got a horse running on Boxing Day at Wincanton. Have a tenner on it Chris. You might win a few bob because I fancy it."* And so I did. Now I know nothing about gambling, horseracing or whatever and found that even putting the £10 bet on was a little bit taxing to me – tax being the operative word with gambling. Apparently you pay the tax on the bet and if it wins you don't have to pay tax on the winnings. I learnt this much to my cost many years before with another bet that I had with a friend and it won, but we didn't pay the tax. We won 300-odd quid apiece minus tax. You live and you learn.

Rupert was always so kind, so friendly and his sidekick Nigel treated me better, I think, because Rupert was my... I don't wish to say the word friend; that's making me a lot more important than I was. My acquaintance. Now that it's all done and dusted and the fat lady's sung the song and I've finished and retired, and most of these people, if this book is of any sort of success, if it goes to print, I'll probably end up giving most of them away, but if ever you get to read this Rupert and Nigel, I'd love to tell you something. If ever you think that or thought that Nigel has spent a little bit longer in Hong Kong than was perhaps justifiable, but you didn't like to ask him because he fulfilled such a vital role within your organisation, I can tell you the reason now Rupert, for why he spent a little bit longer than normal.

I'm not saying anything wrong occurred, but I don't know whether you ever met the lady who worked for him in Hong Kong. I met her by sheer chance at the Hong Kong Lighting Show one year. I was sat on somebody's stand where I thought it might be interesting but it was totally boring, but because they'd poured me a drink, I was obliged to stay until I'd drunk it. The drink was water by the way. It's okay, it was water. The fact that it tasted a bit like gin is a total coincidence.

And I was sitting there thinking, *"Well I'll just get down this water and move along to somewhere else"*, and out of the corner of my right eye, I see one of the most attractive Chinese ladies wearing a... what do they call it for a skirt? A pelmet? Yes, a pelmet. And she was heading straight towards me. I didn't take much notice. The legs were just driving me into another world. She was absolutely fabulous. I didn't notice the man next to him until he said, *"And how's Barnsley going on these days then?"* And then I turned my head slightly to the left and it was Nigel. Rupert, the reason he spends the time in Hong Kong is because with legs like that they're a damn sight better than anything you've seen on your horses. And I don't blame him. I can't remember what on earth we talked about because I couldn't manage to get my eyes much above waist height. It was her fault. She chose the dress. Not me. And I'm sure it wasn't Nigel. Was it??

I've said earlier in the book that apart from one scary moment in an aeroplane flying down from Ningbo to Hong Kong and that's it as far as untoward happenings 35,000/40,000 foot up in the air. Well it is, I suppose. But the one thing that I would warn anybody of, is that flying back from Hong Kong to the UK through the air lanes provided for you by... when I say for you, I mean for the airlines themselves and the pilots flying the planes, I'm advised about a ten-mile wide lane up and over China. And then you get near to, not so far from mountains. I take it they must be the Himalayas.

And the one thing that you... well I got used to it, if you ever get used to it... the one thing was the immense amount of turbulence that occurs for about a 30-minute stretch of this journey. You always know when you get on a plane in Hong Kong to fly back here whether the turbulence is going to be worse than normal. You know because if it is going to be worse, then by the time you've got to the end of the runway they've got the trolley out serving the drinks and getting the dinner ready. That's so that they can get it all away and get into their little beds wherever they are. I think they're

337

above your head somewhere aren't they, on these large airlines? The staff I'm talking about. And the quicker they do all that, then the worse you know the turbulence is going to be. Regular travellers like me are aware of this. People who've just gone out for an odd journey for a holiday are not aware of this.

They show you a great map on a screen on the bulkhead which divides the classes of seats, and wherever you go, if you look at the film screen on the seat that's in front of you, you can see that you are coming up to a sort of a white area which is indicating snow which indicates mountains and the nearer you get to that, then the bumpier it gets. And some nights it's got very bumpy and it only goes to show what magnificent machines these aeroplanes really are because they are thrown about all over the sky – or it seems that way; it feels that way. I'm quite sure if you were outside looking in you wouldn't even be able to notice it. But there is turbulence galore up there and it's always on the return journey. It's never on the outward journey. I take it that that must be because the return journey is nearer to the mountains and I assume that the air rising up from the ground, mountains et cetera, is hitting you rather forcibly and throws you about all over the sky, or seems to do. It only lasts half an hour. You can always tell when it's over because the captain's told the staff you can come back out of your hidey-hole now if you want and wander around smiling at the passengers.

The journey was always so long, I could sleep. I used to think that when I came out of the hotel in Hong Kong – or Shanghai for that matter – when I came out of the hotel in Shanghai to get in a taxi to take me down to a shuttle station which took you out to the airport, I used to think that, as near as damn it, give or take, it was 24 hours from coming out and getting in that taxi and the taxi driver would invariably say the same thing, *"I take you all way airport."* *"No, you don't take me all way airports. You take me to the airport something or other station, which is only five minutes away and drop me off and then I'll buy a ticket for 50 Hong Kong dollars which is about a fiver and I'll get myself out, thank you very much, out to the airport."* 24 hours I always used to think from the door of the airport to getting out the taxi here that had picked me up at Manchester Airport. 24 hours was about par for the course.

And that's about the only golfing expression you'll ever get out of me because along with racing round in circles, I regard golf as being... well, what did Dr Johnson say, 'the best way ...' I'll not quote him exactly, but the best way he knew of spoiling a damn good walk. Or as I always say to a friend of mine, *"You'll never knock that stick down with that little white ball if you play until you're a thousand."* It's not my game, as you can probably gather. That sort of issue is for another book and another time. It's just given me a clue why I might go for a 'sporting likes and dislikes' book. There'll be more dislikes than likes, but nonetheless who the hell cares?

You get to Paris and then you have to... oh, because you've already been up there 11 hours, you have to drag yourself over to another Terminal for the flights to the UK and there's always one to London next to the one to

Manchester. The north-south divide is alive and kicking in Charles de Gaulle Airport or Roissy. Roissy is the name of the village which was destroyed – flattened – to build Charles de Gaulle Airport. That's why a lot of people refer to it as Roissy. Then there's a north-south divide because the Manchester flight is always a further walk along the gates than the London one. You get to Manchester, you queue up to go through the immigration, although I believe today you can do it automatically with the new passport that I have. By the way, talking of passports, my passport was always 46 pages. I bet yours isn't. That's not because I'm anything particularly clever, but at the rate of stamping that goes along in China and Hong Kong for that matter, it's necessary to have a 46-page book because these Chinese insist that you must have X number of clean pages in your passport after your Visa has been issued. Why they do all this I really don't know, but they're great lovers of paperwork, stamping things and presumably saving all this stuff for posterity.

I always found the French lovely people, except the ones who worked – not all of them – worked by the security apparatus in Charles de Gaulle Airport. It's a bit off at half past five in a morning after a tremendously long journey to be pushed and shoved like Gert and Daisy were on the cattle trailer. It's a bit odd, a bit uncomfortable, but nonetheless you put up with it because you know that once you're through, that's the end of them and you wait for your plane and an hour later you're in Manchester where they are just as bad because, well it's Lancashire isn't it, so what do you expect? Come through there, taxi home.

I've always come out of the taxi into the house completely shattered. I know that they say that there are cures for jetlag. Well, all I will say is - show me one please, that works. Over the years I have suffered from jetlag to a considerable extent. I've never found a way round it and I could no more come out of Manchester Airport, go in the car park and get in my car at round about eight o'clock in the morning when the traffic is heavy, no more do that and drive safely than I could fly to the moon. I know some people who do and I admire them. I don't think they're foolish. I admire them. They obviously feel they're up to it and they do it. I know people who come from as far as Heathrow to up here, straight off the plane, land in Heathrow, a shuttle bus out to whichever car park you're going to, find your car, which is hopefully still there, and I've known people then... well Graham Allen in Kent certainly does that and he definitely drives from Heathrow to where he lives in Folkestone. But Folkestone isn't Barnsley. It's a darn sight further is Barnsley and I just do not know how people do it. They are made of something stronger and different to me. I just simply couldn't do it. Jetlag was certainly something that I never, never overcame. And I don't believe that now with my dickie ticker I'll do a great deal of flying again and if I do, it won't be long-haul, so consequently I'll never have to contemplate the possibility of driving such distances when jetlagged.

# Chapter Forty-Two

There's only one sad additional aside to this story of Foshan and Tim and the other people that I met there and that was that... and it's only a very brief remark. I picked up a rather large order for a customer in the Leeds area for which I make no bones about it, it's so many years ago now it doesn't matter. My commission was $7,000 and you can work out from that, at 5% the value of the order. And the man in Leeds paid Timothy the full amount and that meant that I was due $7,000 which would have been, as luck would have it and history would prove if you were to look at the books of the company, the largest amount that I ever made on one order. And it took an awful lot of work to get that order together and to then make sure that I convinced a man in Leeds to pay an enormous amount of money over to China on a wing and a prayer that the goods would follow.

Now, to be frank and to be honest and to be truthful, the man in Leeds paid his money, the man in Leeds got his goods. He never lost a red cent. Timothy never took a penny piece out of the value of the order, but as I've said on several occasions, his major weakness was gambling and the easiest man to take it off wasn't the people in Leeds who would be demanding their goods, the easiest one to take it off was the softest link in the chain – me. And he never paid me. I never saw him again.

He was ashamed, I'm sure, at what he'd done, but I never saw him again. He never answered his phone to me again. From one day being my friend in China, he disappeared totally from view and the only time I ever spoke to him was when one day I rang and he must have not noticed that it was me and it was my number and he answered. He wasn't apologetic. He simply promised that he would pay me when he could. Well if you ever get to read this Tim, the bank account hasn't changed and if you'd care to transfer the $7,000, I'd be very, very grateful. It was just one of those things.

Only twice in over 16 years did I ever not get paid. The total amount that I was defrauded of – I think there's no better word – was probably about $11,000 – a lot of money to a self-employed man who worked basically... well no, who worked entirely on commission. $11,000 made a big hole in the profit and they were both done at the same time in the same financial year, so it made a big hole in the turnover, the profit for that financial year. I'll never forgive him for it, but I don't suppose that's worrying him. Today I suppose, what will he be? When I first met him, he'd be a young lad of about 25. Today, he'll be in his middle 40s. I don't wish him harm. I don't have that sort of bone in my body. I don't wish him harm. I just wish he'd paid me what was due.

Do you know, if I'm absolutely honest, if Timothy had said, who was a very good friend of mine or seemed to be; I'm sure he really was, if Timothy had said to me, *"Chris, I've got myself into a state,"* through this never-ending gambling habit that he had, *"the $7,000 that I owe you, I need to keep the wolf from the door,"* me being me, I'd have let him keep it on the understanding that one day... a thousand dollars every other month until it got paid off, he could pay me back. He never gave me chance to say that. And I'm sad about that. I'm very sad about that. But that was just a sad moment in China.

I'll finish by saying this part of the book that I asked you at the very beginning to put yourself in my shoes and see things through my eyes, you can't because you've never seen what I've seen. You've never heard what I've heard. You've never experienced a fire 19 floors up and no firemen to be seen. How can you possibly have experienced that? How can you possibly know what it's like? How can you possibly know what a near-miss on an aeroplane coming down from Ningbo to Hong Kong is like if you haven't been through it yourself?

But you can try and you can try to realise that the old expression of things being worlds apart has never been truer than when I was taken out of my home, comfortable, safe, certain environment and on my own suddenly put into the middle of a culture I did not understand and a culture I will never understand because I will never go back. In many ways I sometimes think whether I would like to go back. I'd love to re-live the pleasant times and the nice times and I'd love to meet again the men who were very honest, very decent with me because there could have been lots more $7,000s. There could have been a lot more $7,000s had they not trusted me to get orders for them and had I not trusted them to pay me for my efforts.

I can't say it's a country I can recommend to you. When I hear of people going on holiday and I always think, ah yeah, the Bund in Shanghai, Tiananmen Square, the Great Wall of China, the Terracotta Soldiers. I've been 64 times and seen one of those. I've seen the Great Wall of China from the air and it is some sight. The others I never got the time for. I have never been to Beijing. Well, not unless you count sitting on the tarmac in an aeroplane – once. That is my total amount of visits to one of the world's greatest capital cities. Did I miss it? At the time, no. Do I realise what I missed out on? Today, yes. But it's no good crying over spilt milk because that doesn't put it back in the jug. It never has in my experience and I've been around quite a while.

# Chapter Forty-Three

In March of 2013, I was rapidly approaching my 66th birthday. I'm getting a little tired by all the travelling, both inside and outside the United Kingdom, so I decided that I would sell the business, if I could. I approached a company in Leeds who specialised in selling businesses of my type and they did the necessary and they found me a buyer and the buyer took it and a fee was agreed. There's no need to go any further than that except that that was the end of that in terms of a negotiation.

I had at that time already arranged another journey over to the Far East; to China. This time I decided to go, on the advice of my travel agent, from Manchester by Qatar Airlines through the Middle East and on to Hong Kong. I went as normal by taxi to Manchester to get onto this flight and of course by now I'd made a few bob and I was using business class just to make it a little easier for me in both directions. Went through all the nonsense and got onto the plane and I'd asked deliberately for an aisle seat in business class. And I went onto the plane, I showed my boarding card to the hostess. She pointed me in the general direction of row, whatever it was. I walked down the plane on my own with my briefcase, found the seat, put the briefcase in the locker above and sat down. There was at that time nobody in the window seat. I was in the aisle seat. I suppose a little selfishly I was hoping that the window seat wouldn't have been sold and that I would get more room to stretch out during the flight to the Middle East.

So I'm watching all the people come on and seeing these people walk on and find their seats and find his seat and find her seat and nobody came to this particular seat of mine until a man got on the plane who I recognised absolutely immediately as being the ex-Captain of Lancashire County Cricket Club and probably more importantly, the ex-Captain of the West Indies International Cricket Team, Sir Clive Lloyd. And my attitude towards whether anybody had got the window seat changed immediately, in the sense that, *"Oh, I hope he's got it."* Well as luck would have it, he had. He came up to me and said, *"Excuse me, but can I bother you? That's my seat."* I was absolutely delighted when he sat down. This is one of the... I won't say cricketing heroes because he played for all the wrong teams, one in particular, but you can't deny this was a man of extreme ability as a batsman. Bowled a bit as well when he was younger. But towards the latter years his legs weren't so clever and he concentrated on batting.

He sat there and we took off and we'd been gone about... it's about eight hours out to Qatar and we'd been going about half an hour and I hadn't spoken to him except when he passed me to get into the seat. And I'm thinking should I or shouldn't I? Do I pretend I don't know him? Do I pretend I don't recognise him? Or do I speak? And I took the latter option. I said something like, *"I can't help but notice... I recognise who you are,"* and he smiled and we just chatted a little bit. And they came round with the lunch menu – one for him, one for me and I looked at mine and I turned to him and I said, *"What do you fancy off here?"* And he gave me an answer. I said, *"Do me a favour before you get off the plane; would you autograph your menu and give it to me? I'd very much appreciate it."*

Sir Clive turned out to be one of the most pleasant, if not the most genuinely pleasant, travelling partners of the world (if I can put it that way) that I'd had in all those years of going to various parts of the world. And we talked and he told me he'd recently been to the West Indies to... He was working for the ICC, that's the International Cricket Council and he told me that he'd recently been to the West Indies to watch a series and he'd bumped into Geoff Boycott over there who was recovering from cancer and I enquired as to his health and he told me that he was improving. And I thought, well just that quick 'he's improving' phrase from him is worth a load of newspaper nonsense. And I said, *"Where are you going now?"* And he said, *"Oh I've drawn the short straw. There's an international cricket conference in Bangladesh and I got the short straw. So I'm going out to Qatar, changing aeroplanes and flying onto Dhaka..."* I think is the capital of Bangladesh *"... and I'm looking forward to it no end. I don't like Bangladesh and I don't like the food and I shall be wishing I'm coming home from the moment I get there."* I thought, that's pretty straight talking to a total stranger who you've only met a while ago.

And we nodded off and then chatted and nodded off and then chatted and I recall saying to him as we're getting towards... within the last sort of hour of reaching Qatar. I said, *"I've got to say this to you. Watching you on a Saturday afternoon at Headingley or Old Trafford, while you've been knocking hundreds of runs off the Yorkshire bowling attack, you have spoilt more Saturday afternoons than any other cricketer I can ever recall."* And I absolutely loved his response. He turned at me, looked at me, realised I was a Yorkshireman and I was not so keen on Lancashire and he just looked at me and said, *"Shame that wasn't it?"* And I think those were the last meaningful words we ever exchanged, when he said, *"Shame that wasn't it?"* And I thought well that's put me in my place.

And we landed and I shook his hand and he walked off in one direction and I walked off in the other. I went into the business lounge and I'd got a seven-hour wait. Heaven knows why I allowed the travel agent to talk me into this, I really don't know, but anyway there I am. I had a seven-hour wait in the business lounge at Qatar.

A great deal of the time when I was in China I was accompanied by Job. Intelligent lad, clever lad and has now I believe from what he says, a business with about 20 to 25 workers making various types of lighting which he sells into hotels like the Hilton, but all of them are in south-east Asia I believe. I don't think he does much here, although I can think of one customer that he does deal with.

I recall the day that I arrived at Shanghai to meet him. Prior to this particular visit, we'd always had to go anywhere by taxi or hire a car or do something with a driver because he couldn't drive. But this particular day I touched down in Shanghai and he's there waiting for me beaming all over his face because he's got the news for me that he's learnt to drive and he's got a car. So we walk with the suitcases, my suitcase and his because we were going to one or two towns – we walked to the car and when I get there, he's bought a Rover. He told me that he'd bought the Rover to impress me. It was a British car. I said, *"Well they've gone bust."* He said, *"Well that doesn't matter. I can still get the parts if I need any."* He'd bought the Rover to impress me.

We got in the car and we set off to leave the car park and then like in most car parks there is a pay desk. He gave the man the ticket and paid. The barrier went up and he put the car into second gear, and the car didn't like this a great deal and we chugged forward with the car protesting desperately that 'there is a first gear on me and I suggest that you use it from time to time'. But he kept his foot down until the car eventually picked up and off we went.

When we got out of the car park we were straight onto the motorway and he got up to about 30 miles an hour I should have thought in second gear before he threw it straight into fifth. No third, no fourth – fifth. And the car again didn't like it and we had a four-hour journey and we drove for four hours using second and fifth gears. On these motorways there are several – the French would call them 'péages' – tolls and we pulled up at every one by putting it into fifth gear, so that the car stalled when we eventually got to pay the money.

Then he put it into second and started the engine up again and tried to move off. We kept doing this repeatedly and I kept explaining to him that he should use all the gears and why did he think that Rover had put on the top of the gearstick the numbers 1, 2, 3, 4 and 5 and the letter R. But for goodness sake don't put it into R because we don't want to go backwards. But it didn't work. We drove for hours in second and fifth. We never changed. And I said to him, *"Last time I came you weren't driving but now you are and you've got a car. You must have passed your test."* This is me thinking my way, our way; you must have passed your test in the meantime.

And he said to me, *"Oh no, I haven't had a test."* I said, *"You haven't had a test? Well how did you learn to drive?"* He said, *"Well I haven't learnt to drive. I've just bought the car, got in it and driven off."* I said, *"What, without a driving licence?"* *"Yeah. But I've got one now."* I said, *"Well, I'm dying to know where the driving licence came from."* *"Oh..."* he said, *"... that was easy. I just bribed a policeman."* I said, *"You're going to say that again. Run that past me again. You bribed a policeman?"* *"Yeah,"* he said, *"I went down to the local police station near where I live, told them I wanted a driving licence. They said they wanted so many RMB. I gave it to them and they gave me a driving licence."* *"And you had no lessons, no test and you bought the driving licence purely and simply by giving a policeman some money?"* *"Yes."* *"Oh, most reassuring Job, I'm sure. You feel that you can drive comfortably and correctly."* I said, *"Does it not bother you that you keep stalling the car?"* *"Something wrong with car,"* he said. I said, *"No, nothing wrong with car. Something wrong with driver. You're doing it all wrong."* A bit like you're playing all the right notes but not necessarily in the right order.

I didn't say that to him because I knew it wouldn't make any sense to him, but that was a bit like the way that it really was. I said, *"Does everybody do this? Does everybody simply go to the police station and buy a licence which in effect is like a bribe?"* And he said, *"Yes."* And he could not see why I thought that that was in the slightest bit unusual. He couldn't see why I thought it was strange; odd. To him it was perfectly, perfectly normal.

And for the rest of that week we drove around in second and fifth gear every day. Nothing ever altered. Nothing ever changed. Except when we were in cars owned by other suppliers who he knew and where he took me to and we went out for a meal or whatever with them and I found that the more experienced of them had all got automatics rather than manual cars and that they did know... somebody had told them somewhere along the line how an automatic worked. You put it into drive and it chooses its own gear as the speed increases.

But for all Job's brains and intelligence and all that he could do and all that he knew, he couldn't work that out. He couldn't work that out about a motor car. That was just, way, way, way beyond him. Whether he's still driving a car or... I don't think he is. I think the last time I asked him, he'd packed up with the car because there's too much traffic on Chinese roads and I think he'd packed up with the car and was concentrating very much on public transport. The only thing I can say about that is that he now lives down in the Hangzhou area. He's moved from Shanghai with his wife and two children, down to Hangzhou and the only thing I can say is that it's not Shanghai's loss and it certainly isn't Hangzhou's gain from a driving point of view.

Once we were in Hangzhou, he took me to a hotel called the 'China Hotel'. It's not called that now. They've sold out. They've changed their name, but I can't remember what it's called. And he went off to park the car or somebody did it for him perhaps with a bit of luck, I'm not sure, and I was left sitting in the lobby simply waiting for him to come back and then we'd go up to the two rooms. And as per normal in these places, there's background music. There's always background music. There's always somebody playing something.

Now I'm not a great musician and I'm not a great music fan, but I did like The Beatles. I did like The Beatles. And I was sitting there this particular afternoon and, what was it called? 'When I'm 64'. You know, the one that goes 'Will you still need me, will you still feed me when I'm 64?' And I'm singing along to this and I didn't realise I was getting a little bit loud. But I was giving it some, *"Will you still feed me, will you still need me... when I'm 64,"* et cetera. There was a very good reason why I was singing along actually to it – apart from the fact that I knew it – that it happened to be my 64th birthday that day.

And I thought, *"Well they can't know in the hotel and they're not playing it particularly for me."* It's a pure chance. And there were some Americans there and this American woman came up to me and said, *"You seem to know the words of the tune extremely well. Is there any particular reason?"* And I said, *"Yes dear, there is. Today is my 64th birthday."* I'm sure she thought that I was telling lies and I said, *"No, I'm not. It's quite right. It is. It's true. I am 64 today and it's The Beatles and I'm British and I know the song and I'm singing the words."* And she just said, *"Happy birthday,"* walked away back to the place that she was sat with husband and kids and obviously explained that this crazy Englishman was pretending he was 64 (because he didn't look a day over 50 – ha-ha) and was singing the song because of his birthday. But the reality was, what I said. I don't think there's a word of a lie in the whole book and it definitely is not a lie to say that that was my 64th birthday. You know, they talk about special birthdays. I don't remember much about very many other birthdays, but I do remember, for very good reasons, my 64th birthday.

Have you ever lived at Buckingham Palace or 10 Downing Street? Possibly not. But I have. Well, let's be a bit more accurate on that than I have. Of course, I've never been inside either. Never been anywhere near either. Well I have. I remember going to 10 Downing Street in the days when my dad was alive when you could actually get up to the door and have your photograph taken.

The reality of the situation is quite simple. When you are travelling in and out of China – and I did it sometimes two or three times per visit because if I was in Hong Kong and I went across the sea to China and then came back and then the next day went back again, then my passport was stamped and a form filled in for each visit. And every time you had your passport stamped you had to fill in a form and when you've been as many times as I've been, you do tend to get rather fed up of these forms and you do think, do they really read them? And if they do, do they keep them? And if they do, why? Why on earth do they keep them?

So I thought I would test it out. And once I'd been on a ferry from Hong Kong to China to see Mr. Liang at an emergency lighting factory and they ran me back to the ferry port for me to get the ferry back to Hong Kong. But to go through the immigration to get to the wee boat, I had to fill a form in, which then, accompanied by my passport, they read, stamped and kept – not my passport, the form. And on one day I was really feeling quite happy with the world. I think business was going quite well and we were making a few quid and I was not far off the time that I was going home within a couple of days. So I went to the area where the immigration desk is and on the wall at the side with pens attached are these forms that you fill in.

And so I thought, "Right..." So I filled the form in with my name and I put the passport number on and I put where I was born and all this, that and the other – everything. Then I came to the bit that said address and I thought, go on, just try it. Put an address on that is well known everywhere in the world and see what happens. So I put 'Buckingham Palace, London' on and the guy read it, filed it somewhere and gave me my passport back without so much of a blink of an eye.  To him, even though he was a customs official, Buckingham Palace, London meant absolutely nothing to him.  He'd never heard of it.

The next day I'm going back, but to a different port because I'm going to a different town, but the whole exercise is very much the same.  It's the same form.  So this other factory they run me back to the ferry port and I thought, "*Go on, I'll do it again*", but I thought, "*I won't put Buckingham Palace on this time*".  So I filled the form in and when it came to the part about address I put '10 Downing Street, London'.  Now at this time, Tony Blair was Prime Minister.  Not that I thought that that mattered a great deal, but that's a fact, he was.  And the fact that he was will become evident in a few moments.

I get back to Hong Kong, go into the room, put on the television just to see what the news is.  Are we at war with somebody?   And lo and behold, they were announcing a state visit to China by British Prime Minister Tony Blair and I thought, "*Oh dear, oh dear, what may I have done?  I've put I live at 10 Downing Street and the guy that does live at 10 Downing Street is here and he's looking at me on the television.*"  And then of course common-sense took over and I thought, "*Well surely Tony won't have to fill in a form will he to get in?*"  And I thought, "*Well you never know.  They're just daft enough.*"  But I never heard any more.  I didn't expect to hear any more.  But that just goes to show that you can tell them absolutely anything.  10 Downing Street and Buckingham Palace; my addresses and nobody, nobody queried it, questioned it or even thought I was pulling their leg or even, worse still, made me fill in another form or got me locked up for what I'd done, I don't know. But that was the time I lived at Buckingham Palace and 10 Downing Street.

Another brief story in China was sometimes I had to go to places, and a lot of times in reality, on my own. Job wasn't there; he couldn't make it or whatever and I had to get to wherever I was going the best way I could which was usually to go to the hotel porter. Hopefully he would recognise the address in Chinese and a taxi would take me. This happened on one occasion. I can't remember the town or whatever that I was staying in. It wasn't Ningbo, I can remember that. And the taxi understood. Yes, he saw the address. Yes he knew. And he was telling the truth, he did and I turned up at this factory. They knew I was coming.

And I go in and the girl on the reception spoke enough English to understand and I asked for the name of... I didn't know if it was a man or a woman and I go in and I ask and she nodded her head and everything was okay. And I was escorted to a room and they invited me to sit down and said, *"Would you like a tea?"* and I said, *"No, thank you,"* because it's always that green stuff and that has an unfortunate effect on me. And within a few moments two girls came in who would be, I don't know, 27 and 30-ish. Sometimes it's very difficult to judge ages of Chinese people. They always look so young until they suddenly go old. And I nodded to them and smiled at them and they... *"Hello,"* and all the rest of it.

I used to have red and white cards. Now the reason that my cards were red and white was quite simple. It's all to do with the colour of the local football team's shirts. And I gave them this card with my full address here in Barnsley and I gave one to each of the girls. And everything went silent for a while and it was quite a long while; quite a long time that things went silent. They were whispering to one another and pointing at the card and I said, *"Is there anything wrong? Is there something wrong?"* and they said… in a rather sheepish manner, one said to me, *"You from Barnsley?"*

And I said, *"Yes, I'm from Barnsley, yes. My word, don't tell me you've heard of Barnsley all the way over here? I know it's the centre of the earth, but I didn't realise you'd know where it was."* And I said, *"Can I ask you why it means something to you, the name? Why does the name mean something to you?"* And they looked rather, again, sheepishly around the room and then just said to me, *"You got football team,"* and I thought yes, we have got a football team, yes and I've got a season ticket and they're not that good; and they're still not that good. *"Oh yes, Barnsley football team, yes, yes. Where's the significance in all this? Why does it matter?"* and she said, *"Every week we do football pools. Every week we gamble on English football and we see your town name on football coupon."* I said, *"Oh do you?"* *"Yes, and we bet. You think they're going to win on Saturday?"* I said, *"I doubt it very much, but you should get good odds on betting that they will."* And they just left it at that.

It was fascinating that all that way round the world and there we've got two young ladies who knew of my town because we'd got a football team. I wish I could say that we did any business with them and that I went many a time and that I was still in contact with them occasionally but I'm afraid it would be untrue. Their prices were too high, their quality certainly wasn't very good and despite emails from them et cetera over the years, we never did anything. But they obviously loved their football, didn't they?

One day over there I'd been asked to find a particular product made by a particular company and it meant nothing to virtually anybody. Absolutely nobody had ever heard of this company. They all knew the sort of product that I was looking for and quite a few wanted to offer me theirs, but no, I wanted one which was the same as one being sold by a company in Leeds. I didn't want it copying, I just wanted something similar or of the same quality, shall we say. I'm asking and asking and asking and eventually if you ask enough times you find somebody who knows the answer. And I can't remember who it was who told me the answer to my question, but I do remember that we were taking a journey from one town to another – quite a long journey – and the man who was with me said that this place that I was looking for was exceedingly difficult to find, but that he knew where it was and he would come with me.

So off we go and it was a long, long way. It was a long journey. And it wasn't a motorway and mad driving and veering here and veering there, it was quite a sensible journey. And we eventually came to a rickety old town in

the middle of nowhere with nothing going for it at all
and he told the driver who was... it was a hired car. He
told the driver to turn left, which we did. We turned left.
I'm thinking, well if we've turned left off the main road,
it can't be all that far away. Far away? We drove for
ages. I wouldn't like to put a time on it because I just
was... I was giving up. I really was resigning myself to
this was a wild goose chase and who were they kidding?
There couldn't possibly be a factory out here. We'd left
any sort of resemblance of factories way behind us. We
were out in the countryside where they grew, I presume,
rice and what have you and we were going gradually
up and up and up. We went through a tiny little hamlet
and the road that was going through there was fit for
one vehicle and one vehicle only. Fortunately we didn't
meet anything going in the opposite direction.

And we got so far and I think our friend decided that
the call of nature had overcome him and he nipped
behind some bushes or something like that. And I
looked down at a stream that was down to my right and
unlike the stream where I described where the young
lady was who had all the problems with the baby et
cetera, this was crystal-clear water. I would have drunk
from that. You could see straight to the bottom. And
we were getting higher and higher and higher and the
pollution that you've got in China and such countries
had disappeared. It had gone. We were in an absolutely
beautiful part of the world; a completely unspoilt part
of the world, but with nobody to ask, not a soul.

Our friend seemed to know what he was doing and half
an hour later he did know what he was doing because

we pulled up into a little larger village and on the right-hand side was a new building that hadn't been built more than a few years, we'll say, something like five. And he said, *"That is the factory that you are looking for."* Now this factory, if it was the right place, was making for a lighting company up here in Leeds and I thought, well I've no idea how anybody from that company – and I knew the company; I knew the managing director; I knew him well – I could not work out how anybody from his company would ever have found this place.

And we went in, and inside they were making what exactly I knew that these people in Leeds sold – among other things. They sold thousands of products, but this was one of their major lines. And I went in and they had one huge, new machine. How they got that machine up there, I've no idea how they got it up. I've no idea how they got the orders away or the raw materials in. It was all a complete puzzle. It was all beyond comprehension. There is no way we, in this country, would have stuck a factory like that way out in the middle of nowhere. I nicknamed it Shangri-La because it was so beautiful. It was so beautiful.

And I'm still needing convincing that this is the factory that makes for the firm in Leeds. And I asked through the man who... they said, *"Yes, yes, that's us. No exclusivity. They may say there's exclusivity, but there isn't. You can buy them."* And I thought, yeah, but we'd need to buy tens of thousands and I don't think that the people that we're talking about that I'm sourcing for had got the thought in their mind to buy quite so many as you seem to think that we would need. And then one of the staff came bustling out of the back with an empty box. You know how they make packaging and it's flat. The box was in English and there was a picture and on the reverse was the name of... and I can say the name because they, I'm afraid, have gone bankrupt. They don't exist anymore. Ring Lighting, Gelderd Road, Leeds. And that's the firm that... that's the product that I was looking for. Decisions to make. Got to tell the bloke back here, they're going to want a lot of pieces to deal with you. We've got to mull that over.

Came out and the man said, *"Do you fancy an ice-cream?"* I said, *"An ice-cream? How on earth do we get an ice-cream up here?"* And he said, *"Well look."* At the side of the gate into the factory was a tiny door and the tiny door was the way in to a tiny little corner shop. And I suppose she must have supplied the entire village with everything. When I say she, the lady who ran it and owned it and controlled and was ever so pleasant; she was fantastically pleasant and she told me that she was 90 and I believed her. She had a face like one of those old-fashioned lace-up footballs that you used to get as a kid and the same colour, like a brownie colour. And we bought two ice-creams. I had a raspberry-something and I don't know what the other fella had.

And then all the kids – there must have been some teaching or some means of school up there, I guess in somebody's house – they all had been informed that there was a foreigner in the village and they were let out and they came rushing down and they were wrapped round me like bees round a honeypot. I think they were all expecting me to buy them an ice-cream but I didn't. And do you know, I thought to myself at the time, there's one thing, I'm up here and they're all back at work at home because of the time of day it was. It would be about ten or 11 o'clock in the morning at home and I thought, mm, well there's one thing for sure, my mobile phone won't be ringing for an hour or two. It's an impossibility.

And I am telling you no lie, I had no sooner had that thought when my old friend Neil Mantovani from Doncaster rang and the line was as clear as if he was stood next to me. And there I am three parts of the way up some sort of mountain, nowhere near anywhere, in what I nicknamed 'Shangri-La' and I've got a bloke from Doncaster on the phone.

Some of these things that I say and talk about, you perhaps find difficult to believe, but I swear to you, that the Shangri-La story, Ring Lighting in Leeds and my pal from Doncaster, it's all absolutely true. And sometimes I find it difficult myself to believe, but true I said and true I meant.

I suppose we'd better leave China. I've a thousand stories that I haven't told.

I'll just tell you a brief, final one and that's about coming home from China down to Hong Kong to fly out.

I had so many friends in the Ningbo area; men I've not even mentioned. Alan Yang is one; a great guy.

I could tell you a story about Alan, but another day, another day. A great snooker player, Alan; a great snooker lover. And I can remember one day being taken back by Liu Fei to the airport at Ningbo to catch the flight down to Hong Kong. A couple of days in Hong Kong. I always had a bit of relaxation. I needed it before tackling a flight as long as that to Paris and then another flight to Manchester and then another journey home to here. And I never got used to… and this is not a story about something that happened once, it happened many times. I could never get used to going to the airport in Ningbo, which was a relatively new airport – only about a dozen gates; only one international flight.

Well it's not an international flight, but they called it one, Hong Kong. And you had to go through the emigration and having gone through there, you had to put your briefcase through the detector and go through the detector yourself. If you beeped because you'd got an odd coin or something in your pocket or you'd left your mobile phone in your pocket or you hadn't switched it off or something, they would want to examine you, go through you to find out… examine you all over to make sure that you weren't some sort of smuggler.

And the thing that you find a little difficult to understand is that if that happens here – and I'm a man; it's a man that frisks me. Oh not in China. In China it can be a woman frisking a woman, a woman frisking a man or vice-versa and many a time I've been in Ningbo airport; invariably in Ningbo airport and been frisked by a lady who never batted an eyelid when she got into the nether regions and thought that... and never apologised for giving you a little nudge, shall we say, which I became sure was deliberate but I didn't dare say so.

Now that was a very short, brief little story because it happens. It sums up the total difference between what's acceptable there and acceptable here. I was telling a very dear friend of mine, a lady called Jackie – short for Jacqueline – Jackie Beighton, lives opposite here, a very nice lady; a very good friend of my wife and a very good friend of mine and I've played bits of this saga of mine to her.

And I can only finish this book by telling you what she said after hearing, not all of it, but some of it and most particularly, the Chinese bit.

I remember Jackie looking me straight in the eye and saying, *"Well, would you do it again Chris?"*

**"NOT FOR ALL THE TEA IN CHINA."**

9 781839 753